TABLE OF CONTENTS

Fall 2020
Volume 1, Number 1

EDITOR
LEON WIESELTIER

MANAGING EDITOR
CELESTE MARCUS

PUBLISHER
BILL REICHBLUM

JOURNAL DESIGN
WILLIAM VAN RODEN

WEB DESIGN
HOT BRAIN

Liberties is a publication of the Liberties Journal Foundation, a nonpartisan 501(c)(3) organization based in Washington, D.C. devoted to educating the general public about the history, current trends, and possibilities of culture and politics. The Foundation seeks to inform today's cultural and political leaders, deepen the understanding of citizens, and inspire the next generation to participate in the democratic process and public service.

Engage
To join the discussion please go to libertiesjournal.com

Subscribe
To subscribe or any questions about your subscription, please go to libertiesjournal.com

ISSN 2692-3904

EDITORIAL OFFICES
1604 New Hampshire Avenue NW
Washington, DC 20009

DIGITAL
@READLIBERTIES
LIBERTIESJOURNAL.COM

Liberties

MICHAEL IGNATIEFF

Liberalism in the Anthropocene

In the more innocent time before the pandemic, we already knew that we were living in an era with a new name. We had entered the Anthropocene — a new epoch in which the chief forces shaping nature are the work of our own species. Some date the dawn of the Anthropocene to the beginning of the Industrial Revolution, others to 1945 and the detonations at Hiroshima and Nagasaki. While we may disagree about when this epoch began, we are beginning to understand, and not a moment too soon, its moral imperative. It requires that humans must assume responsibility for natural phenomena — the weather, sea levels, air quality, soil fertility, species survival, and viruses — that we once left in the hands of God or fate. This is a genuinely momentous alteration in our worldview. We have for centuries boasted of our mastery of nature, but the time has come for Prometheus to shoulder the responsibility that comes with mastery, and to make our mastery wiser.

We may be lords and masters of nature, but as philosophers have been telling us, we must learn to master our mastery. It is dawning on us that this so-called mastery could kill us, and not only us. According to what we currently know, a virus leaps from a non-human to a human in a wet market in Wuhan: a tiny entity composed of RNA acid and protein jumps the gap between species, and within eight weeks, thanks to the malign interaction between the global economy and the global biosphere, the entire world was in lock-down, parents and grandparents were dying and the young adults, who came to majority in the new precarious economy, were wondering whether they would ever know economic security again.

Naturally enough, the idea of the Anthropocene no longer awakens only a sense of mastery and control, but also a terrible fear. We fear our own powers and their consequences; we fear our world ending, going dark in environmental collapse and plague, followed by that old evil stand-by, barbarism. Ecological pressure has ended other great civilizations: if Easter Island, why not us? If viruses finished off the Mayans, the Incas, the tribes who so innocently greeted Columbus, why not us?

The Anthropocene — and the fear that now haunts our mastery of nature — is putting enormous pressure on the whole spectrum of modern political beliefs. Some American progressives accept the ecological facts, but they blame everything on capitalism, demonstrating pattern blindness towards the environmental devastation and public health incompetence in the command economies of Russia, China, and Eastern Europe for two generations after 1945. Ideologically hostile to markets, militant progressives are also giving away significant ameliorative tools such as carbon pricing that may be crucial to any solution to the climate crisis.

At the other end of the political spectrum, there are still many conservative parties — Republicans in the United States prominently among them — who are in double denial about the risk to the environment and the risks to human health, vitiating environmental controls on polluting industries and unlocking their local economies before it is safe to do so. Sometimes this know-nothingism derives from a larger hostility to science and objectivity that has emerged from the cultural and political agenda of the American right. It is just possible that the scale of the crisis of the Anthropocene will awaken conservatives from their dogmatic slumbers, because if they do not awaken they will lose the power they live for. (And the eventual catastrophe will hardly be a good business environment.) There are also populists of the right — Salvini, Orban, Wilders — who prefer to change the subject, who tell their voters that the thing to fear is not climate change or pandemics but immigrants and foreigners. But a politics that changes the subject does not have much of a future either.

In a host of countries — the United States, Canada, Germany, the Netherlands, and the Nordic states — a new politics has been taking shape that identifies climate change as the central political issue of our time and argues, cogently, that species destruction and environmental wastage have rendered us also more vulnerable to pandemics. Before the pandemic broke, however, this politics seemed stuck, unable to achieve electoral breakthrough anywhere except in Germany and Scandinavia. It was asking for more change than most electors were ready to vote for. Now the question is whether the pandemic, combined with the increasing threat of climate change as it is quantitatively measured, will lure voters out of cautious complacency and pull them towards what the times seem to be calling for — a revolutionary politics.

So should we ready ourselves for a revolutionary politics? Does the threat to the natural environment deserve to erase what we know about revolutions and revolutionaries? For the dystopian imagination, the temptation is very great. Panic is not the friend of patience, and there are more and more voices urging us to panic. But if revolution is not the answer, and we should not throw away the wisdom about politics that we have gained from our experience of other historical emergencies, what would a non-revolutionary climate- conscious politics look like? That is the question that liberalism must answer now. By liberalism, I mean any politics that as a matter of principle prefers reform to revolution, puts its trust in political institutions as instruments of change, and develops policies within the checks and balances of a liberal democratic system and with the market signals of a capitalist economy. This kind of liberalism has depended for its success on its association, since the Enlightenment, with precisely the historical story that climate change and pandemics put into question: the story of progress, the tale that says that science and the mastery of nature, married to the capitalist profit motive and free markets, have created an upward spiral in which political freedom advances hand in hand with economic liberty and technological change, all three combining in a successful synthesis that preserves our natural habitat and increases our life-span.

This, understand, is not a "neoliberal" story, one that supposes that markets left to themselves, disencumbered

9

Liberalism in the Anthropocene

from regulation, will automatically create a society that reconciles freedom, equity and environmental responsibility. That faith is absurd. The only morally supportable capitalism is a regulated capitalism. Nor will all the essential values of an open society ever go together perfectly or without dissonance. A properly liberal story is very different: it contends that politics — collective public action in the name of citizens and the state — is essential if technological progress can ever be made to serve human ends like freedom, justice, and the preservation of our habitat. Activism, representation, debate, compromise, reason, law: those are the elements of the liberal idea of public action against public harm. But will these suffice against the harm we are causing to our climate? Liberalism's historical story — politics taming the capitalist Leviathan — seems complacent in revolutionary times, or so many people think. Liberalism is not just associated with a story of progress that is now on trial; it is also associated with a style of politics — meliorist, gradual, compromising — that is now held to be unfit for a time that requires radical solutions. Liberal convictions seem out of step with the prevailing end-times mood that warns we are headed for apocalypse. And in the face of a great fear, liberal politics may be swept aside.

Yet the liberal tradition happens to know something about fear. There once was a great liberal who knew about fear all the way down, so let's begin with him. There is nothing to fear, he famously said, but fear itself; and he said so when the fear of his time was universal and truly terrifying. Roosevelt's adage is more than just uplift. It recommends an analytical approach to the causes of fear. Following FDR, a liberal believes that the first thing to do about fear is to disaggregate. Break it into little pieces. Attempt to distinguish what you fear most

10

from what you fear less and least. The one big problem is in fact many smaller problems. If there is no quick and effective and salvific way to address the one big problem, there are ways to address the smaller problems, and this is a more likely way of solving them. Once you disaggregate, you can prioritize. Once you prioritize, a politics begins to take shape. In the case of climate change: first recycling, then road pricing; then carbon pricing; then subsidize renewables; when they are competitive, withdraw the subsidy; then, take coal-fired and gas-fired stations off line; then, when renewables start generating sufficient load, start decommissioning nuclear; and so on. This liberal politics — as opposed to the progressive summons to the barricades — we might call the politics of policy.

In pandemics, disaggregation is also the key. Break the problem down into the pieces you can fix: tracing, masks, ventilators, personal protective gear, distancing. As Jacinda Ardern of New Zealand observed, you go early and you go hard. In the absence of a vaccine, you shut your borders, your schools, your whole economy, and you keep it down till the infection dies for lack of carriers. In the process of additively applying these partial solutions to this lethal problem, liberal societies have demonstrated once again the falsity of a very old canard: that capitalist societies value profits more than lives. (I know, some capitalists do.) As President Macron recently said, in shutting down economies in their entirety, capitalist society revealed its deepest anthropological commitments. It imperiled its economy to save its society.

Dissolving a big problem into little steps is the essence of a liberal politics. Radical environmentalists like to scorn gradualism and incrementalism, but working with incentives and markets, liberal gradualism is on the cusp of transforming

11

Western energy systems. Look around at all those windmills and all those solar panels. Look at the way renewables are competing with fossil fuels on price. This is how regulated markets can work. It turns out that the environmental emergency does not refute liberal politics: far from being bankrupted by climate change, liberalism has turned out to be the only politics that has made substantive progress thus far. It has the eloquence of actual changes. Both the environmental crisis — and even more so the pandemic — have vindicated the liberal belief in government. Only a central government can enact the policies and enforce the regulations that will make a decisive difference. Who, worried about the fate of the earth, could oppose the regulatory state? Who, worried about protecting their families from infection, will not want competent government? Against such threats the private sector is a reed in the wind. Competence, simple competence, on the part of public officials, governmental power used responsibly and effectively for the public good, has a way of vindicating liberal gradualism and of taking away the sting of fear.

It is important to understand that fear is a political phenomenon. It is organized by interests whose purpose is to drive public opinion for profit, political gain, or public benefit. Fear is not only a feeling; it is also a strategy. We need to regard the tribunes of fear as political actors, to test their assertions, especially, as in the case of environmentalists, when we support their objectives. We need to be aware of our own susceptibility to fear. There is a voluptuous quality to it: we like to be afraid, even very afraid, as every Hollywood producer knows. Fear is also an industry: intellectuals build careers upon it; newspapers build circulation upon it; demagogues amass power upon it. Nothing sells like fear: it is a brand. Even a sincere fear may be politically constructed and politically manipulated.

Liberalism is the sworn adversary of such a politics. A liberal knows that the only antidote to fear is knowledge. While there may be legitimate controversies about what is true and what is not, the possibility of truth, the reality of verifiable facts, is — at least for liberals — the foundation of political action. But here we get to the heart of the problem. The reliance upon the facts is most often celebrated when truths are deployed against falsehoods, so that prevailing misconceptions are corrected by accurate information. But what if the prevailing conceptions are not misconceptions? What if fear is warranted by the facts? What if the nightmares have a basis in reality?

After all, fear about climate change and pandemics is not a delusion. We all know (unless we choose not to know) the facts already. Millions of human beings are carrying an infection for which there is no cure yet. The polar ice caps are melting. Sea levels are rising. Sea water is acidifying. Coral reefs are dying. Air and water temperatures are rising, accelerating the violence of storms, flooding, and wildfires. It is no wonder that the narrative of doom is penetrating our psyches, leaving us with a grim sense that our virtuous behaviors — and the politics of little steps — are now beside the point.

And yet. Even when hysteria may seem like a plausible feeling about a problem, it is not a plausible feeling for the discovery of its solution. We need to keep faith with little steps — not despite the magnitude of the crisis but because of it. The environmentally progressive actions of individuals are more than just "virtue signaling." All these small gestures certainly have "big number effects" when millions of strangers, uncoordinated, all join their little efforts to our own. In lockdown,

13

we discovered the immense impact — we called it "flattening the curve" — that individual behaviors such as staying at home could have in reducing risk for us all. Little efforts scaled up are among the central tools of a liberal politics. They are also antidotes to despair.

Despair may be a way of simply registering, at the level of feeling, the gravity of the facts. But it is one thing to face the facts and another to question or even abandon the hope of remedies. Fear in the Anthropocene is also challenging the relevance of the very frame in which liberal politics operates: the nation-state. It is easy to believe that pandemics and environmental crisis overrun the capacities of our sovereign actors. Climate change makes it easy for the powerful to claim that they are powerless, while their private planes idle not far from the conference center, but it also makes it easy for activists to believe that the tactics of liberal gradualism, focused as they are on local, regional, and national governments, are irrelevant. When a problem as big as climate change, as global as a pandemic, enters the political agenda, the advanced chatter begins to claim that only global solutions matter — whereas in reality it is national authorities who actually have the power to close borders, quarantine their citizens, force the transition to sustainable energy. The grueling months of pandemic crisis, far from demonstrating the irrelevance of liberalism's chosen site for politics — the nation-state — have shown that it is the site that actually matters.

These narratives about the irrelevance of national politics should be seen for what they are: alibis for inaction. Those who do have power still make a huge difference, for good or for ill. Every day that President Trump dismantles the environmental protections built up since Nixon's time, every time he contradicts common sense in public health matters, he shows us what malevolence and incompetence in public office can do. Xi Jinping makes an equally malign difference, as 56% percent of the increase in CO2 emissions comes from China and a good proportion of the misinformation about covid19 as well. Ditto Narendra Modi in India. Indeed, climate change and the pandemic — contemporary life in the Anthropocene — has also exposed the price we have paid for the shredding of what once passed for a liberal international order. We mock that phrase at our own peril. International climate change conferences — Paris, Copenhagen, Madrid — are easily dismissed, but for all their faults they did edge states towards action, and for all the suspect friendliness of the WHO towards China, does anyone, apart from the president of the United States, seriously believe the world is a safer place without the WHO?

So we desperately need competent national governments to protect us, but also governments smart enough to learn from each other and share knowledge — open governments, empirical governments. The time left for this mixture of national and international action keeps getting shorter. If concerted and scientifically based action fails to address climate challenge, if the oceans keep rising, if the fires keep getting worse, if infections spike again, we may reach a moment when democratic citizens will demand that their leaders acquire autocratic powers to protect us from further harm: governments of national salvation, in the old expression. The pandemic has already demonstrated the use that authoritarians have for such crises. Climate change, if sufficiently terrifying, could cause us to vote ourselves into an authoritarian state.

Thus the climate emergency and the pandemic may test the viability of liberal democracy even more than populism has. Yet before we allow ourselves to be rushed towards the authoritarian exit, let's ask a simple question: which global leader would you rather have in charge of your climate emergency and your pandemic? Xi Jinping or Angela Merkel? Jair Bolsonaro or Jacinda Ardern? Far from demonstrating that liberal democratic leaders are not up to the crisis, climate change and the pandemic have vindicated democratic leadership and demonstrated what it consists in: trusting your citizens, believing in reason and research, marshaling the forces of government to support them, and having the courage to tell your citizens the truth.

Yet even this is not the core challenge. Liberals face a deeper crisis — in our confidence in our stories about the past. It was technology and political reform that lifted the burden of labor off the backs of men and women; it was science that enabled women to face childbirth without fear and gave us the prospect that everyone could have a full and longer life-span, free of hunger and disease. This is the Enlightenment story, the saga of the empowering relationship between knowledge and freedom. It is the only good story left. It is the narrative that made us feel that all the senseless hustle and brutality of capitalist modernity served a higher purpose, even if we could not see it ourselves. We were bound on the wheel of progress, and it was inexorably moving uphill. Or so we thought.

Now we are told that it is rolling downward towards the abyss. Radical environmentalism, reinforced by covid19, has become the glamorous pessimism of our time. It has become an identity and a style: an opportunity to demonstrate one's own righteousness, to express disgust at politicians, to give shape, however dark, to time. Better a master narrative that predicts doom than no narrative at all. To dissent from this view is to take upon oneself a whole lot of trouble. My own dissent is in fact pretty limited. I do not dispute the facts, of course — shame on those who do. I dispute the attitude. What I dislike is the pessimism, the misanthropy, the wholesale indictment of progress and humanism, the tendentious re-writing of modern history, the impatience with liberal half-measures, which — I insist — are the only ones that have made any constructive difference.

It is common these days to read that our species is a cancer upon the planet, a virus, an infestation, or to change metaphors, that we are the chief serial killers on earth. Thanks to this dire and defeatist mental agitation, many people worry aloud whether we even deserve to survive. Young people actually ask themselves whether they should bring children into such a benighted world. The fight for life is damaging the appetite for life. Instead of feeling empowered by what we have come to know about the climate and about epidemics, the more we know, the worse we feel.

Are we guilty of crimes against our environment? Of course we are. (We are guilty also of crimes against each other.) Being human demands that we take responsibility for what we have done to the planet. But being human also means keeping faith with our species' staggering and proven resourcefulness. In a crisis of these dimensions, misanthropy becomes a fatal spiritual temptation. Radical environmentalists understandably wish to shake us awake, but the language they commonly use fosters only despair and disengagement. The pandemic has given life to this new rhetoric of repentance and flagellation. Fire-and brimstone language that calls for apocalyptic change has a long and unappetizing history: in the Protestant Reformation, in the French Revolution, and in the chiliastic fervor of the Russian revolution. In all three it led to a betrayal of the goals that revolutionary change sought to achieve. Our past should have taught us by now to recognize and reject such impulses.

Incredible as it may seem, after hundreds of thousands of people across the world have already died of the pandemic, there are some environmentalists who argue that this is a necessary wake-up call, even a price worth paying if it induces us to turn away, before it is too late, from the path of profligacy, waste, and consumerism. As in heartless religions of old, we are encouraged to make this suffering redemptive. Once again radicals have uses for our terror. Surely there is something indecent about celebrating the desolation of city streets as good for us, and something morally decadent about seeing the quiet of lockdown as a harbinger of a better world when freezer trucks are parked outside our hospitals.

In this new talk about how the pandemic points us towards environmental resurrection, there is a very disreputable idea about human wants and preferences. This is Marx' idea of false consciousness, according to which this vast world of capitalist consumption is an orchestrated delusion, in which capitalism creates counterfeit needs and desires which then enslave us and lead us to environmental perdition. Liberalism's belief about human beings could not be more different. We accept that people have the needs and desires they have and we believe that a free society must respect these needs and desires for what they are. People want pleasure, cars, goods, vacations; they derive comfort and consolation from possessions. They are willing to spend money, lots of it, in pointless but amiable sociability in restaurants, bars, cafes, and holidays on far-away beaches. All this is not decadent, it is human. And the vast machine of capitalism exists to serve these wants. The market does not distinguish between those wants that are noble and those that are trivial, those that are conducive to the survival of the species and those that are hostile to it. These are choices that free men and women make for themselves, not least through their political choices. The world that results is only partly free, since the combined effect of these wants can create externalities which then plague us and diminish our enjoyment, but still, fundamentally, the order of our world is created by human desire.

This set of ideas makes a liberal deeply resistant to an environmental moralism that implies that there is a sustainable world to be had if only we could realize that our desires are false. From a conviction that actual human wants are destroying the planet to the premise that human beings should not be allowed to want what they want is but one small step. Most environmentalists are democrats, but if they take that step they will cease to be democrats and cease to be liberals. Pandemics and the climate crisis do not just empower autocrats. They can also corrupt democrats.

For what real alternative is there, except to place our faith and direct our energies where they always should have been: in knowledge, reason, science, persuasion, and policy — in the imperfect and constantly adapting tools that we have used, since the beginning, to gain such mastery as we have of ourselves and of our world? What real alternative is there, what greater engine of mitigation, to democratic politics? Does anyone doubt that the planet will not be saved by dictators? Recall the earlier fascist enemies of democracy, who thought that it was feckless — only to discover how formidable a democratic people can be when their survival depends upon it.

A liberal's critique of radical environmentalism is that it is essentially a religious movement, in its absolutism, in its exclusive claims to virtue, in its contempt for differences of opinion, in its call for salvation. The pandemic has made these calls for salvation more insistent. Instead of a new secular religion, however, what the environment actually needs is a new politics. For any strategy that will get CO_2 and pollution under control is bound to be deeply divisive. To deal with these divisions, green activism must become properly political, seeking the compromises between energy producing regions and energy consuming regions, between workers in smokestack industries and workers in the new economy, between those who benefit from green change and those who may be hurt in the long transition to a sustainable future. The pandemic, likewise, forces choices upon us. Neither the absolutism of public health nor the absolutism of the economy is any kind of guide to our perplexities.

The very idea of compromise sounds scandalous in the face of our emergency, but the core of a liberal politics, surely, is that there are no absolute claims — not even the melting glaciers, not even the spread of a pandemic — that clear the table in democratic debate. We must argue about everything if we wish to stay free. Experts must be heard but they do not rule. Majorities rule, but minorities have to be protected. Legislatures pass laws, but courts have to rule on their lawfulness and constitutionality. All this slows down a liberal polity's capacity to act, but that is the price of freedom — and also the condition of effective action against complicated problems. Above all, citizens matter, one by one. Energy workers and energy producers, in smokestack industries and regions, are citizens like the rest of us, and their claims deserve something better than moral derision. They need help, they need time, and like all of us they need jobs.

Liberal institutions can handle climate change and

pandemics, but only if they are honest and free. Here liberals should confront some hard truths. We need to face up to the reality of how tarnished our chosen instruments have become. The climate crisis is exposing just how many of our institutions have been captured by the interests they purport to regulate. Liberals have to acknowledge in particular the distorting impact of energy oligopolies on market prices for carbon intensive goods, and the equally distorting impact of big energy money in politics. Equally, the pandemic has exposed, at least in the United States, the fearful way in which a private health industry weakened the capacity of states and governments to maintain a public health infrastructure that protects everyone regardless of their ability to pay.

Liberalism is an elite politics in the sense that representative democracy consists in the appointment of a governing class or echelon by popular ballot — and that echelon, that elite, has become much too cozy with big money, whether it be from the pharmaceutical industry or big oil. Here the climate change protesters have been proven right: we will not get climate policies that work if the legislation is written by the energy companies. Likewise, we will not get health care policy that protects all of us, especially the poorest and most vulnerable, if policy is written by health care companies. So the liberal counter-lobby, in favor of sensible and attainable policy, will have to be as well financed and as relentless as the forces it is up against.

It is commonly feared that liberal democracy may not be up to the challenge of cleaning its own house and making the right choices to protect nature and our lives. Yet before we give up on liberal democracy, we should observe a significant fact — noted by the historian Niall Ferguson — that it is only in liberal democracies that CO_2 increase has halted. To be sure, these societies are still emitting CO_2, too much of it, but they have stopped its increase and with good leadership they can attain carbon neutrality. Where CO_2 continues to increase, by contrast, is in authoritarian societies such as China and Russia. So the argument that liberal democracy is too paralyzed by polarization to meet the climate crisis may be wrong. Action on climate change needs more democracy, not less — it needs open societies that empower from the ground up, and favor initiatives at every level, especially the municipal, and enable all of us as citizens to act, to protest, to represent, and to invent solutions.

It is also in open societies that basic knowledge about climate change and pandemics has spread most quickly. Only democratic societies can guarantee the freedom that knowledge requires, though the political and economic pressures on science and free public debate have lately been growing. Despite the counter-attack of the know-nothings, we should remember how far we have come. Mass public awareness of the environmental crisis dates no further back than Earth Day 1970. Mass awareness of the existential lethality of pandemic is no older than HIV, SARS, and ebola. But now we know, and there is no going back. We are closer now, in the early twenty-first century, to a mass politics, based on environmental and epidemiological science, than at any time in history. The new politics has begun, and we must give it time to have its effect, to make its way to government.

Radical environmentalists are already warning us that this is all too little too late. In life, as in politics, it is never too late, and the suggestion itself encourages inaction. Already the next generation grasps that this will be the political challenge of their age, to which they must rise if they are to have a future to hand on to their own children. The politics of environmental correction and global health will not succeed if its core message is to hate ourselves for what we have done.

In finding the balance of activism and understanding, we need to remember how deeply men and women have loved the natural world and have ardently portrayed it in their culture, so that their fellow creatures would love it as they do. We forget how deep the respect for nature's limits and nature's laws goes in the anthropological record. We forget how epidemiology has enabled us to see that we are creatures whose survival depends on respect for our habitat and for other species. We walked away from this wisdom, but we are now walking back to what our aboriginal and peasant ancestors knew.

Let us face up to the whole complex story of how we became lords and masters of nature. The celebration of progress since the Enlightenment, the historical script that we inherited from Kant and Hegel, Smith and Marx, made sense of time for us, but it was always in part a myth, concealing the dark side of our conquest of nature. Yet let us also remember that an astounding amount of material, scientific, and moral progress was made, and remember also that the mythical dimension of the story of progress was an ennobling myth, which taught us to believe in our agency for good, in our capacity to become masters of our fate rather than slaves of gods and nature. We must be unafraid to confront the dark side of progress now, but without losing faith in the human campaign to make life better. *This* is the conviction that we need to save our planet and ourselves.

Liberalism in the Anthropocene

LAURA KIPNIS

Transgression, An Elegy

24

Sade does not give us the work of a free man. He makes us participate in his efforts of liberation. But it is precisely for this reason that he holds our attention.

SIMONE DE BEAUVOIR, *"MUST WE BURN SADE?"*

Vito Acconci, later to be known as the art world's "godfather of transgression," is crouched under a low wooden ramp constructed over the floor of the otherwise empty Sonnabend Gallery in New York. Apparently he's masturbating to sexual fantasies about the visitors walking above him, the soundtrack of which is projected through loudspeakers installed in the corners of the gallery. "You're on my left . . . you're moving away but I'm pushing my body against you, into the corner . . . you're bending your head down, over me . . you're pushing your cunt down on my mouth... you're pressing your tits down on my cock... you're ramming your cock down into my ass..." Now and then gallery goers can hear him come. The piece is titled *Seedbed.*

It was 1971, Nixon was in the White House, and artists were shooting, abrading, exposing, and abjecting themselves, deploying their bodies to violate whatever proprieties had survived the 1960s, and shatter the boundaries between art and life. This would, in turn, rattle and eventually remake sclerotic social structures and dismantle ruling class hegemony, or so I learned later that decade from my Modern Art History instructor, a charismatic Marxist-Freudian bodybuilder who fulminated about Eros and Thanatos and seems never to have published a word, but greatly influenced my thinking on these matters.

Transgression had been so long implanted into the curriculum that it had become a tradition — a required introductory course at the art school I attended as an undergraduate. Transgression was the source of all cultural vitality, or so it seemed. We learned that aesthetic assault was the founding gesture of the avant-garde, which had been insulting the bourgeoisie for over a century, dating back in the visual arts to 1863 and the Salon des Refusés in Paris. The classic on exhibit was Manet's *Le Déjeuner sur l'herbe*, previously rejected by the jury of the annual sponsored Salon de Paris. Manet was his day's godfather of transgression, though the real scandal of the painting wasn't that a nude woman was casually picnicking with two clothed men and gazing directly at the viewer. No, according to my instructor, it was that Manet let his brushstrokes show, an aesthetic offense so great that visitors had to be physically restrained from destroying the painting. It seemed like an enviable time to have been an artist.

In this lineage, we took our places. I felt it was my natural home, a mental organizing principle. It augured freedom, self-sovereignty — I was angry at the world's timid rule-followers and counted myself among the anti-prissy, though my personal disgust threshold has always been pretty low. Acconci I found both disgusting and intriguing. The heroic transgressor mythology, I eventually came to see, definitely had its little vanities, its preferred occlusions. Even the origin story was dodgy; in fact the Salon des Refusés was itself officially sponsored, something I don't recall my instructor mentioning. Hearing of complaints by the painters who were rejected by the Salon de Paris, Emperor Napoleon III had given his blessing to a counter-exhibition, cannily containing the backlash by accommodating the transgressors. Possibly there's always a certain complicity between the transgressive and the covertly permitted — shrewd transgressors, like court jesters, knew which lines *not* to cross.

A few years before *Seedbed*, Acconci had performed his equally notorious *Following Piece,* which involved randomly selecting and then stalking a different unwitting person through the streets of New York City until they entered a locale — an office, a car — where they could not be trailed. He did this every day for a month. The duration of the artwork was effectively controlled by the individual being pursued though their participation was not, which gave the piece its edge of creepiness. The documentation now resides in The Museum of Modern Art's permanent collection — count Acconci among the shrewd transgressors.

Of course, terms like "consent" were heard infrequently in

26

arty-leftish circles in those days and the idea that it could be unambiguously established had yet to be invented. Eros itself seemed less containable, which was among the things people mostly liked about it in the years after the sexual revolution and before HIV. Even sexual creepiness seemed less malign: sex was polymorphous and leaky, aggression was inseparable from sex and its attendant idiocies, this was largely understood as the human condition, also a big wellspring of artistic inspiration. Anyway, *Seedbed*'s audience would have presumably been wise to the content of the piece before entering Sonnabend and being enlisted for roles in Acconci's onanistic scenarios, though from today's vantage "implied' consent is no sort of consent at all. About *Seedbed,* Acconci was prone to explanations such as "my goal of producing seed led to my interaction with visitors and their interaction, like it or not, with me." The extended middle finger of that "like it or not" (and the unapologetic prickishness of "producing seed") now seems — to borrow my students' current terminology — a little "rapey." But from the new vantage, the entire history of the avant-garde can seem a little rapey.

What was the turning point? When did transgression go south? Even by 2013 damage control was required. When *Following Piece* was displayed at a MOMA exhibition that year, a nervously disingenuous caption was posted to mitigate potential umbrage: "Though this stalking was aggressive, by allowing a stranger to determine his route the artist gave up a certain degree of agency." As if getting to determine the route neutralized the piece's aggression, like carbon offsets for polluters are meant to do for the environment? The artist gave up nothing that I can see, but that was the basic job description for artists from the Romantic era on: give up *nothing*.

The wrestling match between the caption and the photos now seems emblematic. If "like it or not" was the master trope of the Manet-to-Acconci years, today's would have to be *encroachment*. Transgression has been replaced by trauma as the cultural concept of the hour: making rules rather than breaking them has become the signature aesthetic move, that's just how it is, there's no going back. New historical actors have taken up places on the social stage and made their bids for cultural hegemony, having sent the old ones to re-education camp. These days it's the *transgressed-upon* who are the protagonists of the moment: the *offended*, people who are *very upset* by things, their interventions a drumbeat on social media, their tremulous voices ascendant. (Online cultural commissar is now a promising career path.) And the mainstream cultural institutions are, on the whole, deferring, offering solace and apologias, posting warning signs and caveats to what might cause aesthetic injury. Aesthetic injuries flourish nonetheless.

Sure, there have always been offended people, but those people used to be conservatives. Who cared if they were offended, that was the point. What has changed is the social composition of the offended groups. At some point offendability moved its offices to the hip side of town. The offended people say they're progressives! Which requires some rethinking for those of us shaped by the politics of the previous ethos.

After a century and a half of cultural immunity, transgression has started smelling a little rancid, like a bloated roué in last decade's tight leather pants. But okay, change happens, the world is in flux, life is a river, nothing stays the same. Let's try not to get defensive about it. Okay yes, I'm talking to myself, it's me who feels defensive. But what's the point of clinging to superseded radicalisms in a different world and time? Please be patient as I attempt to wrestle myself out of a long-term romance with a dethroned idea. I'm doing my best. I'm a bit conflicted.

It was never precisely said that I recall, but it seems evident in retrospect that there was a particular idea of the self that was embedded in the aesthetics of transgression: a self *too* buffered against the blows of the world, *too* stolid. It was an artistic duty to shatter this securely integrated self. The role of the authoritarian personality in the rise of European fascism, as analyzed by Wilhelm Reich and his Frankfurt School counterparts, was still in the air at the time of my inculcation into the cult of transgression, its tentacles still wrapped around the counterculture and the antiwar movement. Character rigidity was the signature feature of the political right, we learned, who were despicable moral cops with sticks up their asses. In the version of twentieth-century art history that I was taught, art audiences and upright citizens generally were all deeply in need of psychical jolts and emetics. These benighted people needed to have their complacencies rattled; as an artist, you were meant to take up that task, defy the censors, search out and assault social norms and conventions, especially the ones embedded deepest within our (or their) sensibilities.

Art had already abandoned objecthood by then; now the mission was plumbing your depths and darkest instincts, then assaulting the audience with the ickiest stuff. Art was supposed to be perilous and messy. Psychoanalysis had long ago told us that the modern personality structure was a hardened carapace formed around traumatic memories or fantasies that had become bottled up and fetid, and had to be manumitted. Sure this was aggressive, but sublimating aggression into art was what made art feel alive, a collective therapeutics, maybe not unlike love: potentially transcendent. It was a world peopled by depressives and jerks who doubled as therapists, putting culture on the couch and then joining it there; we diagnosed its pathologies and our own, we invented curatives. Sometimes those were painful: success was measured in outrage generated.

People understandably howled when their carapaces were under assault, but that wasn't *bad.* Violation was an ethical project. Censorship was a tool of the death drive and the authoritarians, but luckily there was no such thing as successful repression anyway — lectured my instructor. The festering stuff was always leaking out, which the Surrealists understood, along with other leaky heroes such as Jackson Pollock, who started flinging paint at a canvas on the floor, liberating it once and for all from the falsehoods of representation and the prison of the picture plane. It was the wild men and (occasional) women who changed the world — by breaking rules, not following them! As with Pollock, who upended painting entirely, but it was his psyche that had to get released first, thanks to Jungian analysis. We pored over Jung looking for backdoors to the collective unconscious, we memorized Reich, another wild man always making another comeback for whom character was itself a kind of defense.

The point is that there was an ethics to transgression. As for us aspiring artists, our own defenses needed to be punctured too, our own inflexibilities shattered. Boundaries made us ill. Humans were armored: not only superegos but also bodies needed to be broken down and realigned. Being permeable was good for you. Another of Acconci's performances from 1970 was *Rubbing Piece.* This one involved him rubbing his left forearm with his right hand for an hour until he got a horrible

30

sore, his skin angry and abraded. We all needed to shed our skins, give up our self-protections.

To be sure, these skins were by default white — race wasn't yet part of the curriculum, though another of my teachers was Robert Colescott, who was at the time painting massive and funnily bitter canvases substituting African-Americans for whites in reprises of iconic history paintings (*George Washington Carver Crossing the Delaware*). In quest of whatever permeability was available I underwent Rolfing, a sadistic form of therapeutic massage designed to dislodge and release the emotional injuries stored in your connective tissues; this entailed paying to have someone grind the heel of his hand and occasionally an elbow into the soft parts of your corpus until you cried. It really hurt. But how was anything going to get transformed socially and politically if our rigidities remained intact, bolstered by aesthetic politesse and safety-mongering?

The possibility of smashing everything, your own boundaries included, made for a wonderful political optimism. Aesthetic vanguards and political vanguards seemed like natural allies — the revolutions to come would be left-wing ones, or so we assumed. What innocent times those now seem, when "right-wing radical" was still an oxymoron. Aesthetic conservatives were political conservatives, that was the assumption. The disrupters were on the left; disruption was a left-wing idiom. It was very heady: signing on to the avant-garde linked you to a revolutionary past and future, from the barricades to Duchamp's urinals to Mai 68. Everywhere the mandate was to dismantle the art-life distinction, and to embrace whatever followed.

Yes, I do now see there were some convenient fictions embedded in the romance with transgression. For one thing, as much as we hawked dismantling the art-life boundary, we also covertly relied on it: artistic transgressions were allowed to flourish because the aesthetic frame was itself a sort of protective shield. In 1992, in an aptly titled essay "The Aesthetic Alibi," Martin Jay, while naming no names, gently mocked the whole genre of performance art, invented, he says, to permit behaviors that would put artists in jail or mental wards if art and life were *not* distinct realms of experience. In other words the transgressions of Acconci and his ilk coasted on the inviolability of art while getting acclaim for appearing to militate against it.

As a nineteen-year-old aspiring artist I worshipped Vito Acconci, I wanted to be Acconci, though in pictures he looked hairy and unkempt. I thought *Seedbed* was artistically brilliant. I looked up his address in the New York phone book and thought about dropping by (he lived on Christie Street, I even now recall), or maybe stalking him through the streets of New York and then documenting it — transgressing the transgressor! — to what I imagined would be art world acclaim. It wouldn't have occurred to me to try to pull off public masturbation, even concealed under a platform; there were limits to the transgressions I could imagine.

The gender politics of transgression was not initially much on my horizon. Not that there weren't some stellar female transgressors on the scene: there was Lynda Benglis, for example, who ran a mocking ad in *Artforum* of herself nude except for white-framed sunglasses, wielding an extra-long dildo like a phallus. (It was a commentary on the art world.) But you didn't need to appropriate the phallus to be transgressive, you could daintily repudiate it in the manner of the feminist artist Judy Chicago and others, who were reclaiming maligned "feminine" crafts such as china-painting and needlepoint to contest the macho grandiosities of minimalism.

In some ways of telling this story, feminism and transgression were always on a collision course. For one thing, and needless to say, women's bodies were pretty often transgression's raw material, in art and in life, on canvas and in the bars. I recall reading the painter Audrey Flack on her first meeting with Jackson Pollock at the Cedar Tavern decades before — he pulled her toward him as if to kiss her, then burped in her face. Flack, twenty at the time, wasn't particularly offended, she just saw him as desperate. De Kooning chopped women up on canvas, charged early feminist art historians. The artist Ana Mendieta either fell off her 33rd floor balcony or was pushed by minimalist superstar Carl Andre, who was tried for it and found not guilty.

By the time #MeToo hit, transgression's sheen was already feeling pretty tarnished. #MeToo was about a lot of things and among them was a cultural referendum on the myth of male genius, which as thousands of first-person accounts have elaborated over the decades, is pretty frequently accompanied by sexual grabbiness and bad breath. Sexual transgressiveness has always been the perquisite of gross men in power, but there is also an added perk, which is that treating the boundaries of less powerful people as minor annoyances makes insecure men feel like creative geniuses, like artists and rock stars. Post #MeToo, the emblematic transgressor was starting to look less like Vito Acconci at Sonnabend and more like Dominique Strauss-Kahn at the Sofitel.

Apropos my young reverence for Acconci and his idioms, I didn't at the time ponder my own real-life experiences with real-life masturbators and stalkers. A committed truant and

Transgression, An Elegy

somewhat feral adolescent loner, I could often be found weekday afternoons in one or another of Chicago's seedy downtown movie palaces, where I would park myself in a mostly deserted theater to enjoy a double feature, or the DIY version, sitting though the same movie twice. The raincoat brigade had their plans, meaning solo men not infrequently scurrying into seats within my eyeline once the movie had started and commencing frantic activity in their laps. It took me a while to figure out what was going on — such things weren't covered in my junior high sex-ed classes. I would gather my belongings and move seats or sometimes flee to the ladies room.

Once, feeling aggrieved at having to move seats yet again, I deliberately dumped a large icy soda into the lap of a man I had taken for one of the miscreants. He yelped in outrage, which was thrilling and terrifying, though I wondered for long after whether I had possibly made a mistake. Maybe those teenage experiences of male performance art were buried somewhere in my psyche when I put together my undergraduate thesis show, a semiotic analysis of an obscene phone call I had received, accompanied by deliberately ugly staged photographs of what the caller said he wanted to do. Structuralism and semiotics were then conquering the art world and I liked the intellectual distance they provided, the tools to be cool about a hot subject. I liked the idea of transgressing the transgressor. On to grad school, triumphantly.

In the following years much of my work, even after decamping the art world, was ambivalently fascinated with transgression, sometimes the aesthetic version, sometimes the true-life exemplars. Critical theories that read real life as a "text" helped to blur the distinction, but so did everything else in the culture. I wrote about *Hustler* magazine, I wrote books devoted to adulterers, scandalizers, male miscreants, and the professor-student romance crackdown. Though I think of myself as a generally decorous person — only ever arrested once (teenager, charges expunged) — something drew me to indiscretion and imprudence. Envy, sublimated rage, desire, male impersonation? Let me get back to you on it.

The cultural genres that have flourished in the last few decades have likewise been the ones most dedicated to muddying the art-life distinction: the memoir explosion, autofiction, the psychobiographical/pathographical doggedness in criticism, confessional standup and the heirs of Spaulding Gray, along with the relentless first-person imperatives of social media, where everyone's now a "culture worker," everyone "curates" every-day life into pleasing tableaux for public display. Which means what for the fate of transgression, whose métier, as Martin Jay intimated, covertly relied on keeping the distinction intact?

The concurrent notable trend has been the outperfor-mance of the offense and umbrage sector, now overtaking pretty much everything in the cultural economy. To be sure, umbrage can be a creative force in its own right, as when in 2014 at Wellesley, a woman's college, students protested a painted bronze statue of a sleepwalking man in his underpants located outside the art museum, because it was regarded as potentially harmful to viewers. The man was balding, eyes closed, arms outstretched — not an especially imposing or threatening figure, in fact he appears quite vulnerable. A petition to move the statue inside the museum got over a thousand signatures.

Creative umbrage flourished more flamboyantly in 2013, when the Metropolitan Museum staged an exhibit of the

35

painter Balthus' work and included *Thérèse Dreaming*, with its notorious flash of the pubescent Thérèse's white panties smack in the center of the canvas. As to be expected, the Met attempted to accommodate offended sensibilities by posting a safety warning at the entrance to the exhibit advising that "some of the paintings in this exhibition may be disturbing to some visitors." Though the image of Thérèse is quite stylized, a petition called for the painting's removal because of "the current news headlines highlighting a macro issue about the safety and wellbeing of women of all ages." You'd have thought there was a living, breathing pubescent girl flay-legged in the museum (over eleven thousand signatures to date have concurred).

Speaking of artistic choices, I noted that the anti-Balthus petition was written in the first person, an aesthetic decision that every creative writer faces — whether or not to deploy that all-powerful "I." "When I went to the Metropolitan Museum of Art this past weekend, I was shocked to see a painting that depicts a young girl in a sexually suggestive pose," it read, in bold type and melodramatic prose as aesthetically stylized as Balthus' rendering of Thérèse, the degree of effrontery so precisely calibrated. If the painting was not going to be removed, the petition-writer offered another option: the museum should provide signage indicating that "some viewers find this piece offensive or disturbing, given Balthus' artistic infatuation with young girls."

The demand was that the painting be repackaged as a cautionary tale. And since we live in culturally democratizing times, *Thérèse Dreaming* now comes swathed in lengthy explanations. From the Met's website: "Many early twentieth-century avant-garde artists, from Paul Gauguin to Edvard Munch to Pablo Picasso, also viewed adolescent sexuality as a potent site of psychological vulnerability as well as lack of inhibition, and they projected these subjective interpretations into their work. While it may be unsettling to our eyes today, *Thérèse Dreaming* draws on this history." No longer will a viewer's eye be drawn to that glimpse of white panties and be unsettled, and wonder what to make of it. Goal to the offended, who have seized the license to be outrageous and impose their stories and desires on the polis, much as the transgressor classes once did. But let's not imagine there is any less cultural aggression or cruelty being unleashed here than before.

Trying to construct a timeline for this art-life blur, I recalled an earlier similar remonstrance, one that startled me at the time, given the source — but it now reads like a bellwether. This was Martin Amis, in his literary critic guise, grappling with what he named a "problem from hell" upon the publication in 2009 of his literary hero Nabokov's unfinished novel *The Original of Laura*. The problem wasn't precisely that the subject was the desire to sexually despoil very young girls, a preoccupation it shared with the canonical *Lolita* and four of Nabokov's other books, six in all. It was that as the aging Nabokov's talents drastically waned those "unforgivable activities" — the sexual despoiling stuff — were no longer absolved or wrestled with by the usual stylistic firepower, and what remained on the page was dismal squalor. Worse, *Laura's* stylistic failures, along with *Ada* before it — another late-career nymphet-obsessed ponderous mess — taints the other books. Even the great ones start feeling squalid by proximity, don't they?

Though Amis insists that he is making an aesthetic case and not a moral one — "in fiction, of course, nobody ever gets hurt" — as you watch him valiantly trying to pry the two apart, the critical performance is palpably anxious. He feints, he deflects, he finally states outright that it comes down to the truism that writers like to write about the things they like to think about, and without sufficient stylistic perfume to offset the foulness of the subject matter, what Nabokov was thinking about just smells bad. But admitting this means, effectively, retracting the license to transgress that Amis (and most of the literary world) once so appreciatively granted Nabokov, leaving the critic (and the rest of us) wallowing in "a horrible brew of piety, literal-mindedness, vulgarity and philistinism."

My own question is, what in the cultural ether pushed this anxiety to the forefront? Had the protective blockades once erected around the aesthetic become that much more porous since Nabokov's heyday? Literary criticism has always had the sociological move up its sleeve, available to whip out and flay transgressors as necessary — Irving Howe indicting Philip Roth as bad for the Jews, and so on. But when such a prominent writer decides, so late in the day, that Nabokov is bad for pre-teens, it does seem like some major sands have shifted. Reading Amis reread Nabokov's oeuvre through the lens of *Laura*, you notice the transgression jumping from the art to the artist, like a case of metaphysical fleas. We have left literature behind and been plummeted into the sphere of moral contagion. The anxiety isn't just that our glimpses of the violated bodies of pubescent girls have arrived too stylistically unadorned. I wonder if it is also that whatever's corrupt and ignoble in there will seep out and taint the reader.

If I understand him correctly Amis' problem from hell is something like this: What if there resides at the center of this deeply transgressive oeuvre not the "miraculously fertile instability" he reveres about Nabokovian language but, rather, the rigidity of a repetition compulsion?

Is this a general condition? I'm not sure, but other such "problems from hell" certainly seem to dot the recent social landscape, especially at the art-life checkpoints. When the comedian-genius Louis C.K. was exposed as a compulsive masturbator and encroacher on women in the wake of #MeToo, it naturally brought back my long-ago teenage movie theater experiences. I was fascinated by his fellow comedian Sarah Silverman's insouciant response. When asked by Louis if he could do it in front of her, Silverman would sometimes respond — at least so she reported — "Fuck yeah, I want to see that!" As she told it, it was a weird, interesting aesthetic experience, and she was Louis' equal in weirdness, no one's victim. Silverman had to quickly apologize to all the women who had not felt similarly — for one thing, it wasn't clear that everyone upon whom this lovely sight was bestowed had been asked for permission or felt able to refuse. Pathetic C.K. may have been, but he was still a comedy gatekeeper.

Of course he'd also been telling the world for decades exactly who he was, namely a self-loathing guy who was obsessed with masturbation. He did innumerable comedy routines and episodes of various shows devoted to masturbation. Apparently many of his fans — let's call them the aesthetic-autonomy diehards — thought this was "art," just a "bit," and were deeply disappointed in C.K. He was supposed to have been a feminist ally! He was supposed to be fucked up about women, but self-aware! He did comedy routines about how terrible men were at sex, and how grossly they behaved to women — and then he turned around and was gross!

The world is becoming a tough place for anyone who still wants to separate the artist from the art — then again, pretty few people any longer do. Creative writing students across the country now refuse to read Whitman, a man of the nineteenth century who, they believe, said some racist things in addition to the great poetry. I guess reading him now feels disgusting, as though a cockroach had crawled in your ear and deposited a bunch of racism that you are helpless to expunge.

Things were much less confusing when the purists were right-wingers, when the "moral majoritarians" railed against cultural permissiveness while concealing their private transgressions behind facades of public rectitude. I loved the last few decades of the twentieth century, when one after another fundamentalist minister was exposed as a scummy lying adulterer and the world made sense. The right was still at it throughout the 1990s, waging their losing culture wars — it was almost too easy to get them to huff and puff. When none other than the reptilian Rudolph Giuliani, then mayor of New York, threatened to shut down the Brooklyn Museum in retribution for an art exhibit he deemed offensive, the museum produced a yellow stamp announcing that the work in the exhibit "may cause shock, vomiting, confusion, panic, euphoria and anxiety." Note that as of 1999 it was still possible to be ironic about offending people, because offended people were generally regarded as morons.

The rise of identity politics, it is widely agreed, introduced a far more granular vocabulary of umbrage. Now it is the social justice left wielding the aesthetic sledgehammers and "weaponizing" offense. (Note, for the record, that the socialist left, young and old, those for whom class remains the primary category and think identity politics is just corporate liberalism, are not particularly on board with the new umbrage.) There was already a general consensus that pernicious racial and

40

ethnic stereotypes have been among the factors impeding social equality for marginalized groups. The last few decades have introduced a new vocabulary of cultural must-nots: cultural appropriation, microaggression, insensitivity. New prohibitions keep being invented, and political coherence is not required. An obviously antiracist artwork like Dana Schutz's painting *Open Casket*, which depicted Emmett Till's mutilated face and body and was included in the Whitney Biennial in 2017, could be accused by its critics of attempting to transmute "black suffering into profit and fun," because in the new configuration the feeling of being offended licenses pretty much anything. (Schutz had made it clear that the painting would not be sold.) Protestors blocked the painting from view and petitions demanded that it be destroyed. Offended feelings are like a warrant for the summary arrest of the perps, and prior restraint is expected: the offending thing should never have been said or seen. Culture is no longer where you go to imagine freedom, it's where you go for scenes of crime and punishment.

Speaking of political incoherence, the irony of the charges against Schutz was the degree to which they echoed the old miscegenation codes, as if Emmett Till's murder wasn't itself spurred by fears and prohibitions about racial mixing. It was the "one-drop rule" in reverse, except now a white woman was being accused of crossing the color line, of positioning herself too intimately to a black male body. The extremity of the accusations made the identity politics of the left seem stylistically indistinguishable from the identity politics of the right, both spawned from the same post-truth bubble — as with Swiftboating, Pizzagating, and "Lock Her Up." Throw some dirt around and see what sticks.

Meanwhile more terrible things have been happening.

"Transgression" has become the signature style of the alt-right and "alt-light" (those are the slightly less anti-Semitic and white supremacist ones). Now *they* are the rebellious, anti-establishment ones, gleefully offending everyone. Some even lay the blame for the stylistics of online troll culture — the alt-truth shitposting adopted so successfully by the current president and his basket of deplorables (to borrow Hillary Clinton's supremely self-annihilating phrase) — at the doorstep of the avant-garde. In *Kill All Normies*, Angela Nagle traces their antecedents to Sade, the Romantics, Nietzsche, the Surrealists, the Situationists, the counterculture and punk — culminating with far-right culture hero Milo Yiannopoulos, who also extolled the virtues of disrupting the status quo and upsetting the liberals, whom he saw as hegemonic. All was going well for Milo, the self-proclaimed "dangerous faggot," until he got a smidgen too dangerous by commending pedophilia, or so said his former patrons who quickly smote him into oblivion. Haha, their transgressive spirit is about an inch deep.

Yet the longstanding association of transgression with the left was always superficial and historically accidental. In Nagle's version, the alt-right crowd have simply veered toward nihilism in lieu of revolution. She even intimates that it was the virtue-signaling and trigger warnings of the touchy-feely left that gave us Donald Trump and the rest of the destructive right- wing ids; and this has made her persona non grata in certain leftish circles. However you draw your causality arrows, there's no doubt that the more fun the right started having, the more earnestly humorless the social justice types became, and the more aesthetically conservative. Especially problematic for the younger crowd are jokes: every comedy routine was now examined for transgressions, like a team of school nurses checking kindergarteners for head lice. Comedy is no longer any sort of protected zone, it's the front lines, with id-pol detectives on house-to-house searches to uncover humor offenses from decades past. Old jokes are not grandfathered in, obviously; old jokes are going to be judged by current standards. Irony has stopped being legible — it puts you on "the wrong side of history," a phrase you suddenly hear all the time, as though history always goes in the right direction.

In sum, transgressors are the cultural *ancien regime* who have reaped the spoils for far too long, and now had better watch their steps. Even France, proud home to Sade and Genet, is dethroning its transgressors and putting them on trial. This includes that most literary of pedophiles, the award-festooned novelist Gabriel Matzneff, currently in hiding in Italy, who used to have a lot of friends in high places despite (because of?) habitually foisting his sexual desires on teenage girls and under-age boys, then writing detailed accounts of his predilections. One of his former conquests, fourteen at the time of their affair, recently wrote her own bestselling book, titled *Consent*. Another, fifteen when they were involved and whose letters Matzneff appropriated and published (even putting her face on the cover of one of his novels — no, he didn't ask permission or even inform her), has also gone public. She attempted to do so previously, in 2004, but no one then cared or would publish her account.

But it's a new era: the transgressed-upon of the world are speaking, and the world is listening. This changes many things, profoundly. It's been a long time coming. As to whether injury will prove a wellspring of cultural vitality or a wellspring of

43

platitudes and kitsch, that is what's being negotiated at the moment. At the very least, trauma is more of an equal-opportunity creative force than inspiration or talent, which were handed out far more selectively. Trauma is a bigger tent. The injury and the wound — and importantly, the socially imposed injuries of race, ethnicity, gender, queerness — have long been paths to finding a voice, an intellectual "in." This is hardly new: wounds have long been sublimated into style or form — so argued Edmund Wilson, and before him Freud. It seems like injuries more frequently enter the cultural sphere minus the aesthetic trappings these days — perhaps there is more patience or attention for unembellished pain. The question we're left with is how much of the world can be understood from the standpoint of a personal injury: does it constrict or enlarge the cultural possibilities?

Reading about Matzneff, I'd been wondering what the French plan to do about Sade in the post -#MeToo era and was happy to stumble on an essay by Mitchell Abidor pondering the same question. An American who has translated many French avant-gardists and anarchists into English, Abidor rereads Sade through the lens of Jeffrey Epstein, concluding that it is impossible not to see Sade as Epstein's blueprint. His point is that Sade did not just fantasize on the page, he acted out what he wrote, kidnapping, sexually abusing, and torturing young girls, also numerous prostitutes, and a beggar named Rose Keller — women who supposedly didn't count, and don't count to Sade's legions of readers. Epstein's victims were, likewise, financially needy teenagers. Two sexually predatory rich guys separated by a few centuries, both monsters of privilege: Sade had his chateau, Epstein his townhouse and his island. Both were arrested and tried; both got out or escaped prison and did more of the same.

What is inexplicable for Abidor is how many of his fellow intellectuals fell under Sade's spell and became his great defenders, despite what a verbose and repetitive writer he is. They see him as an emissary of freedom — or as in Simone de Beauvoir's reading, at least it's on the itinerary. Abidor says that Sade's freedom is the freedom of a guard in a concentration camp who does what he likes to his victims because they cannot escape. It's not just the liberties of surrealism that Sade heralds, but also the death trap of fascism.

I arranged a coffee date with Abidor not long ago, wanting to meet this assassin of the avant- garde; he suggested a spot where old Brooklyn socialists congregate. He had become a despised figure on the Francophone left, he told me, glancing around nervously and spotting a few former compatriots. The old guard was furious at him for putting their revered transgressive lineage — Apollinaire, Bataille, Barthes, the heirs of Sade, to which they still cling — in such an ugly light. It is the question of our moment: who gets to play transgressor, and who is cast in the role of the transgressed upon. When transgressions — in art, in life, at the borders — repeat the same predictable power arrangements and themes, what's so experimental about that?

Yet putting it that way gives me a yucky tingle of sanctimony, a bit of the excess *amour-propre* that attends taking the "correct" position. What's left out of the anti-transgression story are the *rewards* of feeling affronted — how takedowns, shaming, "cancelling," the toolkit of the new moral majoritarians, invent new forms of cultural sadism rather than rectifying the old ones. All in a good cause, of course: inclusiveness, equality, cultural respect — so many admirable reasons!

The truant in me resents how much cultural real estate the anti-transgressors now command, while positioning

Transgression, An Elegy

themselves as the underdogs. Witness the new gatekeepers and moral entrepreneurs, wielding not insignificant amounts of social power while decrying their own powerlessness. And thus a new variety of hypocrite is born, though certainly no more hypocritical than the old hypocrites.

We used to know what transgression was, but that's not plausible anymore. Maybe violating boundaries was a more meaningful enterprise when bourgeois norms reigned, when liberal democracy seemed like something that would always endure. The ethos of transgression presumed a stable moral order, the disruption of which would prove beneficial. But why bother trying to disrupt things when disruption is the new norm, and permanence ever more of a receding illusion?

DAVID GROSSMAN

The Human Infinity: Literature and Peace

Writers often talk of the torments of writing, of "the fear of the blank page," of nights waking in a cold sweat because suddenly they see the weaknesses, the vulnerabilities, of the story that they have been writing, sometimes for years. This distress is certainly real, but I insist also upon the pleasures of creation, of inventing an entire fictional world out of thousands of facts and details. There is a particular kind of wonder that I feel when a character I have invented begins to overtake me, to run ahead and pull me forward: suddenly this imagined character knows more than I do about its own fate, its own future, and also about other characters in the story, and I must learn to follow, to catch up. In a way that I do not fully understand, my invented person infuses me with the materials of life, with ideas, with plot twists, with understandings I never knew I possessed.

A creative work represents, for me, the possibility of touching infinity. Not mathematical infinity or philosophical infinity, but human infinity. That is, the infinity of the human face. The infinite strings of a single heart, the infinity of an individual's intellect and understanding, of her opinions, urges, illusions, of his smallness and greatness, her power to create, his power to destroy — the infinity of her configurations. Almost every idea that comes to my mind about the character I am writing opens me up to more and more human possibilities: to a lush garden of forking paths.

"To be whole, it is enough to exist," wrote the poet Fernando Pessoa. This wonderful observation pours salt on the wounds of every writer who knows how difficult it is to translate a character born in the imagination into a character that contains even a particle of the Pessoan "wholeness," even a fraction of the fullness of life that exists in one single second of a living person. It is this wholeness — made up also of infinite flaws, with defects and deficiencies of both mind and body — to which a writer aspires. This is the writer's wish, this is the writer's compulsion: to reach that alchemical development at which suddenly, through the use of inanimate matter — symbols arranged on a page in a particular order — we have conjured into being a life. Writers who have written characters and dissolved into them and then come back into themselves; who have come back to find themselves now composed in part of their character; who know that if they had not written these characters they would not truly know themselves — these writers know the pleasures to be found in the sense of life's fullness that lives inside each of us.

It is almost banal to be moved by this, but I am: we, each and every one of us, are in fact a plenitude of life. We each contain an infinity of possibilities and ways of being inside life. Yet finally such an observation is not banal at all. It is a truth of which we regularly need to remind ourselves. After all, look how cautiously we avoid living all the abundance that we are, how we dodge so many of the possibilities that are broached by our souls, our bodies, our circumstances. Quickly, at an early age, we ossify, and diminish ourselves into a single thing, a "one," a this or a that, a clearly delineated being. Perhaps it is our desire not to face this confusing and sometimes deceptive welter within us that makes us lose some part of ourselves.

Sometimes the unlived life, the life we could have lived but were unable to live, or did not dare to live, withers inside us and vanishes. At other moments we may feel it stirring within, we may see it before our eyes, and it stings us with regret, with sorrow, with a sensation of squandered chances, with humiliation, even with grief, because something, or someone, was abandoned or destroyed. It might be a passionate love that we renounced in favor of calm. Or a profession wrongly chosen, in which we molder for the rest of our lives. Or an entire life spent in the wrong gender. It could be a thousand and one choices that are not right for us, which we make because of pressures and expectations, because of our fears, our desire to please, our submission to the assumptions and the prejudices of our time.

Writing is a movement of the soul directed against such a submission, against such an evasion of the abundance within us. It is a subversive movement of the writer made primarily against himself. We might imagine it as a tough massage that the writer keeps administering to the stale muscles of his cautious, rigid, inhibited consciousness. In my own case,

The Human Infinity: Literature and Peace

writing is a free, supple, easy movement along the imaginary aces between the little boy I still am and the old man I already am, between the man in me and the woman in me, between my sanity and my madness, between my inner Jew-in-a-concentration-camp and my inner commander of that camp, between the Israeli I am and the Palestinian I might have been.

I remember, for example, the difficulties I experienced when I wrote Ora, the main character in *To the End of the Land*. For two years I struggled with her, but I was unable to know her completely. There were so many words surrounding her, but they had no living focal point. I had not yet created in her the living pulse without which I cannot believe in — I cannot be — the character I am writing. Finally I had no choice but to do what any decent citizen in my situation would do: I sat down and wrote her a letter, in the old fashioned way, with pen and paper. Ora, I asked, what's going on? Why won't you surrender?

Even before I had finished the letter, I had my answer. I grasped that it was not Ora who had to surrender to me, but I who had to surrender to her. In other words, I had to stop resisting the possibility of Ora inside me. I had to pour myself into the mold of she who was waiting deep inside me, into the possibility of a woman within me — more, the possibility of this particular woman within me. I had to be capable of allowing the particles of my soul — and of my body too — to float free, uninhibited and incautious, without narrow-minded, practical, petty self-interest, toward the powerful magnet of Ora and the rich femininity that she radiates. And from that moment on she practically wrote herself.

There are extra-literary implications to my discovery of another interiority, a human plenitude, within my writing self. A few years ago, I gave a speech on Mount Scopus in Jerusalem. It was late afternoon, the sun was preparing to set. The mountains of Moab behind me, at the edge of the horizon, would soon be painted red, and gradually turn paler until their outlines blurred and darkness finally descended. I spoke about my submission to Ora, and then I turned to the reality of our lives here in Israel — to what we Israelis somewhat grimly call *hamatzav*, or the Situation. It is a word that in Hebrew alludes to a certain stability, even stasis, but is in fact a euphemism for more than a century of bloodshed, war, terror, occupation, and deadly fear. And most importantly, fatalism and despair.

Perhaps there is no more appropriate place to talk about the Situation than on Mount Scopus, because I find it difficult to gaze at that beautiful landscape in a way that is disconnected from reality, from the fact that we are looking a what is called, in conflict-speak, "Ma'aleh Adumim and Zone E-1." That location is precisely the point at which many Israelis, including government officials, wish to begin the annexation of the West Bank. Others, myself included, believe that such an act would put an end to any chance of resolving the conflict and doom us all to a life of ceaseless war.

On Mount Scopus our reality seems all the more densely present, containing not only the Hebrew University, with all the wisdom, knowledge, humanity, and spirit of freedom that it has amassed for almost a century, but also the three thousand Bedouins in the adjacent desert — men, women and children, members of a tribe that has lived there for generations, who are denied their rights and citizenship, and subjected to constant abuses, the purpose of which is to remove them from

51

this place. They, too, are part of the Situation. They, too, are our situation: our writing on the wall.

Fifty years ago, after the end of the Six-Day War, in the amphitheater on Mount Scopus, Lieutenant-General Yitzhak Rabin, the Chief of Staff who oversaw Israel's victory, accepted an honorary degree, and his speech on that day reverberated throughout the country. Rabin's address was an attempt — a successful attempt — to construct the collective consciousness and the collective memory of his contemporaries. I was thirteen at the time, and I still remember the chills it sent down my spine. Rabin articulated for us Israelis the sense that we had experienced a miracle, a salvation. He gave the war and its results the status of a morality tale that almost exceeded the limits of reality and reason.

When we said "The finest to the Air Force," Rabin said in his speech, referring to a famous recruitment slogan, "we did not mean only technical aspects or manual skills. We meant that in order for our pilots to be capable of defeating all the enemies' forces, from four states, in a matter of hours, they must adhere to the values of moral virtue, of human virtue." He continued: "the platoons that broke enemy lines and reached their targets..... were borne by moral values and spiritual reserves — not by weapons and combat techniques."

It was a breathtaking speech. (It was written by Chief Education Officer Mordechai Bar-On.) It was impassioned but not over the top, although those were euphoric days. God is not mentioned even once. Nor is religious faith. Even the experience of finally touching the stones of the Western Wall is described not in a religious context, but rather in an historical one: "the soldiers touched right at the heart of Jewish history." Just imagine the florid prominence that would be given to religion, to holiness, to God, in such a speech today.

Rabin also declared that "the joy of victory seized the entire nation. But despite this, we have encountered..... a peculiar phenomenon among the soldiers. They are unable to rejoice wholeheartedly. Their celebrations are marred by more than a measure of sadness and astonishment... Perhaps the Jewish people has not been brought up to feel, and is not accustomed to feeling, the joy of the occupier and the victor," But as Rabin uttered those words, the embryonic occupation had already begun to grow. It already contained the primary cells of every occupation — chauvinism and racism, and in our case also a messianic zeal. And there also began to sprout among us, without a doubt, "the joy of the occupier" which Rabin believed we were incapable of feeling, and which ultimately led, through a long and torturous path, to his assassination twenty-eight years later.

It appears that no nation is immune to the intoxication of power. Nations stronger and more steadfast than ours have not been able to withstand its seductions, much less the small state of a nation such as ours, which for most of its history was weak and persecuted, and lacked the weapons, the army, the physical force with which to defend itself. A nation that in those early days of June, 1967 believed it was facing a real threat of annihilation, and six days later had become almost a small empire.

Many years have passed since that victory. Israel has evolved unrecognizably. The country's accomplishments in almost every field are enormous and should not be taken for granted. And neither should the larger saga: the Jewish people's return to its homeland from seventy diasporas, and the great things it has created in the land, are among humanity's most incredible and heroic stories. Without denying the tragedy that this historical process has inflicted upon the Palestinians, the natives of this land, the Jewish people's transition from a people of refugees and displaced persons, survivors of a vast catastrophe, into a flourishing, vibrant, powerful state — it is almost incomprehensible.

In order to preserve all the precious and good things that we have created here, we must constantly remind ourselves of what threatens our future. I am not referring only to the external dangers that we face. I have in mind, first foremost, the distortion that damages the core of Israel's being — the undeniable fact that it is a democracy that is no longer a democracy in the fullest sense of the word. It is a democracy with anti-democratic illusions, and very soon it may become an illusion of democracy.

Israel is a democracy because it has freedom of speech, a free press, the right to vote and to be elected to parliament, the rule of law and the Supreme Court. But can a country that has occupied another people for fifty years, denying its freedom, truly claim to be a democracy? Can there be such an oxymoronic thing as an occupier democracy?

A hundred years of conflict. Fifty years of occupation. Beyond the details of the political debate, we must ask: what do those fifty years do to a person's soul, and to the soul of a nation? To both the victim and the victimizer? I return here to the process of artistic creation that I described earlier — the axiomatic sense of a person's infinity, whoever that person may be. In the context of our present historical circumstances, I summon back the writer's understanding that beneath every human story there is another human story. I insist again upon the archeological nature of human life, which is composed of layers upon layers of stories, each of which is true in its own way. The imagination of all these layers and truths, upon which the writer relies for the richness of his creation, has another name: empathy.

But a life lived in constant war, when there is no genuine intent to end the war — a life of fear and suspicion and violence — does not recognize or encourage or tolerate this abundance of human realities. It is by definition a morally unimaginative life, a life of restriction. It narrows the soul and contracts the mind. It is a life of crude stereotypical perceptions, which in denying another people's humanity promotes a more general denial of all otherness and difference. This is the sort of climate that finally gives rise to fanaticism, to authoritarianism, to fascist tendencies. This is the climate that transforms us from human beings into a mob, into a hermetic people. These are the conditions under which a civil, democratic, and pluralistic society, one that draws its strengthen from the rule of law and an insistence on equality and human rights, begins to wither and fray.

Can we say with confidence that Israeli society today is sufficiently aware of the magnitude of *these* dangers? Is it fully capable of confronting them and contending with them? Are we sure that those who lead us even want to contend with them?

I began with the literary and I end with the real — with the reality of our lives. In my view they are inseparable. We do not know, of course, who will stand here fifty years from now. We cannot predict the problems that will consume them and the hopes that will animate them. To what extent, for example, will technology have changed people's souls, and even their bodies? Which dimensions and dialects will have been added to the Hebrew language that they will speak, and

The Human Infinity: Literature and Peace

which will have disappeared? Will they utter in their daily speech the world *shalom*? Will they do so happily, or with the pain of disappointment and squandered opportunities? Will *shalom* be spoken naturally, with the ease of the commonplace — routinely, as if peace had become a way of life?

I do not know what sort of country the Israel of the future will be. I can only hope with all my heart that the man or woman who will stand in my place will be able to say, with their head held high and with genuine resolve: *I am a free person, in my country, in my home, in my soul.*

RAMACHANDRA GUHA

The Indian Tragedy

Earlier this year, the Republic of India turned seventy. On
January 26, 1950, the country adopted a new Constitution,
which severed all ties with the British Empire, mandated multi-
party democracy based on universal adult franchise, abolished
caste and gender distinctions, awarded equal rights of citizen-
ship to religious minorities, and in myriad other ways broke
with the feudal, hierarchical, and sectarian past. The chairman
of the Drafting Committee was the great scholar B. R. Ambed-
kar, himself a "Dalit," born into the lowest and most oppressed
strata of Indian society, and representative in his person and
his beliefs of the sweeping social and political transformations

that the document promised to bring about.

The drafting of the Constitution took three whole years. Between December 1946 and December 1949, its provisions were discussed threadbare in an Assembly whose members included the country's most influential politicians (spanning the ideological spectrum, from atheistic Communists to orthodox Hindus and all shades in between) as well as leading economists, lawyers, and women's rights activists. When these deliberations concluded, and it fell to Ambedkar to introduce the final document — with 395 Articles and 12 Schedules, the longest of its kind in the history of the democratic world — to the Assembly, he issued some warnings, of which at least one was strikingly prophetic. He invoked John Stuart Mill in asking Indians not "to lay their liberties at the feet of even a great man, or to trust him with powers which enable him to subvert their institutions." There was "nothing wrong," said Ambedkar, "in being grateful to great men who have rendered life-long services to the country. But there are limits to gratefulness." His worry was that "for India, *bhakti*, or what may be called the path of devotion or hero-worship, plays a part in its politics unequalled in magnitude by the part it plays in the politics of any other country. Bhakti, in religion, may be a road to the salvation of the soul. But in politics, bhakti or hero-worship, is a sure road to degradation and to eventual dictatorship."

When he spoke those words, Ambedkar may have had the possible deification of the recently martyred Mahatma Gandhi in mind. But his remarks seem uncannily prescient about the actual deification of a later and lesser Gandhi. In the early 1970s, politicians of the ruling Congress Party began speaking of how "India is Indira and Indira is India," a process that culminated, as Ambedkar had foreseen, in political degradation and eventual dictatorship. In June 1975, Prime Minister Indira Gandhi suspended civil liberties, jailed all opposition politicians, and imposed a strict regime of press censorship. This was a time of fear and terror, which lasted almost two years, and ended when Mrs. Gandhi — provoked in part by criticism from Western liberals and in part by her own conscience — ended the Emergency and called for fresh elections, which she and her party lost.

If one is reminded of Ambedkar's warning when reflecting on the career of Indira Gandhi, it brings to mind even more starkly the career of India's current Prime Minister, Narendra Modi. In terms of their upbringing and ideological formation, no two Indian politicians could be more different than Modi and Mrs. Gandhi. One witnessed enormous hardship while growing up; the other was raised in an atmosphere of social and economic privilege. One had his worldview shaped by the many years he spent in the Hindu supremacist organization, the Rashtriya Swamaysevak Sangh (RSS); the other was deeply influenced by her father, Jawaharlal Nehru, India's first Prime Minister, who detested the RSS. One has no family; the other had children and grandchildren. One had to work his way up the ladder of Indian politics, step by step; the other had a lateral entry into a high position purely on account of her birth.

And yet there are significant commonalities. These very different personal biographies notwithstanding, it has long seemed to me that there are striking similarities in their political styles. Back in 2013, I wrote in *The Hindu* that "neither Mr. Modi's admirers nor his critics may like this, but the truth is that of all Indian politicians past and present, the person Gujarat Chief Minister most resembles is Indira Gandhi of the period 1971-77. Like Mrs. Gandhi once did, Mr. Modi seeks to make his party, his government, his administration and his country an extension of his personality." At the time the article was published, the Chief Minister of the western state of Gujarat was making his national ambitions explicit. Fifteen months later, Narendra Modi became Prime Minister of India, his Bharatiya Janata Party (BJP) winning, under his leadership, the first full majority in Parliament of any party since 1984. Modi's time in office has seemed to confirm the parallels between him and Indira Gandhi. As she had once done, he cut the other leaders in his party down to size; sought to tame the press; used the civil services, the diplomatic corps and the investigative agencies as political instruments; and corralled the resources of the state to build a personality cult around himself.

In January 2020, when the Republic of India turned seventy, Narendra Modi was facing his first serious challenge since he became Prime Minister six years earlier. Modi's ideological formation in the RSS had convinced him that India's destiny was to be a "Hindu Rashtra" — a theocratic state run by Hindus and in the interests of Hindus alone. In his first term as Prime Minister, Modi had kept these beliefs largely under wraps. But when he was re-elected with a large majority in May 2019, the majoritarian agenda came strongly to the fore. On August 5, 2019, the government of India abrogated Article 370 of the Constitution, which accorded cultural and political autonomy to the state of Jammu and Kashmir. This was done unilaterally, without consulting the people of the state (as the law required them to do). It was a wanton intervention in one of the most dangerous areas of contention in the world. The state of Jammu and Kashmir was abruptly converted into a mere "Union Territory." It was henceforth to be ruled directly by New Delhi, preparatory to what the rulers of India called a "full integration with the Nation," which the people of the Kashmir Valley feared would result in an invasion of their land by grasping outsiders and a transformation of this Muslim-majority state into a Hindu colony.

Worse was to follow. In early December, the Parliament passed the Citizenship Amendment Act (CAA). This sought to give Indian citizenship to people fleeing religious persecution in three countries: Bangladesh, Pakistan, and Afghanistan. The Act was illogical — it ignored the largest group of stateless refugees in India, the Tamils from Sri Lanka; and it was also spiteful, for it had carefully specified that Muslims from any country, however persecuted they might be, would not get refuge in India. Moreover, the Modi government announced that the CAA was to be accompanied by a National Register of Citizens (NRC), which would demand, from everyone living in India, documentary proof of Indian parentage, length of residence in India, and so on. Those who were unable to "prove" to the government's satisfaction that they had these papers would be declared illegal immigrants. But if they had the good luck to be Hindu, Buddhist, Jain, Sikh, Parsi, or Christian — that is, anything other than Muslim — they could apply to become Indians under the Citizenship Amendment Act. The CAA was a clear violation of Articles 14 and 15 of the Constitution, which promised equality before the law and prohibited discrimination on the grounds of religion. Following on the downgrading of Jammu and Kashmir from full statehood to Union Territory status, the passing of the CAA represented a further — and fuller — ethnonationalist step towards the construction of a Hindu State. Were it to be implemented along with the NRC, as top government ministers had repeatedly threatened, Muslims would become, formally as well as legally, second-class citizens.

61

The abrogation of Jammu and Kashmir's statehood was met with muted protest by intellectuals and human rights activists, and little else. Prime Minister Modi and his hardline Home Minister, Amit Shah, clearly hoped that these new changes in the citizenship laws would likewise go uncontested. They were wrong. There were widespread protests across India, led at first by students, but then with a wide cross-section of the citizenry joining in. Elderly Muslim women staged a peaceful sit-in for weeks in South-East Delhi, this act inspiring many similar sit-ins in other cities and towns. The state sought to suppress the protests through colonial-era laws prohibiting gatherings of more than five people, but the non-violent and collective civil disobedience continued. Although the Acts targeted Muslims specifically, many non-Muslims participated in the protests, outraged at this whole stigmatization of their fellow citizens merely on account of their faith. The countrywide upsurge within India was accompanied by widespread condemnation of the Modi Government in the international press. This intensified when President Donald Trump visited India in late February, his visit coinciding with religious rioting in Delhi, the country's capital, in which radical Hindus were the main perpetrators and Muslims the main sufferers.

At this time, it seemed that the degradation of Indian democracy had been arrested. The pushback against the cult of personality and the ideology of Hindu supremacy had begun and seemed as if it might perhaps accelerate. Then came the pandemic, and India, and the world, gasped in wonder and horror. I shall return to the consequences of covid19 for my country at the end of my essay. But first I wish to outline the historic roots of the struggle that has been unfolding within India, between the capacious ideals with which the Indian republic was founded and the majoritarian tendency that seeks to replace it. We must begin with the intellectual and moral origins of the Constitutional idea of India, which Narendra Modi and his party wish to consign to the ash heap of history.

Like the railways, electricity, and the theory of evolution, nationalism was invented in modern Europe. The European model of nationalism sought to unite residents of a particular geographical territory on the basis of a single language, a shared religion, and a common enemy. To be British, you had to speak English, and minority tongues such as Welsh and Gaelic were either suppressed or disregarded. To be properly British you had to be Protestant, which is why the king was also the head of the Church, and Catholics were distinctly second-class citizens. Finally, to be authentically and loyally British, you had to detest France.

Now, if we go across the Channel and look at the history of the consolidation of the French nation in the eighteenth and nineteenth centuries, we see the same process at work, albeit in reverse. Citizens had to speak the same language, in this case French, so dialects spoken in regions such as Normandy and Brittany were sledgehammered into a single standardized tongue. The test of nationhood was allegiance to one language, French, and also to one religion, Catholicism. So Protestants were persecuted. Likewise, French nationalism was consolidated by identifying a major enemy, although who this enemy was varied from time to time. In some decades the principal adversary was Britain; in other decades, Germany. In either case, the hatred of another nation was vital to affirming faith in one's own nation.

This model — a single language, a shared religion, a common enemy — is the model by which nations were created throughout Europe. And it so happens that the Islamic Republic of Pakistan is in this respect a perfect European nation. Pakistan's founder, Mohammad Ali Jinnah, insisted that Muslims could not live with Hindus, so they needed their own homeland. After his nation was created, Jinnah visited its eastern wing and told its Bengali residents they must learn to speak Urdu, which to him was the language of Pakistan. And, of course, hatred of India has been intrinsic to the idea of Pakistan since its inception.

Indian nationalism, however, radically departed from the European template. The greatness of the leaders of our freedom struggle — and Mahatma Gandhi in particular — was that they refused to identify nationalism with a single religion. They further refused to identify nationalism with a partic-ular language, and — even more remarkably — they refused to hate their rulers, the British. Gandhi lived and died for Hindu-Muslim harmony. He liked to emphasize the fact that his party, the Indian National Congress, had presidents who were Hindu, Muslim, Christian, and Parsi. Nor was Gandhi's nationalism defined by language. As early as the 1920s, Gandhi pledged that when India became independent, every major linguistic group would have its own province. But perhaps the most radical aspect of the Indian model of nationalism was that hatred of the British was not intrinsic to it. Indian patriots detested British imperialism, they wanted the Raj out, they wanted to reclaim this country for its residents — but they did so non-violently, and while befriending individual Britons. (Gandhi's closest friend was the English priest C.F. Andrews.) Moreover, they wished to get the British to 'Quit India' while retaining the best of British institutions. An impartial judiciary, parliamentary democracy, the English language, and not least the game of cricket; these are all aspects of British culture that Indians sought to keep after the British had themselves left.

British, French, and Pakistani nationalism were based on paranoia, on the belief that all citizens must speak the same language, adhere to the same faith, and hate the same enemy. Indian nationalism, by contrast, was based on a common set of values. During the non-cooperation movement of 1920-1921, people all across India came out into the streets, gave up jobs and titles, left their colleges, and courted arrest. For the first time, the people of India had the sense, the expectation, the confidence that they could create their own nation. In 1921, when non-cooperation was at its height, Gandhi defined *Swaraj* (Freedom) as a bed with four sturdy bed-posts. The four posts that held up Swaraj, he said, were non-violence, Hindu-Muslim harmony, the abolition of untouchability, and economic self-reliance.

When the Republic of India was created in 1950, its citizens sought to be united on a set of ideals: democracy, religious and linguistic pluralism, caste and gender equality, and the removal of poverty and discrimination. The basis of citizenship was adherence to these values, not to a single religion, a shared faith, or a common enemy. I would describe this founding model of Indian nationalism as constitutional patriotism, because it is enshrined in our Constitution. Its fundamental features are outlined below.

The first feature of constitutional patriotism is the acknowledgement and appreciation of our inherited and shared diversity. In any major gathering in a major city — say, in a music concert or in a cricket match — people who compose the crowd carry different names, wear different clothes, eat different kinds of food, worship different gods (or no god at all), speak different languages, and fall in love with different kinds of people. They are a microcosm not just of what India is, but of what its founders wished it to be. For the founders of the Republic had the ability (and the desire) to endorse and emphasize our diversity. Multiethnicity was not the problem, it was the solution. As the poet Rabindranath Tagore once said about my country, "no one knows at whose call so many streams of men flowed in restless tides from places unknown and were lost in one sea: here Aryan and non-Aryan, Dravidian, Chinese, the bands of Saka and the Hunas and Pathan and Mogul, have become combined in one body." An appreciation of this rich inner diversity means that we understand that no type of Indian is superior or special because they belong to a particular religious tradition or because they speak a certain language. Patriotism was defined by the allegiance to the values of the Constitution, not by birth, blood, language or faith.

The stress on cultural diversity and religious pluralism was all the more remarkable because it came in the wake of the savage rioting of Partition. Gandhi and the Congress had hoped for a united India, but in the event, when the British left in August 1947, they divided the country into two sovereign nations, India and Pakistan. The division was accompanied by ferocious clashes between Hindus and Muslims, in which an estimated one million people died and more than ten million people were made into refugees. But Pakistan was explicitly created as a homeland for Muslims, whereas India resolutely refused to define itself in majoritarian terms. As the country's first Prime Minister, Jawaharlal Nehru, wrote to the Chief Ministers of States in 1947, "We have a Muslim minority who are so large in numbers that they cannot, even if they want to, go anywhere else. They have got to live in India. ... Whatever the provocation from Pakistan and whatever the indignities and horrors inflicted on non-Muslims there, we have got to deal with this minority in a civilized manner. We must give them security and the rights of citizens in a democratic State."

The second feature of constitutional patriotism is that it operates at many levels. Like charity, it begins at home. It is not just worshipping the national flag that makes you a patriot. It is how you deal with your neighbors and your neighborhood, how you relate to your city, how you relate to your state. In America, which is professedly one of the most patriotic countries in the world, every state has its own flag. And some states of India also have their own flag, albeit informally. Every November 1, when the anniversary of the formation of my home state, Karnataka, is celebrated, a red-and-yellow flag is unfurled in many parts of the state. It is not Anglicized upper-class elites such as myself who display the state flag of Karnataka, but shopkeepers, farmers, and autorickshaw drivers.

Patriotism can operate at multiple levels. The Bangalore Literary Festival (which is not sponsored by large corporations but is crowd-funded) is an example of civic patriotism. The red-and-yellow flag of Karnataka is an example of provincial patriotism. Cheering for the Indian cricket team is an example of national patriotism. This patriotism can operate at more than one level — the locality, the city, the province, the nation. A broad-minded (as distinct from paranoid) patriot recognizes that these layered affiliations can be harmonious, complementary, and reinforce one another.

67

The model of patriotism advocated by Gandhi and Tagore was not centralized but disaggregated. And it helped make India a diverse *and* united nation. Look at what is happening in Spain today. Why are so many Catalans keen on a nation of their own? Because they believe that they have been denied the space and the freedom to honorably have their own language and culture within a united Spain. The centralized Spanish state came down so hard that the Catalans had a referendum in which many of them insisted upon nothing less than independence. Had the Republic of Spain been founded and run on Indian principles, this may not have happened. Had Pakistan not imposed Urdu on Bengalis, they may not have split into two nations a mere quarter of a century after independence. Had Sri Lanka not imposed Sinhala on the Tamils, that country may not have experienced thirty years of ethnic strife. India has escaped civil war and secession because its founders wisely did not impose a single religion or single language on its citizens.

One can be a patriot of Bangalore, Karnataka, and India — all at the same time. Yet the notion of a world citizen is false. The British-born Indian J.B.S. Haldane put it this way: "One of the chief duties of a citizen is to be a nuisance to the government of his state. As there is no world state, I cannot do this.... On the other hand I can be, and am, a nuisance to the government of India, which has the merit of permitting a good deal of criticism, though it reacts to it rather slowly. I also happen to be proud of being a citizen of India, which is a lot more diverse than Europe, let alone the U.S.A, USSR or China, and thus a better model for a possible world organization. It may, of course, break up, but it is a wonderful experiment. So I want to be labelled as a citizen of India." A citizen of India can vote in local, provincial and national elections.

In between elections he or she can affirm their citizenship (at all these levels) through speech and (non-violent) action. But global citizenship is a mirage, or a cop-out. It is only those who cannot or will not identify with locality, province, or nation who accord themselves the fanciful and fraudulent title of "citizen of the world."

The third feature of constitutional patriotism, and this again comes from people such as Gandhi and Tagore, is the recognition that no state, no nation, no religion, and no culture is perfect or flawless. India is not superior to America necessarily, nor is America superior to India necessarily. Hinduism is not superior to Christianity necessarily, nor is Islam superior to Judaism necessarily. The fourth feature is this: we must have the ability to feel shame at the failures of our state and society, and we must have the desire and the will to correct them. The most egregious aspects of Indian culture and society are discrimination against women and the erstwhile "Untouchable" castes. A true patriot must feel shame about them. That is why our Constitution abolished caste and gender distinctions. Yet these distinctions continue to pervade everyday life. Unless we continue to feel shame, and act accordingly, they will continue to persist.

The fifth feature of constitutional patriotism is the ability to be rooted in one's culture and one's country while being willing to learn from other cultures and other countries. This, too, must operate at all levels. Love Bangalore but think what you can learn from Chennai or Hyderabad. Love Karnataka, but think what you can learn from Kerala or Himachal Pradesh. Love India, but think of what you can learn from Sweden or Canada. Here is Tagore, in 1908: "If India had been deprived of touch with the West, she would have lacked an element essential for her attainment of perfection. Europe now has her lamp ablaze. We must light our torches at its wick and make a fresh start on the highway of time. That our forefathers, three thousand years ago, had finished extracting all that was of value from the universe, is not a worthy thought. We are not so unfortunate, nor the universe so poor." And here is Gandhi, thirty years later: "In this age, when distances have been obliterated, no nation can afford to imitate the frog in the well. Sometimes it is refreshing to see ourselves as others see us."

As a patriotic Indian, I believe that we must find glory in the illumination of any lamp lit anywhere in the world.

The crisis of contemporary India may be described succinctly: the model of constitutional patriotism is now in tatters. It is increasingly being replaced by a new model of nationalism, which prefers and promotes a single religion, Hinduism, and proclaims that a true Indian is a Hindu. This new model also elevates a single language — Hindi. It insists that Hindi is the national language, and whatever the language of your home, your street, your state, you must speak Hindi also. Thirdly, this model luridly presents a common external enemy — Pakistan.

Whether they acknowledge it or not, those promoting this new model of Indian nationalism are borrowing (and more or less wholesale) from nineteenth-century Europe, where nationalism, for all its cultural riches, culminated in disaster. And to the template of a single religion, a single language, and a common enemy they have added an innovation of their own — the branding of all critics of their party and their leader as "anti-national." This scapegoating comes straight from the holy book of the RSS, M.S. Golwalkar's *Bunch of Thoughts*, which appeared in 1966. In his book Golwalkar identified three "internal threats" to the nation — Muslims, Christians, and Communists. Now, I am not a Muslim, a Christian, or a Communist, but I have nonetheless become an enemy of the nation. This is so because any critic, any dissenter, anyone who upholds the old ideal of constitutional patriotism, is considered by those in power and their cheerleaders to be an enemy of the nation.

In the wonderful Hindi film *Newton,* one character says, *"Ye desh danda aur jhanda se chalta hai,"* the stick and the flag define this country. This line beautifully captures the essence of a paranoid and punitive form of nationalism, based on the blind worship of the sole and solitary flag, and on the use of the stick to harass those who do not follow or obey you. This new nationalism in India is harsh, hostile, and unforgiving. The name by which it should be known is certainly not patriotism, and not even nationalism. It should be called jingoism.

The dictionary defines a patriot as "a person who loves his or her country, especially one who is ready to support its freedoms and rights and to defend it against enemies or detractors." Note the order: love of country first, support of freedom and rights second, and defense against enemies last. And what is the dictionary definition of jingoist? One "who brags of his country's preparedness for fight, and generally advocates or favors a bellicose policy in dealing with foreign powers; a blustering or blatant 'patriot'; a Chauvinist." The order is reversed: first, boasting of the greatness of one's country; then advocating attacking other countries. No talk of rights or freedom, or of love either. Patriotism and jingoism are antithetical varieties of nationalism. Patriotism is suffused with love and understanding. Jingoism is motivated by hatred and revenge.

71

I have already outlined the founding features of constitutional patriotism. What are the founding features of jingoism? First, the belief that one's religion, culture, and nation (and leader) are perfect and infallible. Second, the demonization of critics as anti-nationals and Fifth Columnists. Rather than engage critics in debate, hyper-nationalists harass and intimidate them, through the force of the state's investigating agencies and through vigilante armies if required.

In recent years, Indian nationalism has been captured by its perverted jingoist version. But the country remains some sort of democracy, where the jingoist version is popular among a large section of the population and has been brought to power through the ballot box. How did this come to pass? Why is it that the party of the Hindu Right has so many supporters in India today?

I believe there are four major reasons why jingoism is ascendant in India, while constitutional patriotism is in retreat. The first is the hostility of the Indian left to our national traditions. The Communist parties are still an important political force in India. They have been in power in several states. Their supporters have historically dominated some of our best universities, and been prominent in theater, art, literature, and film. But the Indian left, sadly and tragically, is an anti-patriotic left. It has always loved another country more than its own.

That country used to be the Soviet Union, which is why our Communists opposed the Quit India Movement, and launched an armed insurrection on Stalin's orders in 1948, immediately after Gandhi was murdered. Later the country that the Communists loved more than India was China; and so, in 1962, they refused to take their homeland's side in the border war of that year. Still later, when the Communists became disillusioned with both Soviet Union and China, they pinned their faith on Vietnam. When Vietnam failed them, it became Cuba; when Cuba failed them, it became Albania. When I was a student in Delhi University, there was a Marxist professor who taught that Enver Hoxha was a greater thinker than Mahatma Gandhi. But then Albania failed, too. So now the foreign country that our comrades love more than India is — what else? — Venezuela. The late (and by me unlamented) Hugo Chavez was venerated on the Indian left. If you think Modi is authoritarian, then Chavez was Modi on steroids — the ur-Modi. The megalomaniac Chavez destroyed the Venezuelan economy and Venezuelan democracy, and yet he continued to be worshipped by Indian leftists young and old.

The degradation of patriotism in India has also been abetted by the corruption of the Congress Party. The great party which led India's freedom movement has in recent decades been converted into a single family. I have spoken of how the Left chooses its icons, but in some ways the Congress is even worse. When it was in power, it named everything in sight after Jawaharlal Nehru or his daughter or his grandson. Why couldn't the new Hyderabad international airport have been named after the Telugu composer Thyagaraja or the Andhra patriot T. Prakasam? Why Rajiv Gandhi? Likewise, when the new sea link in Mumbai had to be given a name, why couldn't the Congress consider Gokhale, Tilak, Chavan, or some other great Maharashtrian Congressman? Why Rajiv Gandhi again?

Many, indeed most, of the icons of the national movement belonged to the Congress party. But the Congress has abandoned and thrown them away because it is only Nehru,

73

Indira, Rajiv, Sonia, and now Rahul that matter to them. (The only Congressman outside the family they are willing to acknowledge is Mahatma Gandhi, because even they can't obliterate him from their party's history.) If someone like Hugo Chavez is adored so much by Indian leftists, then obviously this will help the jingoists — and likewise, if the Congress government named all major schemes and sites after a single family, ignoring even the great Congress patriots of the past, then that would give a handle to the jingoists, too. The corrupt and sycophantic culture of the Congress Party is a disgrace. When I made a sarcastic remark on Twitter about Rahul Gandhi becoming Congress president, someone put up a chart listing the presidents of the BJP since 1998 — Bangaru Laxman, Jana Krishnamurthi, L.K. Advani, Rajnath Singh, and so on, the last name on the list being Amit Shah, followed by "party worker," whereas the presidents of the Congress in the same period were "Sonia Gandhi, Sonia Gandhi, Sonia Gandhi...Rahul Gandhi...."

A third reason for India's jingoist fate is, of course, that jingoism is a global phenomenon, manifest in the rise of Trump, Brexit, Le Pen, Erdogan, Putin, Bolsonaro, Orban, and the rest, all of whom pursue a xenophobic, paranoid, often hateful form of nationalism. The rise of such narrow-minded nationalism elsewhere encourages the rise of jingoism in India to match or rival it, and friendships between the authoritarians are naturally formed. And finally we must note the rise of Islamic fundamentalism in our own backyard. Over the decades, the state and society of Pakistan have become dangerously and outrageously Islamist. Once they persecuted Hindus and Christians; now they persecute Ahmadiyyas and Shias, too. And Bangladesh is also witnessing a rising tide of violence against religious minorities. Since religious fundamentalisms are rivalrous and competitive, every act of violence against a Hindu in Bangladesh motivates and emboldens those who want to persecute Muslims in India.

The Bharatiya Janata Party, Modi's party, and its mother organization, the RSS, claim to be authentically Indian, and damn the rest of us as foreigners. Intellectuals such as myself are dismissed as bastard children of Macaulay, Marx, and Mill. As an historian, however, I would say that it is the ideologues of the RSS who are the true foreigners. Their model of nationalism — one religion, one language, one enemy — is foreign to the Indian nationalist tradition, to the Gandhian model of nationalism which was an innovative indigenous response to Indian conditions, designed to take account of cultural diversity and to tackle caste and gender inequality.

If the RSS model of nationalism is inspired by Europe, their model of statecraft is Middle Eastern in origin. From about the eleventh to the sixteenth century, there were states where monarchs were Muslims and the majority of the population was Muslim, but a substantial minority was non-Muslim, composed mainly of Jews and Christians. In these medieval Islamic states, there were three categories of citizens. The first-class citizens were Muslims, who prayed five times a day and went to mosque every Friday, and who believed that the Quran was the word of God. The second-class citizens were Jews and Christians whose prophets were admired by Muslims, as preceding Mohammed, the last and the greatest prophet. Third-class citizens were those who were neither Jews nor Christians nor Muslims. These were the unbelievers, the Kafirs.

In medieval Muslim states, Jews and Christians, the 'People of the Book', were defined as 'Dhimmi', which in Arabic means 'protected person'. As a protected person, they had certain rights. They could go to the synagogue or church; they could own a shop; they could raise a family. But other rights were denied them. They could not enroll in the military, serve in the government, be a minister or prime minister. Nor, unlike Muslims, could they convert other citizens to their faith. Such was the second-class status of Jews and Christians in medieval Islam. This model was applied in Medina and Andalusia, and in Ottoman Turkey. While Kafirs (including Hindus) had to be suppressed and subdued, Jews and Christians could practice their profession and raise their family, so long as they did not ask for the same rights as Muslims.

This is precisely how the Hindu Right wants to run politics in the Republic of India today. Muslims in modern India now must be like Jews and Christians of the medieval Middle East. If Muslims accept the theological, political and social superiority of Hindus they shall not be persecuted or killed. But if they demand equal rights they might be.

The new jingoism in India is a curious mixture of outdated ideas of nationalism mixed with profoundly anti-democratic ideas of citizenship. And yet it finds wide acceptance. But its popularity does not mean that we should surrender to it, or that it is legitimate, or that it is genuinely Indian. For the Republic of India is an idea as well as a physical and demographic entity. Those of us who are constitutional patriots must continue to stand up for the values on which our nation was nurtured, built and sustained. If the BJP and the RSS are to continue unchecked and unchallenged, they will destroy India, culturally as well as economically.

The political and ideological battle in India today is between patriotism and jingoism. The battle is currently asymmetrical, because the jingoists are in power, and because they have a party articulating and imposing their views. The constitutional patriotism of Gandhi, Tagore, and Ambedkar has no such party active today. The Communists followed Lenin and Stalin rather than Gandhi and Tagore, and the Congress has turned its back on its own founders. But while Indians patriots may not currently have a credible party to represent them, they are — as the protests in December 2019 and January 2020 showed — willing to carry on the good fight for constitutional values even in its absence. Those protests admirably demonstrated that citizenship is an everyday affair. It is not just about casting your vote once every five years. It is about affirming the values of pluralism, democracy, decency, and non-violence every day of our lives.

It was ordinary citizens, not opposition parties, who presented the Modi government with the first major challenge since it came to power in 2014. The challenge was political, it was moral, it was constitutional. But then came the pandemic, and the balance shifted once more, back in favor of the ruler and the regime.

In the beginning of this essay I spoke of how Narendra Modi's was the second great personality cult in the history of the Indian republic. The first, that of Indira Gandhi, had led to the imposition of a draconian Emergency. When Modi became Prime Minister, I myself had no illusions about his centralizing instincts, yet the historian in me was alert to how the India of 1975 differed from the India of 2014. When the Emergency was imposed by Indira Gandhi, her Congress Party ruled the Central Government in New Delhi, and also enjoyed power — on its own or in coalition — in all major states of the

Union except Tamil Nadu. On the other hand, when Narendra Modi became Prime Minister, many states of the Union were outside the control of his Bharatiya Janata Party.

My hope therefore was that our federal system would serve as a bulwark against full-blown authoritarianism. In Narendra Modi's first term as Prime Minister, the BJP won elections in some major states while losing elections in other major states. Even after Modi and the BJP emphatically won re-election at the national level in 2019, they could not so easily win power in the state Assembly elections that followed. The anti-CAA protests further strengthened one's faith in the democratizing possibilities of Indian federalism. Large sections of the citizenry rose up in opposition to a discriminatory act that seemed grossly violative of the Constitution. The Chief Ministers of several large states were also opposed to the new legislation. This seemed like further confirmation that the present was not the past. Indira Gandhi could do what she did only because her party controlled both the Center as well as all the states in India (Tamil Nadu's DMK Government having been dismissed a few months after the Emergency was promulgated). But this was not the case with Modi and his BJP.

The covid19 pandemic has changed this calculus. It has given Narendra Modi and his government the opportunity to weaken the federal structure and radically strengthen the powers of the Center vis-a-vis the States. They have used a variety of instruments to further this aim. They have invoked a "National Disaster Management Act" to suspend the rights of States to decide on the movement of peoples and goods, the opening and closing of schools, colleges, factories, public transport, and so on, and to centralize all these powers in the Central Government, effectively in the person of the Prime Minister. They have further postponed the disbursal of funds already due to the States as their share of national tax collections — substantial revenues, amounting to more than Rs 30,000 crores ($40 billion), which, if released, could greatly alleviate popular distress. They have created a new fund at the Centre, the so-called PM-CARES, which discriminates against the States in that it gives special exemptions (to write off donations as "Corporate Social Responsibility") that are denied to those who wish to donate instead to the Chief Minister's Fund of their own states. This fund gives the Prime Minister enormous discretionary power in disposing of thousands of crores of rupees as he pleases. The functioning of the fund is shrouded in secrecy, with even the Comptroller and Auditor General are not allowed to audit it.

This heartless exploitation of the covid19 pandemic to weaken federalism has been accompanied by a systematic attempt to further build up the personality cult of the Prime Minister. State-run television, senior Cabinet Ministers, and the ruling party's IT Cell have all been working overtime to proclaim that only Modi can save India. Even as lives are lost and livelihoods are destroyed by the pestilence, the Prime Minister is going ahead with an expensive plan to redesign India's capital, New Delhi. This will destroy the historic centre of one of the most beautiful cities in the world, and replace it with a series of concrete and glass blocks. The showpiece of this project is a grand new house for the Prime Minister himself. As one writer has remarked, "the biggest irony remains that a prime minister from the humblest of backgrounds should yearn for a house on Rajpath, no less, to endorse his vision of personal greatness and legacy. Would Emmanuel Macron demand and, more importantly, *get* a house on the Champs Elysées? Can even Trump order himself a second home on the Mall?" The Prime Minister's own justification of the project is that it was to mark not a personal but a national milestone—the seventy-fifth anniversary of Indian independence. This is disingenuous, because past anniversaries overseen by past Prime Ministers had not called for such a spectacular extravaganza. Apparently, what was good enough for Indira Gandhi and I. K. Gujral won't quite do for the great Narendra Modi.

The architecture of power reveals a lot about those who wield it, and Modi's redesign of New Delhi brings to mind not so much living Communist autocrats as it does some dead African despots. It is the sort of vanity project, designed to perpetuate the ruler's immortality, that Felix Houphouet-Boigny of the Ivory Coast and Jean Bédel-Bokassa of the Central African Republic once inflicted on their own countries. (I refer readers to V. S. Naipaul's great essay "The Crocodiles of Yamoussoukro.") And as this wasteful and pharaonic self-indulgence proceeds, an economy that was already flailing has been brought to the brink of collapse by the pandemic. The ill-planned lockdown has led to enormous human suffering. Working-class Indians, already living on the edge, are now faced with utter destitution. In his speeches to the nation since the pandemic broke, the Prime Minister has repeatedly asked Indians to sacrifice — sacrifice their time, their jobs, their lifestyles, their human and cultural tendency to be gregarious. Surely it is past time for citizens to ask the Prime Minister to sacrifice something for the nation as well. Anyway, he won't.

When he was first elected Prime Minister in 2014, Narendra Modi said that he wished to redeem India from the thousand years of slavery it had suffered before his election. My son, the novelist Keshava Guha, commented at the time that Modi saw himself as the first Hindu leader to have the entire country under his command. Nehru and Indira —

the two prime ministers of comparable popularity before
him — were to him fake Hindus, their faith corrupted by
their English education and what he and his party saw as an
unconscionable partiality towards Muslims. My son is right.
Narendra Modi thinks of himself as doing what medieval
chieftains such as Shivaji and Prithviraj Chauhan could
not do — make the whole country a proud Hindu nation.
His followers call him *Hindu Hriday Samrat,* the Emperor
of Hindu Hearts, but it would be more precise to call him
Hinduon ka Samrat, an Emperor for and of Hindus. He is, to
himself and millions of others, Emperor Narendra the First.
The history of personality cults tells us that they are always
disastrous for the countries in which they flourished.
Narendra Modi will one day no longer be Prime Minister, but
when will India recover from the damage he has done to its
economy, its institutions, its social life, and its moral fabric?

The Indian Tragedy

THOMAS CHATTERTON WILLIAMS

The Peripheralist

During Black History Month earlier this year, the New York City streetwear boutique Alife brought to market a limited set of six heather grey hooded sweatshirts made of heavyweight, pre-shrunk fourteen-ounce cotton fleece, with ribbed cuffs and waist. The garments, whose sole decorative flourish were the names of black cultural icons — from Harriet Tubman to Marcus Garvey — screen-printed in sans-serif across the chest, retailed for $138 a pop and sold out promptly. Of the six men and women featured in the campaign, there was only one writer: James Baldwin.

On Instagram, to promote its product, the brand deployed

a short clip of Baldwin's extraordinary debate against William F. Buckley, Jr., on the theme "Is the American Dream at the Price of the Negro?" at the Cambridge Union in 1965 — a grainy YouTube gem beloved by aficionados that was recently brought to mainstream attention in Raoul Peck's documentary *I Am Not Your Negro*. A friend messaged the post to me accompanied by the Thinking Face emoji, finger and thumb against the chin, a look of skepticism. I responded differently. I wasn't incredulous about this cultural commoditization: Baldwin's name had long since become a kind of shorthand, an emblem of a position — a way, increasingly fashionable in its own right, to signal which side of any number of contested issues of the day one wishes to come down on.

Jean-Paul Sartre once described the young Albert Camus as "the admirable conjunction of a man, of an action, and of a work," by which he meant, simply, that there was no daylight between his life and his ideas, and it was impossible to think of one without conjuring the other. In an essay for the *New York Review of Books* in 1963, in which she contrasted morally virtuous if artistically second-tier writers ("husbands") with perverse and reckless but exciting geniuses ("lovers"), Susan Sontag took Sartre's observation as a springboard for a merciless review of Camus' posthumously published *Notebooks*. "Today only the work remains," she asserted. "And whatever the conjunction of man, action, and work inspired in the minds and hearts of his thousands of readers and admirers cannot be wholly reconstituted by experience of the work alone." Elsewhere she expanded the critique:

> Whenever Camus is spoken of there is a mingling of personal, moral, and literary judgment. No discussion of Camus fails to include, or at least suggest, a tribute to

his goodness and attractiveness as a man. To write about Camus is thus to consider what occurs between the image of a writer and his work, which is tantamount to the relation between morality and literature. For it is not only that Camus himself is always thrusting the moral problem upon his readers. ... It is because his work, solely as a literary accomplishment, is not major enough to bear the weight of admiration that readers want to give it. One wants Camus to be a truly great writer, not just a very good one. But he is not. It might be useful here to compare Camus with George Orwell and James Baldwin, two other husbandly writers who essay to combine the role of artist with civic conscience.

What occurs between the image of a writer and her work: the same problem afflicts the reception of Sontag herself. Still, she has a point. She writes elsewhere that Camus, as a novelist, attained a different altitude than either Orwell or Baldwin, but I have never been able to unsee that dressing down of all three "husbandly" men, Baldwin in particular, or to entirely dislodge him from her framework. As the years accumulate and Baldwin's image and moral authority become ever more flattened, ever more frequently appropriated for the preoccupations of the present moment — with the most casual assumption of self-evidence — something in Sontag's refusal to play along nags at me. In any event, and even though Baldwin, later in his career, wrote that he had "never esteemed [Camus] as highly as do so many others," I have always found it useful to think of him as a kind of Harlem companion to the scholarship student from Algeria who became — and then failed to remain — his nation's moral compass, who was blessed with the same gift of preternatural eloquence, and who struggled mightily and elegantly and perhaps vainly to bridge the disparate worlds that he straddled.

Like Camus, a decade his senior, James Baldwin was born in the first quarter of the twentieth century in squalor, about as far as possible — spiritually if not physically — from the glittering intellectual circles that he would come to dominate. Both young men were total packages, publishing stories, novels, plays, essays, reviews and reportage after having exploded on the scene fully formed in their twenties. Likewise, both men rose to global stardom outside their home countries, specifically in Paris, and peaked at an age when others only start to hit their stride — more or less around forty. Unlike Camus, Baldwin was not exactly fatherless, but it was necessary for him to eliminate one such figure after another to make space in his life for his own prodigious talent. In this sense, he was every bit the "first man" that Camus intended. By the time that Baldwin died of stomach cancer in the sunbaked Mediterranean village of Saint-Paul-de-Vence — not so far from the equally picturesque medieval town of Lourmarin, where Camus invested his Nobel money and is buried—he too was regarded as *passé* by a generation of readers no longer interested in reconciling differences or avoiding conflict. "Unfortunately, moral beauty in art — like physical beauty in a person — is extremely perishable," Sontag warned.

Baldwin did have the good fortune to have won at least two very influential younger champions in Henry Louis Gates, Jr. and Toni Morrison. But it was not at all a foregone conclusion that he would become, in the next three decades, nothing less than the pop culture patron saint of an entire generation of black (and increasingly non-black)

The Peripheralist

artists, activists, and writers, in America and beyond. I am referring to the generation that came of intellectual age during the Obama presidency and the Black Lives Matter movement, which defined this decade's response to the spate of highly publicized police and vigilante killings of unarmed African Americans, beginning with Trayvon Martin's murder in Sanford, Florida in 2012. The enormous renewal of attention paid to Baldwin — which, at least until the coronavirus catapulted *The Plague* back onto bestseller lists around the world, had eluded Camus — has certainly been merited and illuminating. It has also been reductive and disturbing.

Poor, black, and not straight — intersectional *avant la lettre* — Baldwin fits seamlessly, as very few icons from the past are able to do, into the readymade template of our era's obsession with identity. (Even Sontag, a near-exact contemporary who outlived him by almost twenty years, could not entirely bring herself to admit that she was gay.) Books about Baldwin abound, biographical and literary and political studies, and films too: a cottage industry of Baldwiniana has emerged over the past decade. The most sensational entry in the contest for Baldwin's halo would have to be Ta-Nehisi Coates' *Between the World and Me*, his letter to his teenaged son that was formally modeled on the first section of Baldwin's book *The Fire Next Time*, called "My Dungeon Shook: an open letter to my nephew." The motor of Coates' essay was the question that Baldwin debated with Buckley — is the American Dream at the price of the Negro? In his own response to that question, Coates divided America into two essentialized camps, the "Dreamers" and a permanent black underclass. *Between the World and Me* went on to become one of the most widely read and discussed works of nonfiction in the new century.

In the book's sole blurb, the late Morrison herself enthused: "I've been wondering who might fill the intellectual void that plagued me after James Baldwin died. Clearly it is Ta-Nehisi Coates." More than anything else, that endorsement bound the two men together in the public's imagination. In his biography of Balwin, which appeared last year, Bill V. Mullen goes so far as to argue that *Between the World and Me* "was singularly responsible for the rediscovery of Baldwin by the Black Lives Matter movement." Whether or not that is true, five years out a certain irony is clear: Morrison's remark and Coates' success had an even greater impact on the way we perceive Baldwin than the way we do Coates.

Despite the hard-won optimism and ardent emphasis on reconciliation and regeneration through love that distinguishes his work, there is an undeniably pessimistic strain in Baldwin that often rings prophetic today. Drawing on this latter element alone, Coates captured and vocalized the profound disappointment provoked by the many limitations of the first black presidency. *Between the World and Me*, which so frankly and forcefully embodied the rage and justifiable frustration of an historically oppressed people with a rising set of expectations, rhetorically homed in on a single (mostly but not entirely late-phase) blue note in Baldwin's catalogue of sonorities. If there is a problem here, it is not that Coates' version of Baldwin rings altogether false. But it is tendentiously selective. It is a simplifying and coarsening distillation of a versatile and multifaceted writer, a supple and self-contradictory writer, into a single dark and haranguing register. In the process we are made to sacrifice a large amount of the complexity that made the author of *Giovanni's Room* and *Another Country* so special and difficult to pin. Baldwin is revered, but he is lost.

Consider also that Oscar-nominated Baldwin documentary, *I Am Not Your Negro*. Though a decade in the making, the project arrived at and helped to define the Baldwin renaissance. The film takes as its impetus Baldwin's thirty-page unfinished manuscript, *Remember This House*, which he described in a letter to his agent in 1979 as an exploration of race in America told through the assassinations of three prominent Civil Rights leaders: Medgar Evers, Malcolm X, and Martin Luther King, Jr. Onto this frame Peck grafts footage of Baldwin at roundtables and debates, familiar and jarring archival clips of violent white reaction to Civil Rights progress, such as school and bus integration, as well as contemporary shots of charged police confrontations with activists in Ferguson and elsewhere. There are no interviews with scholars and experts, no talking heads. Peck calculates correctly that Baldwin's words alone will carry the film (he is the sole writer credited on the project), whether spoken directly or read with understated authority by the actor Samuel L. Jackson. The effect is exhilarating — Baldwin's language is always captivating and lucid; he needs no translation or amplification. Even the wildly charismatic Jackson refrains from any attempt to compete with the words that he reads, which were written by a former child preacher in Harlem who was one of the few great writers in recent memory to be an equal or better public speaker, a distinction that the film makes thrillingly apparent.

Yet *I Am Not Your Negro* inadvertently makes manifest some of the incongruities between the smooth new radical mythology of the writer and the man as he actually existed and co-existed with the cultural forces and major personalities of his era. Though it purports to tease out important connections — "I want these three lives to bang against each other," Baldwin writes of the project — we learn very little about the relationship between him and the trio of martyrs he set out to examine in *Remember This House*. This is both because those leaders, while they knew and understood each other, did not really constitute a fraternity of any sort, and also — perhaps more importantly — because it can be expedient to avoid the complexity and contradictions of Baldwin's own insecure position within the actually existing black America, to and from which he remained throughout his adulthood a permanent "transatlantic commuter."

Of the three, he may have experienced the most straight-forward fellowship with the Mississippi activist Medgar Evers, the youngest of the group and the first to be murdered. Malcolm X was explicit, however, that what he sought was a "real" revolution, not the "pseudo revolt" of someone like James Baldwin. And Martin Luther King, Jr., as Douglas Field shows in *All Those Strangers: The Art and Lives of James Baldwin*, once balked — in a conversation taped by the F.B.I. — at appearing alongside the writer on television, claiming to be "put off by the poetic exaggeration in Baldwin's approach to race issues." It is hard to imagine that he could have been unaware that Baldwin was being denigrated as "Martin Luther Queen" in civil-rights circles.

89

Baldwin himself was understandably eager to emphasize and even embellish his connection to such extraordinary and sacri-ficial figures, especially King, but their realities were highly incommensurate on a variety of levels. In his memoir *No Name in the Street*, in 1972, there is a revealing set piece in which Baldwin writes about buying a nice dark-blue suit for a sched-uled appearance with King at Carnegie Hall. Two weeks later, after the latter was brutally assassinated, it would be Baldwin's attire for his funeral. Early in the Peck film we hear Baldwin worry over his role as a "witness" and not an "actor" in the convulsions of his time, only to resolve the apparent discrepancy by declaring that the two roles are separated by a "thin line indeed." In his attempts to write himself over that line and into proximity with men like Evers, King, and Malcolm and by extension into the center of the civil rights struggle — to collapse that space between man, action, and work — Baldwin at once underestimated a crucial distinction (as well as his own specialness) while also betraying his insurmountable distance from all of them. Darryl Pinckney, in a review of the Library of America's edition of Baldwin's writings, kindled to Baldwin's comment to a newspaper journalist that he would never be able to wear that suit again:

> A friend of Baldwin's, a US postal worker whom he rarely saw, had seen the newspaper story and, because they were the same size, asked for the suit that to Baldwin was "drenched in the blood of all the crimes of my country." Baldwin went up to Harlem in a hired "Cadillac limousine" in order to avoid the humiliation of watching taxis not stop for him, a black man. His life came into the "unspeakably respectable" apartment of his friend like "the roar of champagne and the odor of brimstone." He characterizes himself as he assumes he must have appeared to his friend's family: "an aging, lonely, sexually dubious, politically outrageous, unspeakably erratic freak."

> His friend had also "made it" — holder of a civil-service job; builder of a house next to his mother's on Long

90

Island. Baldwin was incredulous that his friend had no interest in the civil rights struggle. They got into an argument about Vietnam. Baldwin says he realized then that the suit belonged to his friend and to his friend's family. "The blood in which the fabric of that suit was stiffening was theirs," and the distance between him and them was that they did not know this.

The story is tortured and yet, regardless of Baldwin's outrage at indifference or his identification with slain civil rights leaders, there is something wrongly insinuating about his depicting his scarcely worn suit as drenched and stiffening with blood, even metaphorical blood. People still remember what Jesse Jackson's shirt looked like after King was shot.

This slightly frivolous side of Baldwin can just be glimpsed in *I Am Not Your Negro* (and is almost totally absent from the new hagiography). "I was never in town to stay," he admits on the film, and after Evers' death we do hear Jackson read, "Months later, I was in Puerto Rico, working on a play," as the camera reveals a sparkling beachscape. But he assumes his comparative privilege in *No Name in the Street,* where he notes that, when King was murdered, he was ensconced in Palm Springs, working on an unrealized screenplay for *The Autobiography of Malcolm X.* After the emotional and rhetorical shift to Black Power at the end of the '6os, many of Baldwin's contemporaries and descendants wrote him off — much the same way that intellectuals and radicals in Algeria and Paris turned their backs on Camus — considering him too enamored of his own voice and far too comfortable in the white world. *No Name in the Street,* like much of Baldwin's later output, can be read as a kind of overture to these critics, a capitulation to the new rules of engagement.

"I was in some way in those years, without realizing it, the great white hope of the great white father," Baldwin concedes. "I was not a racist, or so I thought. Malcolm was a racist, or so they thought. In fact we were simply trapped in the same situation." In actual fact their situations were very different and those differences are worth thinking through — not wishing away — because they help to explain why their worldviews differed, too. Baldwin was in London when Malcolm was murdered. In the epilogue of *No Name in the Street*, just a beat after he writes that "the Western party is over, and the white man's sun has set. Period," he signs off "New York, San Francisco, Hollywood, London, Istanbul, St. Paul de Vence." Unlike Malcolm X, there were plenty of lovely and welcoming places where James Baldwin could go, Pinckney mordantly notes, "to remind himself that he felt trapped."

Yet he did not invent his own marginality. It is no exaggeration to say that he was in some crucial ways homeless. In 1950, with a reasoning that anticipates the desire of today's #ADOS movement to disentangle the all-American experience of descendants of slaves from any larger pseudo-biological notion of international blackness — to say nothing of that infinitely fuzzier category "people of color" — Baldwin wrote in his essay "Encounter on the Seine" that "they face each other, the Negro and the African, over a gulf of three hundred years — an alienation too vast to be conquered in an evening's good will, too heavy and too double-edged ever to be trapped in speech." In Paris, he discovered what he could not recognize under the specific conditions of racial bigotry in New York City, and what he could never entirely disavow once he had experienced it: "I proved, to my astonishment, to be as

American as any Texas G.I. And I found that my experience was shared by every American writer I knew in Paris."

That revelation comes in *Nobody Knows My Name*, his phenomenal second essay collection: "Like me, they had been divorced from their origins, and it turned out to make very little difference that the origins of white Americans were European and mine were African — they were no more at home in Europe than I was." *This* is the Baldwin that the new revival has tended to gloss over or outright ignore. It is what distinguishes Baldwin from so many of his contemporaries and ours. This is the mature Baldwin, the wise Baldwin, the Baldwin who seethes at injustice but is not duped by the excesses of radicalism. It is the writer whose message — while not quite tailor-made to sell sweatshirts — is ultimately persuasive and always necessary. There can be an uncanny Benjamin Button-sense to reading Baldwin in chronological order: it can feel as if the young man and not the elder is the all-accomplished, all-knowing sage. Here is that young-old man in his astonishing debut collection, *Notes of a Native Son*, recalling his birthday in 1943, which also happened to be the day that his father died and his sister was born. Riots in Harlem had erupted after a white police officer and a black soldier clashed in a hotel lobby in a dispute over a woman:

> Negro girls, white policemen, in or out of uniform, and Negro males — in or out of uniform — were part of the furniture of the lobby of the Hotel Braddock and this was certainly not the first time such an incident had occurred. It was destined, however, to receive an unprecedented publicity, for the fight between the

The Peripheralist

policeman and the soldier ended with the shooting of the soldier. Rumor, flowing immediately to the streets outside, stated that the soldier had been shot in the back, an instantaneous and revealing invention, and that the soldier had died protecting a Negro woman. The facts were somewhat different — for example, the soldier had not been shot in the back, and was not dead, and the girl seems to have been as dubious a symbol of womanhood as her white counterpart in Georgia usually is, but no one was interested in the facts. They preferred the invention because the invention expressed and corroborated their hates and fears so perfectly.

Later in the essay, in words he would live by to the end, he writes, "In order really to hate white people, one has to blot out so much of the mind — and the heart — that this hatred becomes an exhausting and self-destructive pose." And he continues, magnificently: "That bleakly memorable morning I hated the unbelievable streets and the Negroes and whites who had, equally, made them that way. But I knew that it was folly, as my father would have said, this bitterness was folly. It was necessary to hold on to the things that mattered. The dead man mattered, the new life mattered; blackness and whiteness did not matter; to believe that they did was to acquiesce in one's own destruction."

I would like to believe that Baldwin never grew out of such views, that he remained an outsider — a peripheralist, as my own father might say — his entire life; and that this is one of the reasons he lived out his final seventeen years in Provence and could never quite bring himself back to America. He paid huge costs to remain semi-aloof, one of which might be the risk of permanent misunderstanding, even in his posthumous

94

homecoming — but I am convinced that this ability to stand apart, this refusal to be completely subsumed and taken over by any group or collectivity, is what ultimately spared him from the all-consuming identity myopia that plagued his era and now plagues ours. He was not a Black Muslim or a Black Panther, he observed, "because I did not believe all white people were devils and I did not want young black people to believe that." The simple decency of that sentence still holds the power to shock. It is the kind of correct-to-the-point-of-seeming-naïve insight that puts me in mind of Camus, the belief of a naturally humane and moral man, which we are desperately in need of in this age of opportunism and distrust.

None of this is to imply that Baldwin was ever less than lucid about the nature and tenacity of American racism. Baldwin in his nobility was nobody's fool. One of the most powerful sequences in *I Am Not Your Negro* is instructive about what makes him, today, such an irresistible figure. Here at last we see him in crackling black-and-white in the company of two of the three martyrs. Here we encounter the "conjunction of man, action, and work" of which Sontag spoke. On a panel moderated by the sociologist E. Franklin Frazier — there was so much aggregated brilliance and iconography assembled there! — a weary-looking King and an implacable Malcolm appear as dignified props for an immensely thoughtful Baldwin, who speaks stirringly of the "vast, heedless, unthinking, cruel white majority." Peck cuts to recent black-and-white images of contemporary American police on a war footing, storming through the streets of Ferguson. "I'm terrified at the moral apathy," Baldwin says, "these people have deluded themselves for so long that they really do think I'm not human. It means that they have themselves become moral monsters." Now the screen floods with color as nostalgic mid-century shots of an all-white beauty pageant, and young white women frolicking in spotless ensembles against a radiant blue sky, wash over the viewer. The dissonance of the juxtaposition is excruciating, undeniable.

How are we ever to find our way out of this conundrum? Baldwin hit upon some of the answers. Late in life he seemed to return to a complex understanding of struggle that contrasts with the victim-oppressor binary to which the discourse that overtook him adheres. "It seemed to me that if I took the role of a victim then I was simply reassuring the defenders of the status quo," he told The *Paris Review* shortly before he died. "As long as I was a victim they could pity me and add a few more pennies to my home-relief check. Nothing would change in that way. ... It was beneath me to blame anybody for what happened to me." And in "Letter from a Region in My Mind," his essay in *The New Yorker* in 1962 that became *The Fire Next Time*, he was even clearer. "For the sake of one's children, in order to minimize the bill that *they* must pay, one must be careful not to take refuge in any delusion," he wrote. "And the value placed on the color of the skin is always and everywhere and forever a delusion," he continued. "I know that what I am asking is impossible. But in our time, as in every time, the impossible is the least that one can demand."

A dozen years later the Israeli-Palestinian writer Emile Habibi coined the wonderful term "pessoptimist" for the title of a satirical novel. I cannot think of a better way to describe the mottled sensibility and variegated conscience that Baldwin brought to black American life and letters. He was repulsed by the stark, cliché-ridden, and fatalistic "Afro-pessimism" that we have become conditioned to espouse, and to tweet; nor was his understanding of race anything like the Panglossian self-hating optimism for which contemporaneous critics such as Eldridge Cleaver excoriated him. To reduce him to either pole in Habibi's paradox is as irresponsible as it is boring. A great deal hangs on the proper interpretation of James Baldwin's work and legacy. Even more than Malcolm X or Martin Luther King, Jr., and certainly more than Ralph Ellison, his principal African American rival in talent, James Baldwin has become one of the primary arenas in which the most urgent questions — the meanings of the past, the possibilities of the future — of black American life are being contested today. These are not idle feuds. The stakes of getting his reputation right extend well beyond literary disputations.

Last May, the excruciating videotaped killing of George Floyd, a forty-six-year-old black man in Minneapolis on whose neck a white police officer kneeled for nearly nine minutes, was yet another brutal and galvanizing cause for pessimism, as Baldwin would rightly have told us. It is at once astonishing and unbearable that our society (and not just white society, as George Zimmerman and other killers "of color" grimly attest) can still produce so many instances of appalling cruelty and injustice, instances which disproportionately target blacks. And yet even as we condemn such evil, our indignation cannot support a total or unending negativity. Baldwin would have admonished us about this, too. It would be just as disastrous a misjudgment of the schizophrenic American reality to argue that nothing (or next to nothing) has changed, that "lynchings" continue to define the black experience some two decades into the twenty-first century, as it would be to dismiss

97

the very specific and incontrovertible familiarity and dread with which so many black Americans viewed that stomach-turning footage from Minneapolis. What is so challenging — but all the more essential for its difficulty — for its absurdity, you could say — is to keep in mind two competing ideas simultaneously. The fight for justice must not end merely in blind revenge or catharsis. The struggle demands not just fury and resentment, but also hope and wisdom.

In maintaining such ambiguity, in defending such complexity, we are left with a single abiding truth: evil is always with us because it is one of the permanent conditions of humankind. Black people — like all other peoples forced to recognize up close the mixed-up character of life, its inextricable tangle of lights and darks — must become connoisseurs of pessimism and optimism to equal degrees. In his moral and intellectual capaciousness, Baldwin models this pessoptimistic mentality on and off the page. In this way his work (as opposed to the compressed and glib image that we are increasingly sold) is mimetic of American reality itself — plenty of which may turn out to be irreconcilable in the end, but none of which is ever enough to justify a single response in every season. Whatever our way out of our racial pain, it will be complicated and fitful and without fully satisfying once-and-for-all resolutions. Much like the context that created him, it is not necessary or even desirable to admire everything that James Baldwin said or did. But he exists to discomfit us, and to call us beyond tidy conclusions and easy emotions. He is forever inconvenient, which is why he is exactly what we need.

HANNAH SULLIVAN

From 2020

1.
The first half having been
given up to space, I decided
to devote my remaining
life to time, this thing we live
in fishily or on like moss
or the spores of a stubborn
candida strain only to be
gored or gaffed, roots
fossicked out by rake or have
our membranes made so permeable
by -azole drugs the contents
of the cell flood everywhere.

The bubble gun I'd bought
on Amazon had come, so
flushed, time's new novitiate,
I stood outside the door
in velour slippers with a plastic
wedge, from M&S, the toes
gone through, and practised
pulsing softly on the trigger,
pushing dribbly hopeless sac
shapes out, dead embryos
that managed all the same
to right themselves to spheres,
and bob as bubbles do, the colour

of a rainbow minced or diced
into the ornamental tree, or else
just brim the fatal fence, most
out of reach of the toddler
capering side to side to keep
his balance on the grass, one
snotty finger prodding like a
rapper turned jihadist's threat
of threat and all, ten seconds in,
unskinned of radiance,
re-rendered air.

This would have been in that
sad hobbled stretch of week
between a Sunday Christmas
and new year, my friends all
40+, harassed by infants, joylessly
still slugging Côte de Beaune
and fennel-roasted nuts, the liver
detox books not downloaded
to app but only browsed by phone
in the dark mornings, slitless.
(I lay there worrying at my own
which had the meaty bigness
underrib of foie gras entier.
The pillow case smelled horsey,
sheets unchanged, the laundry
everywhere, mountainously.)

It wasn't till my birthday,
Jan 3, when schools went back,
search engines saw a volume

spike for 'custody' and gifs of
sullen cats with emery boards
explained the dead-eyed un-
sheathed fear produced by credit
card repayment plans and pissing
on ketosis sticks that the month
could manifest the rawness
of new year: poverty then,
and mock exams; now, enzyme
supplements, and softening
the 11s, scooped one layer
deeper by all that red wine,
by summer's oxidative damage.

2.
The dry trees lolled in drunken
groups outside front gates,
waiting for the council van
to come. Today, which was
my birthday, macerated shit
in nappies from the 24th,
threaded by the bin in links,
by twisting, like short sausages
or poodles fashioned from
balloons, was binned along
with bean tails, tonic bottles,
nails, a mini Lamborghini's
snapped-off wheels, a magnum
bitter round the rim with old
champagne (that halitosis smell),
and twenty near-identical
reception Christmas cards:

a stippled snow-hung tree
a bloated, ravaged robin.

My son propped on one hip,
front door ajar, both shivering
in the not yet dawn, the heating
just about to crackle on,
raised up his palm in silent
pleasure at the work being done.
One man, his shoulders dewy
with reflective strips, waved
back and called him by his name
— the weekly ceremony —
until he bristled in my arms
legs stiffening with joy.

3.
Downstairs I mixed some Movicol
into warm juice and saw a
squirrel run across the grass,
freeze skinny as a meerkat
on the mostly mud I'd tried
to reseed twice last summer.
(After moss killer, waiting,
something ferrous, the shady
lawn seed recommended by
a friend eventually produced,
as if by staple gun, a few sparse
fiercely emerald reeds which died.)

Both boys had scrambled over
Look! and when they turned away

behind the mouth and nose
breath diamonds, fading,
the squirrel was spray-digging,
pelleting again, even though
he must have polished off his nuts
by Halloween. We'd seen him,
bushier then, a baby really,
slyly going back and back,
as we did on school coach trips
to the battlefields of Ypres
ripping through the Monster Munch
long before the sickening ferry
with its waffle smell and slot
machines, the textbook poppy
fields we'd seen on Blackadder,
now stretching flatly, forever.

I suppose the squirrel didn't know
the days would stick like curtains
catching on the outer edge
of the metal track, the yellow
fleur-de-lys a half inch less
wide open every morning.
I knew that I could probe it,
hey Siri, do most squirrels
make it through to spring in their
first year of life in urban
environments, but the fact
that I was always ladling
porridge as he dug, donating
raisins, doing calligraphy
with smooth or crunchy

From 2020

peanut butter — there was
that whole jack-o-lantern
month, involving apricots,
when it rained — only added
to my sense of having been
complicit in his losses:
the bad grass, the Amazon
deliveries that kept coming
in white Toyota vans, the
part-thawed corn cobettes
siloed in their own brown bag,
spongy with a mortuary
softness that repelled me.
He'd seen all that.

The boys must be upstairs
— a long withdrawing roar of
Avalanche! the scuff of
falling cushions — so I grabbed
a handful of cashews and stood,
unseen outside the window,
scattering them contritely on
the mud, around the reeds
now colourless, and the small
quill of his wavering tail.

4.
It being my birthday I was
standing there, lost in the screen,
the screen the same for reading
on and writing this,
for writing to, for finding out

how many steps I'd taken
yesterday/ in March last year,
when I had spotted, bled,
the algorithm always and
upbraidingly concerned
with sensed decline: a higher
average headphone volume,
deafness beckoning,
and fewer steps, an upward
trend in weight from these slack days
around the year's end picking
at the Roses box, and making
desperate cupcakes from a
BBE last August box mix
(the dribbly icing misty
on the spoon, the wafer dog
— a fireman — loosely hanging on)
morbid obesity, then death.

Its view of future time was,
in a sense, so frictionless
I envied it — that whole fin-
de-siècle confidence:
if history wasn't progress
it was *Untergang, Déclin,*
the line traced out as if a ball
dropping from the balltoss
met the racket's sweetspot
swoof and whipped across the net
and up, and up, so rather
than returning it evaded
satellites, fine meteorites,

the rain, all things held still
or left to fall by gravity,
and just went up and up,
and quietly on. In China
health authorities alarm
as virus tally reaches 44
in capital of Hubei province
Wuhan, I could have read,
if I'd read every piece of news
that day. I didn't, of course.

5.
Later, as we watched the moth's
drab plates of wing contracting
on the windowpane or rented
house's limewashed skirting board,
my son would talk of new year
as the time when we had supper
in the living room and 'I
was very 'cited'. After baths,
bedtime, the news, the news,
Zoom wine with friends whose distant
houses were still lapped, dustily,
by sun, I lay unblinking
on the bed, bean-fed again
(shakshuka, quesadillas,
cannellini mulched to paste:
the *NYT* was camping poverty)
and worked the chalky residue
two paracetamols (expired)
had striped across my tongue
with squash, a pint. I searched

for pleurisy, rib pain, cut glass
opacities, read Twitter feeds
of people in Berlin disputing
quarantine R0 pathogen
that ship the Princess Diamond
why cocoons are never safe,
then watched a video of snow
massing right to left across
the scientist's window in Pankow
until it was the only medium
the only crazily still
mobile thing behind the window
flecked with paint chips, greasy
fingerprint galaxies. Beyond,
beyond: the snow did as it pleased
effaced revealed the avenue
he lived on with its scrub of
park, its single taxi, and the lines
of parked-up old estates which
like the broken-backed receding
linden trees reached to the
grey horizon's grainy limit.

MARK LILLA

On Indifference

What blurt is this about virtue and about vice?
Evil propels me and reform of evil propels me, I stand indifferent,
My gait is no fault-finder's or rejecter's gait,
I moisten the roots of all that has grown.

WALT WHITMAN

The Olympian gods are not our friends. Zeus would have destroyed us long ago had Prometheus not brought fire and other useful things down to us. Prometheus was not being benevolent, though. He was angry at Zeus for having locked away the Titans and then for turning on him after Prometheus helped secure his rule. We humans were just pawns in their game. The myths teach that we are here on sufferance, and that the best fate is to be ignored by these poor excuses for divinities. On their indifference depends our happiness. Fortunately we have only minimal duties towards them, so once the ashes from the sacrifices are swept away, the libations mopped up, the festival garlands recycled, we are free to set sail.

The Biblical God requires more attention. Though he is sometimes petulant, his providential hand is always at work for those who choose to be chosen. Providence comes at a price, though. We are obliged to fear the Lord, to obey his commandments, and to internalize the moral code he has blessed us with. For purists, this can mean that virtually every hour of every day is regulated. But that is not how the Bible's protagonists seem to live. They love, they fight, they rule kingdoms, they play the lyre, and only when they lust after a subject's wife and arrange for his death in battle does God stop the music and call them to account. And repentance done, the band strikes up again. The covenant limits human freedom, but it also self-limits God's. Our to-do list is not infinite. Once we have fulfilled our duties, we are left to explore the world. *We good here? Yeah, we're good.* 109

Tut, tut child! Everything's got a moral, if only you can find it.
QUEEN OF HEARTS, *ALICE IN WONDERLAND*

But as a Christian my work is never done. I must have the vague *imitatio Christi* ideal before my eyes at all times and must try to answer the riddle, what would Jesus do?, in every situation — and bear the guilt of possibly getting the answer wrong. Kierkegaard was not exaggerating when he said that the task of becoming a Christian is endless. It can be brutal, too. Jesus told his disciples they must be ready at any moment to drop everything if the call comes, adding, *if any man come to me, and hate not his father, and mother, and wife, and children, and brethren, and sisters, yea, and his own life also, he cannot be my disciple.*

Saint Paul's God has boundary issues. More busybody than Pied Piper, he is always looking into our hearts, parsing our intentions, and demanding we love him more than we love ourselves. That master of metaphor Augustine found a powerful one to describe the new regime: *Two cities have been formed by two loves: the earthly city was created by self-love reaching the point of contempt for God, the Heavenly City by the love of God carried as far as contempt of self.* He hastened to add that the earthly city plays a necessary role in mortal life, offering peace and comfort in the best of times. But over the millennia — such is the power of metaphor over reason — zealots hedging their bets have concluded that if we are to err, it is better to fall into self-loathing than discover any trace of pride within. A moral scan will always turn up something. And so they lock themselves into panopticons where they serve as their own wardens and where nothing is a matter of spiritual indifference.

Subsequent Christian theologians raised doubts about this rigorist picture of the Christian moral life. In the Middle Ages they debated whether there might be such things as "indifferent acts," that is, acts that have no moral or spiritual significance. Scratching one's beard was a common example used by the laxists. Aquinas conceded the point concerning beards, but otherwise declared that if an action at all involves rational deliberation it cannot be indifferent, since reason is always directed towards ends, which can only be good or evil. Q.E.D. And so the class of genuinely indifferent acts was left quite small in official Catholic teaching. That sat just fine with a monastic and conventual elite already devoting their lives to self-abnegating spiritual exercises, accompanied by tormenting doubts about whether such exercises were prideful. But they were a class apart. Ordinary clerical functionaries led more lenient lives, which is how we got cardinals with concubines and with Titian portraits of themselves hanging over the fireplace. Vigilance was not their vocation.

In the Protestant view, that was precisely the problem. Protestantism, and Calvinism in particular, brought back moral rigorism and then democratized it. Now every burgher was expected to frisk himself while meditating on the terrifying mystery of predestination. The anxiety only increased when Protestants faced the choice among different and hostile denominations. Was there only one true church? Or were certain dogmatic disputes among denominations matters of indifference to God? Combatants in the Wars of Religion said no: true Christians must not only walk the right walk, they must talk the right talk. But, over time, as the denominations proliferated like tadpoles in a pond, and the doctrinal differences among them became more abstruse, the rigorist line became more difficult to maintain. Perhaps the Lord's house has many mansions after all.

That thought is exactly what Catholic critics of the Reformation, worried about. If we concede that there are many Christian paths to salvation, people will ask whether there are also non-Christian religious paths. If we concede that there are, they will then ask whether there are decent and admirable non-religious paths to moral perfection. And if we concede that there are — here is the crucial leap — they will be tempted to ask whether there might also be decent and admirable ways of life that do not revolve around moral perfection. The danger would not be that people would abandon morality altogether; no self-declared anti-moralist, not even Nietzsche, has ever renounced the words *must* and *ought*. It would be that they would start considering morality to be just one dimension of life among others, each deserving its due. It would mean the end of morality's claim to be the final arbiter of what constitutes a life well lived.

The gradient on this slope of questioning is steep. Montaigne slid to the bottom of it while the Wars of Religion were still raging and has been dragging unsuspecting readers along with him ever since. He did not openly state the case against the imperialism of conscience; a *bon vivant,* he was in no rush to become a *bon mourant.* Instead he wrote seemingly lighthearted essays full of anecdotes that subtly held up the rigorist life to ridicule or revulsion, implying that there must be a better way to live, without specifying exactly what that might be. He only pointed to himself as a genial, indeed irresistible, exemplar of tolerant, urbane contentment.

Pascal, Montaigne's greatest reader, immediately discerned the threat that the *Essays* posed to the Christian moral edifice: Montaigne inspires indifference about salvation, without fear and without repentance. Atheism is refutable, but indifference is not. The scholastic debate over indifferent acts had presumed a desire to get our moral houses in order. The Reformation and Counter-Reformation debates over justification presumed a desire to get our theological houses in order. Montaigne's indifferentism, as it came to be called, made all well-ordered houses look menacing or faintly ridiculous. That is why indifferentism was denounced along with liberalism as modern "pests" by Pope Pius IX in his Syllabus of Errors of 1864. He understood that there is nothing more devastating to dogma than a shrug of the shoulders.

*It is nonsense and an antiquated notion that the many can do
wrong. What the many do is God's will. Before this wisdom all
people have had to this day bowed down — kings, emperors,
and excellencies. Up to now all our cattle have received
encouragement through this wisdom. So God is damned well
going to have to learn how to bow down too.*

KIERKEGAARD

Americans' relation to democracy has never been an indiffer-
ent one — or a reasoned one. For us it is a matter of dogmatic
faith, and therefore a matter of the passions. *We hold these truths
to be self-evident*: has ever a more debatable and consequential
assertion been made since the Sermon on the Mount? But for
Americans it is not a thesis one might subject to examination
and emendation; even American atheists skip over the *endowed
by their Creator* bit in reverent silence. We are in the thrall of a
foundation myth as solid and imposing as an ancient temple,
which we take turns purifying like so many vestals. We freely
discuss how the *mysterium tremendum* should be interpreted
and which rituals it imposes on us. But the oracle has spoken
and is taking no further questions.

Which is largely a good thing. Not long ago there was
breezy talk of a world-historical transition to democracy, as if
that were the easiest and most natural thing in the world to
achieve. Establish a democratic *pays légal,* the thinking went,
and a democratic *pays réel* will spontaneously sprout up within
its boundaries. Today, when temples to cruel local deities are
being built all over the globe, we are being reminded just how
rare a democratic society is. So let us appreciate Americans'
unreasoned, dogmatic attachment to their own. Not
everything unreasoned is unwise.

But neither are all good things entirely good. This is what

On Indifference

the dogmatic mind has trouble grasping. If some end — the rule of the saints, say, or the dictatorship of the proletariat — is deemed to be worth pursuing, the dogmatist needs to believe it is the only and perfect good, carrying no inherent disadvantages. Blemishes must be ignored so as not to distract the team. But once problems become impossible to ignore, as inevitably they will be, they must be explained. And so they will be attributed either to alien, retrograde forces that have infiltrated paradise, or to insufficient zeal among believers in pursuing the good. The dogmatic mind is haunted by two specters: the different and the indifferent.

Americans' dogmatism about democracy strengthens their attachment to it, but it weakens their understanding of it. The hardest thing for us is to establish enough intellectual distance from modern democracy to see it in historical perspective. (While virtually every American university has courses on "democratic values," I am unaware of any that offers one on "undemocratic values," despite the fact that almost all societies from the dawn of time to the present have been governed by them.) The Framers had experience with monarchy and had studied the failed republics of the European past. They looked upon democracy as one political form among others, a means to particular ends, with strengths and weakness like any other political arrangement. But once Americans in later generations came to know nothing but democratic life, democracy became the end itself, the *summum bonum* from which all discussion and debate about means must flow. When Americans ask *how can we make our democracy better?* what they are really asking is *how can we make our democracy more democratic?* — a subtle but profound difference.

Our dogmatism shows up in other ways, too. Spend some time abroad and you start to notice that Americans rarely

114

express mixed feelings about their country as other peoples do about theirs. We oscillate humorlessly between defensive boosterism and self-flagellation, especially the latter over the past half century. Today there is nothing more American than condemning American democracy or declaring ourselves alienated from it. Yet the only charge we can think of leveling against it is that of failing to be democratic enough. No one appreciates the irony except the alert foreign observer with a sense of humor, like the divine Mrs. Trollope. Foreign anti-Americanism is always, at some level, anti-democratic, which is what can make it enlightening, and useful to us. American anti-Americanism is hyper-American and earnest as dust. We find it virtually impossible to get outside ourselves. We breed no Tocquevilles, we must import them.

Other countries claim to revere democracy, and many do. But few think of democracy as a never-ending moral project, a world-historical epic. And none have considered it their divine duty to bring democracy to the unbaptized. The Protestant stamp on the American mind is so deep that collectively we take on the mantle of the Pilgrim Church marching towards a redemption in which all things will be made new. For much of our history the sacred individual task of becoming a more Christian Christian ran parallel to the sacred collective task of becoming a more democratic democracy. Note that I do not say *liberal* democracy. For there is nothing liberal about Americans when they are on the march. Which is why when conscription begins, the indifferent, who for whatever reason do not feel like marching just now or have other destinations in mind, beat a retreat. Some have sought refuge in rural solitude, some in the American metropolis, some in foreign capitals. Anywhere where they might be free of the unremitting imperative to become a better person or a better American. Anywhere where they could simply become themselves.

The thesis that huge quantities of soap testify to our greater cleanliness need not apply to the moral life, where the more recent principle seems more accurate, that a strong compulsion to wash suggests a dubious state of moral hygiene.

ROBERT MUSIL

—

A hand goes up in the audience: *But we are no longer a Protestant country! We are a secular one that has gotten over religious conformism. What on earth are you talking about?*

Thank you for that question. In one decisive respect we have indeed moved beyond Protestantism: we no longer believe we are fallen, sinful creatures. The Protestant divine was severe with his flock and occasionally with his country, but he was also severe with himself. He was a busybody because his God was a busybody who put everyone, including the clergy, under divine scrutiny. *There is none righteous, no, not one,* says Saint Paul. What a terrible way to start the day.

But in other respects we have retained vestiges of our Protestant heritage and even exaggerated them. Hegel foresaw this. Considering the moral and religious psychodynamics of his time, he observed that the Dialectic has a sense of humor: toss Calvin out the front door and Kant sneaks in through the back. No sooner had the empiricism and skepticism of the Enlightenment disenchanted nature, draining it of moral purpose, than German idealism surreptitiously reestablished the principles of Christian morality on abstract philosophical grounds. And no sooner had Kant midwifed that rebirth than the moral impulse floated free of his universalist strictures and became more subjective, less subtle, more excitable, less grounded in ordinary existence. In a word, it became Romantic. The saints are dead; long live the "beautiful souls."

What is a beautiful soul? For Schiller, who coined the term, it was a person in whom the age-old tension between moral law and human instinct had been overcome. *In a beautiful soul,* he wrote, *individual deeds are not what is moral. Rather, the entire character is...The beautiful soul has no other merit, than that it is.* Schiller imagined individuals who so fully incarnate the moral law that they have no need of moral reasoning and who experience no struggle to surmount the passions. This beautiful soul does not really act morally, it simply behaves instinctively — and such behaving is good. (Ring a bell? *And God saw every thing that he had made, and, behold, it was very good.*) A disciple of Kant, Schiller took the moral law to be by definition universal. What he did not anticipate was that the notion of a beautiful soul could inspire a radical impudence in anyone convinced of his or her own inner beauty. Who would not want to be crowned a moral *Roi Soleil,* absolved in advance of guilt, self-doubt, repentance, and expressions of humility? Who would not want to learn that the definition of righteousness is self-righteousness?

So, in answer to the question, yes, in one sense America is a post-Protestant nation. The uptight Bible-thumping humbug of yore has been shamed off the public square — but only to make room for networks of self-righteous beautiful souls pronouncing sentence from the cathedras of their inner Vaticans. What no one seems to recognize is that they are an atavism, a blast from the past, not a breeze from a progressive future. Like their ancestors, they are prone to schisms and enter civil wars with the giddiness of Knights Templar descending on Palestine. Yet they are bound together by an unshakeable old belief that when it comes to making the world a better place there are no indifferent acts, no indifferent words, no indifferent thoughts, and no rest for the virtuous. Our beautiful souls are Marrano Christians as radical as old Saint Paul. They just don't know it. Yes, the Dialectic really does have a sense of humor.

"Ah," Miss Gostrey sighed, "the name of the good American is as easily given as taken away! What is it, to begin with, to be one? And what's the extraordinary hurry?"

HENRY JAMES

America is working on itself. It is almost always working on itself because Americans believe that life is a project, for individuals and nations. No other people believes this quite the way we do. There is no Belgian project, no Kenyan project, no Ecuadoran project, no Filipino project, no Canadian project. But there is an American project — or rather a black box for projects that change over time. We are always tearing out the walls of our collective house, adding additions, building decks, jackhammering the driveway and pouring new asphalt. We are seldom still and never quiet. And when we set to work we expect everyone to pitch in. And that means *you.*

Which can put *you* in an awkward position. Let's say you are unhappy with the project of the moment. Or you approve of it but think it should be handled differently. Or you appreciate the way it is handled but don't feel particularly inclined to participate right now. Or you even want to participate but resent being dragooned into it or learning that others are being punished for not joining in. Or say that you simply want to be left alone. In any other country these would be considered entirely reasonable sentiments. But not in America when it is at work on itself.

The projects of our moment may sound radical, but they are just extensions of the old principles of liberty, equality, and justice. That certainly speaks in their favor. What is new, thanks to our beautiful souls, is that the task of making this a better America has now been conflated with that of making *you* a better person. In the Protestant age, the promotion of Christian virtue ran parallel to the promotion of democracy but usually could be distinguished from it. Bringing you to accept Jesus as your personal savior had nothing necessarily to do with bringing you to accept William Howard Taft as your national savior. The first concerned your person, the second concerned your country.

In the age of the beautiful soul our evangelical passions have survived and been transferred to the national project, personalizing it. Beautiful souls believe that one's politics emanate from an inner moral state, not from a process of reasoning and dialogue with others. Given that assumption, they reasonably conclude that establishing a better politics depends on working an inner transformation on others, or on ostracizing them. And thanks to the wonders of technology, the scanning of other people's souls has never seemed easier.

These wonders have also landed us in a virtual, and global, panopticon. It has no physical presence, it exists solely in our minds. But that is sufficient to maintain a subtle pressure to demonstrate that we are all fully with the newest American projects. In periods of Christian enthusiasm in the past, elites would make ostentatious gestures of faith in order to ward off scrutiny. They would fund a Crusade, commission an altarpiece, make a pilgrimage, join a confraternity, or sponsor a work of theological apologetics. Virtue-signaling

is an old human practice. Today the required gestures are of
a political rather than spiritual nature. We have all, individ-
uals and institutions, learned how to make them by adapting
how we speak, how we write, how we present ourselves to the
world, and — most insidiously — how we present the world
to ourselves. By now we hardly notice that we are making such
gestures. Yet we certainly notice when the codes are violated,
even inadvertently; the reaction is swift and merciless. Such
inadvertence, even due to temperament or sensibility, is read
as indifference to building a more democratic America, which
ranks very high on the new Syllabus of Errors.

*It is of vital importance to art that those who are made its
messengers should not only keep their message uncorrupted, but
should present themselves before their fellow men in the most
unquestionable garb.*

THE CRAYON (1855)

Aristocracies are aloof and serene. American democracy
is needy and anxious. It wants to be loved. It is like a young
puppy that can never get enough petting and treats. *Who's a
good boy? Who's a very good boy?* And if you repeat this often
enough, eventually the dog will lick your face, as if to say,
and you're a good boy too! The rewards for satisfying this
neediness, and the penalties for failing to satisfy it, are
powerful incentives to conform in just about every sphere
of American life, no more consequentially than in intellec-
tual and artistic matters. Every society, every religion, every
form of government offers such incentives. Since ancient
times worldly intellectuals and artists have understood that
they are never entirely free from the obligation to genuflect

occasionally, and the clever ones learn how to wink subtly at their audiences to signal when they are doing just that. *L'art vaut une messe.* Romanticism in the nineteenth century was the first movement to fuel the fantasy of complete autonomy from society, only to itself become a dogma that all thinkers and artists were expected to profess.

It is one thing, though, to self-consciously genuflect when necessary — and then, just as self-consciously, to stand up when mass is over and return to your workplace. It is quite another to convince yourself that kneeling is standing. Or that you must turn your workplace into a chapel. What Tocqueville meant by the "tyranny of the majority" was exactly this infiltration of public judgment into individual consciousness, changing our perceptions of and assumptions about the world. It is not really "false consciousness," which is the holding of false beliefs that enhance the power of those who dominate others. Rather it is a kind of group consciousness that morphs and re-morphs arbitrarily like cumulus clouds. False consciousness obscures precise class interests. The tyranny of the majority obscures the interests, feelings, thoughts, and imagination of the self.

What is so striking about the present cultural moment is how many Americans who occupy themselves with ideas and the imagination — writers, editors, scholars, journalists, filmmakers, artists, curators — seem to be suffering from Stockholm Syndrome. Rerouted from their personal destinations toward a more moral and democratic America, they are losing the instinct to set their own course. They no doubt believe in what they are doing; the question is whether they are in touch enough with themselves to feel any healthy tension between their presumed political obligations and whatever other drives and inclinations they might have.

On Indifference

Talk to creative young people today and prepare yourself for the patter celebrating the new collective journey, which they have no trouble linking to their personal journeys, however short those still are. The rhetoric of identity is very useful here because it has both individual-psychological and political meaning, blurring the distinction between self-expression and collective moral progress. That is also why identity-talk has become the *lingua franca* of all grant-making and prize-giving bodies in the United States. The committees are much more comfortable exercising judgment based on someone's physical characteristics and personal story than exercising aesthetic and intellectual judgment based on the work. Little do the well-meaning young people drawn into this game suspect that they are not advancing into a more progressive twenty-first century. They have simply been rerouted back to the nineteenth century, where they must now satisfy a newer, hipper class of Babbits. Or, worse, become their own Babbits, convincing themselves that their creative journeys really are and ought to be part of a collective moral journey.

This is not to say that art has nothing to do with morality. Morality in the broadest sense, the fate of having to choose among conflicting ends and questionable means, is one of art's great subjects, particularly the literary arts. But the art of the novelist is not to render categorical moral judgments on human action — that's the prophet's job. It is to cast them into shadow, to explore all the ruses of moral reasoning. Literature and art are not sustenance for the long march toward national redemption. They have nothing whatsoever to do with "giving voice" or "telling our stories" or "celebrating" anyone's or any group's achievements. That is to confuse art with advertising copy. The contribution of literature and art to morality is indirect. They have the power to remind us of the truth that we are mysteries to ourselves, as Augustine put it. Literature is not for simpletons. *Billy Budd* was not written for Billy Budds. It was written for grown-ups, or those who would become one. Which is why the status of literature and the other arts has never been terribly secure in the land of *puer aeternus.*

In the American grain it is gregariousness, suspicion of privacy, a therapeutic distaste in the face of personal apartness and self-exile, which are dominant. In the new Eden, God's creatures move in herds.

GEORGE STEINER

For some, art and reflection have always served as a refuge from the world. In America, the world more often serves as a refuge from art and reflection. We are only too happy when the conversation turns from such matters to those thought to be more practical, more pedagogical, more ethically uplifting, or more therapeutic. The history of anti-intellectualism in America is less one of efforts to extinguish the life of the mind than to divert it toward extraneous ends. (See *On the Usefulness of the Humanities for Electrical Engineering,* 3 vols.) Such efforts reflect a perverse sublimation of the *eros* behind all creative activity, redirecting it from the inner life of the creative person toward some activity that can be judged in public by committees. The result, in intellectual and artistic terms, is either propaganda or kitsch. And we are drowning in both.

123

Censorship in America comes and goes. Self-censorship does too, depending on the public mood at any particular time. The most persistent threat to arts and letters in America is amnesia, the forgetting of just what it is to cultivate an individual vision or point of view in a place where thinking,

On Indifference

writing, and making are judged to be necessarily directed toward some external end. The barriers to becoming an individual in individualistic America should never be underestimated. Tocqueville's deepest insight was into the anxieties of democratic life brought on by the promise and reality of autonomy. Freedom is an abyss; the urge to turn from it is strong. The tyranny of the majority is less a violent imposition than a psychologically comprehensible form of voluntary servitude.

In such an environment, maintaining a state of inner indifference is an achievement. Indifference is not apathy. Not at all. It is the fruit of an instinct *to moisten the roots of all that has grown,* as Whitman put it, and experience one's self and the world intensely without filters, without having to consider what ends are being served beyond that experience. It is an instinct to hit the mute button, to block out whatever claims are being made on one's attention and concern, confident that heaven can wait. It is an instinct for privacy, far from the prying eyes and wagging tongues of beautiful gods and beautiful souls. It is a liberal instinct, not a democratic one.

Liberalism, Judith Shklar once wrote, is monogamously, faithfully, and permanently married to democracy — but it is a marriage of convenience. That is exactly right. The liberal indifference of Montaigne was a declaration of independence from the religious zealots of his time. But zealotry is zealotry, and democracy has its own zealots. We may look more kindly on their aims but they are no less a potential threat to inner freedom than our homegrown messiahs are. The indifferent appreciate democracy to the extent that it guarantees that freedom; they distrust and resist it the moment they are invited down to the panopticon for a little chat. They are not anti-democratic or anti-justice or reactionary. They understand that a liberal democracy requires solidarity and sacrifice. and reforms, sometimes radical ones. They wish to be good citizens but feel no obligation to cast down their nets and join the redemptive pilgrimage. Their kingdom is not of this continent.

It is a paradox of our time that the more Americans learn to tolerate difference, the less they are able to tolerate indifference. But it is precisely the right to indifference that we must assert now. The right to choose one's own battles, to find one's own balance between the True, the Good, and the Beautiful. The right to resist any creeping *Gleichhaltung* that would bring a thinker's thoughts or a writer's words or an artist's or filmmaker's work into alignment with a catechism. Dr. Bowdler be damned.

America is working on itself. Let it work, and may some good come of it. But the indifferent will politely decline the invitation to shake pom-poms on the sidelines or join a Battle for The American Soul just now. Why now? Because the illiberal passions of the moment threaten their autonomy and their self-cultivation, and have formed a generation that fails to see the value of those possessions. That is the saddest part. Perhaps a later one will again find it inspiring to learn what the early modernist writers and artists who fled the country believed: that America's claim on us is never greater than our claim on ourselves. That democracy is not everything. That morality is not everything. That nothing is everything.

125

HELEN VENDLER

Loosed Quotes

THE SECOND COMING

Turning and turning in the widening gyre
The falcon cannot hear the falconer;
Things fall apart; the centre cannot hold;
Mere anarchy is loosed upon the world,
The blood-dimmed tide is loosed, and everywhere
The ceremony of innocence is drowned;
The best lack all conviction, while the worst
Are full of passionate intensity.

Surely some revelation is at hand;
Surely the Second Coming is at hand.
The Second Coming! Hardly are those words out
When a vast image out of Spiritus Mundi
Troubles my sight: somewhere in sands of the desert
A shape with lion body and the head of a man,
A gaze blank and pitiless as the sun,
Is moving its slow thighs, while all about it
Reel shadows of the indignant desert birds.
The darkness drops again; but now I know
That twenty centuries of stony sleep
Were vexed to nightmare by a rocking cradle,
And what rough beast, its hour come round at last,
Slouches towards Bethlehem to be born?

W.B. YEATS

> Turning and turning in the widening gyre
> The falcon cannot hear the falconer;
> Things fall apart; the centre cannot hold;
> . . . .
> The best lack all conviction, while the worst
> Are full of passionate intensity.

In every crisis they appear, those famous and familiar lines from "The Second Coming," written in 1919 by W. B. Yeats. Journalists and critics alike seem to take them as final assertions of Yeats' own beliefs. Such innocent judgments do not ask why those lines open the poem, or for how long their assertions remain asserted. The poem itself has become lost behind the quotability of its opening lines. And Yeats, it seems, wants to be a pundit.

In our ready "yes, yes" to those lines, we think we are accepting the judgment of a sage, but by the time we reach the close of the poem — which is a question, not an assertion — we are driven to imagine the changing states of the writer composing this peculiar poem, and we raise questions. What feelings required Yeats to change his bold initial stance, and in what order did those feelings arise? In order to understand this poem, to free it from its ubiquitous misuses, and to restore it to both its opening grandeur and its subsequent humiliation, those are the questions that we must answer.

Yeats was an inveterate reviser of his own ever-laborious writing: recalling his difficulty in composing "The Circus Animals' Desertion," he confesses, "I sought a theme and sought for it in vain,/ I sought it daily for six weeks or so." (Mention of that poem in his letters of the time prove this no exaggeration: I counted the weeks.) What was the obstacle suspending his progress? (He spends the poem finding out.) In "Adam's Curse" he remarks in frustration, "A line will take us hours maybe." Hours to do what? "To articulate sweet sounds together." Yeats puts the sequence of sounds first; he composed by ear. Are the resulting sounds always "sweet" in the ordinary sense of the word? Not at all; but they are "sweet" in the internal order of rhythms and styles as the poem evolves. When the poet has articulated its theme, its sounds, and its lines to the best of his powers, the ear registers its satisfaction.

"The Second Coming" is a lurid refutation of the lurid Christian expectations of the Second Coming of Christ, which Jesus himself foretells in Matthew 29-3:

Immediately after the distress of those days, the sun will be darkened, and the moon will refuse her light, and the stars will fall from heaven, and the powers of heaven will rock; and then the sign of the Son of Man will be seen in heaven; then it is that all the tribes of the land will mourn, and they will see the Son of Man coming upon the clouds of heaven, with great power and glory.

Yeats proposes a surreal alternative to Jesus' prophecy, proposing that on the Last Day we will see not Christ in majesty but a menacing, pitiless, and coarse beast who "slouches toward Bethlehem to be born." "After us, the savage god," Yeats had said as early as 1896. He watched through the decades, appalled by the sequential horror of world events: The World War from 1914-1918; the failed Easter Rising in Ireland in 1916; the Bolshevik Revolution in 1917. And his first assertions in "The Second Coming" are indeed thoughts prompted by such political upheavals (and by earlier ones — Marie Antoinette appears in the drafts).

But what sort of assertions does he choose to express his thoughts? After the octave of assertions, there is a break not entirely accounted for, since the whole poem is not written in regular stanzas, and there are no further breaks. The compressed sentiments preceding the break are undermined by the unexplained and increasing mystery of the poet's phrases, bringing the reader into the perplexity of the poet. The whole octave is full of riddles: What is a *gyre*? *Whose* is the falcon? What is the *centre* the center *of*? Why all the passive verbs? Who *loosed* the anarchy? Whose *blood, loosed* by whom, has dimmed *what* tide? What is meant by *the ceremony of innocence*? Who are *the best* and who are *the worst*? Such abstract language, such invisible agents, and such unascribed actions persist in Yeats' opening declarations, down to the period that closes the octave.

The quotability of Yeats' opening passage derives, of course, from the total and unmodified confidence of its initial reportage, impersonal and unrelenting, offering a naked list of present-tense events happening "everywhere." Stripped to their kernels, these are Yeats's truculently unmitigated hammer-blows of grammar::

The falcon cannot hear
Things fall apart
The centre cannot hold
Mere anarchy is loosed
The blood-dimmed tide is loosed
Everywhere the ceremony of innocence is drowned
The best lack all conviction
The worst are full of passionate intensity

The break, after Yeats' introductory eight-line block, leads an educated reader to expect that a six-line block will follow, completing a sonnet. Yet the poet finds himself unable to maintain his original jeremiad, which has been aggressive, omniscient, panoramic, and prophetic. Yeats "begins over again," and utters in the fourteen lines following the break a complete second "sonnet," a *rifacimento* of the one originally intended, in which he rejects his earlier rhetoric of impersonal omniscience as inauthentic from his human lips. Who is he to speak as though he could see the world with the panoramic scan proper only to God? That so many successive writers have been eager to reissue his lines reveals how greatly the human mind is seduced by the vanity of the unequivocal. Can we requote without unease what the poet himself immediately rejected?

Although "The Second Coming" begins with an attempt at couplet-rhyme, soon — as Peter Sacks has pointed out to me — the couplets begin to disintegrate, as though they themselves were intent on demonstrating how "things fall apart." After the break, Yeats reveals in its wake a second attempt at a fourteen-line sonnet, one exhibiting a traditional "spillover" octave of nine lines (implying overmastering emotion in the writer) before a truthful closing "sestet" of five lines, making up the desired fourteen. The second, revisionary octave replaces the certainty of the poet's original octave with the self-defensive uncertainty of "Surely." Longing for a revelation more humanly reliable than an unsupported façade of godlike prophecy, Yeats insistently utters his second "Surely," one no less dubious than the first. The second "Surely" attempts to locate a cultural myth to which he can attach the vision vouchsafed to him in a revelation arising within his human consciousness. "Surely the Second Coming is at hand. / The Second Coming!"

For the first time in the poem, we hear Yeats speaking in the first person, declaring that "a vast image out of Spiritus Mundi / Troubles my sight." The poet is the sole spectator of this vast image, and he claims that it stems not from his own bodily sense of sight but from the World Spirit, a universal *Spiritus Mundi* always potentially able to rise into human awareness. (Poets so often describe the initial inspiration for a poem as something coming unbidden that the reader is not troubled by Yeats' myth of a World-Spirit supplying the image for his revelation.) The poet has decided that it is more honest, more tenable, to write in the first person, to present himself as one whose imagination has reliably generated a telling and trustworthy "vast image" of his historical moment. He has forsaken his impressive but fraudulent rhetoric of omniscience for an account of his private inspiration.

Once Yeats has repudiated his initial "divine" posture as a guaranteed seer-of-everything-everywhere, he can take on, in the first person, his limited historical image-making self and create with it a "human" sestet for his newly "remade" sonnet. Admitting the fallibility of any transient metaphorical image, he acknowledges that his image vanishes, "the darkness drops again," and he is left alone. Yet he grandly maintains, in spite of his abandoning a prophetic stance, that he now definitely "knows" something.

The "something" turns out to be a single historical fact: the exhaustion of Christian cultural authority after its "twenty centuries" of rule. His "vast image" — its nature as yet unspecified — has shown him that Christianity will be replaced by a counter-force, a pagan one. Drawing on his reading of Vico and Herbert Spencer, Yeats believed that history exhibited repetitive cycles of opposing forces. Just as Christianity overcame the preceding centuries of Egypt and Greece, now it is time for some power to defeat Christianity.

In his private "revelation" the poet has seen the Egyptian stone sphinx asleep "somewhere" in sands of a desert.

(The uncertain "somewhere" admits the loss of the initial "everywhere" of Yeats' prophetic opening.) The "stony sleep" of the Sphinx has lasted through the twenty centuries of Christianity, but now Fate has set an anticipatory cradle rocking in Bethlehem, birthplace of the previous god, and a sphinx-like creature rouses itself to claim supremacy:

> The darkness drops again; but now I know
> That twenty centuries of stony sleep
> Were vexed to nightmare by a rocking cradle...

Although the poet "knows" that Christianity is undergoing the nightmare of its death-throes, he cannot declare with any confidence what will replace it. He can no longer boast "I know that...": he can merely ask a speculative question which embodies his own mixed reaction of fear and desire to the vanishing of a now outworn Christianity, the only ideological system he has ever known. What will replace the Jesus of Bethlehem, he asks, and invents a brutal and unaesthetic divinity, a sphinx seen in glimpses — "with lion body and the head of a man, / A gaze blank and pitiless as the sun." The desert birds (formerly, it is implied, perched at rest on the immobile stone of the Egyptian statue) are now disturbed by the unexpected arousal of the "slow thighs" beneath them. The indignant birds, their movement in the sky inferred from their agitated cast shadows, "reel about," disoriented, projecting, as surrogates, the poet's own indignation as he guesses at the future parallel upheaval of his own world. Unable to be prophetic, unable now even to say "Surely," the poet ends his humanly authentic but still unsatisfied sestet with a speculative question, one that fuses by alliteration "beast" and "Bethlehem" and "born":

And what rough beast, its hour come round at last,
Slouches towards Bethlehem to be born?

A conventional reading of the poem might take us this far. But no one, so far as I know, has commented that the culminating and ringing phrase, "Its hour come round at last," is an allusion to Jesus' famous statement to his mother at the wedding feast at Cana. When she points out to her son that their host has run out of wine, he rebukes her as he had once done in his youth when she had lost him in Jerusalem and found him preaching to the rabbis in the temple: "Wist yet not that I must be about my Father's business?" (Luke 2: 48-49) At Cana, Jesus is even harsher as he tells his mother that he is not yet willing to manifest his divinity: "Woman, what have I to do with thee? mine hour is not yet come." Not answering her son's austere question, she simply says to the servants, "Whatsoever he saieth unto you, do it." He tells them to fill their jugs with water, yet when they pour it is wine that issues, as, in silent obedience to his mother, Jesus performs his first miracle, even though to do so means changing his own design of when he will reveal his divinity. The evangelist comments: "This beginning of miracles did Jesus in Cana of Galilee, and manifested forth his glory" (John 2: 4-5,11). Unlike Jesus, who wished to delay his hour of divine manifestation, Yeats' rough beast has been impatiently awaiting his own appointed hour, and it has come. His allusion to Jesus' "Mine hour is not yet come" establishes a devastating parallel between the rough beast's presumed divinity and that of Jesus, as the poet quails before the savage god of the future.

One senses there must be a literary bridge between the glorious "hour" of Jesus and the hideous hour of the rough

133

beast. As so often, one finds the link in Shakespeare. In *Henry V*, Shakespeare alludes to Jesus' remark, but adds the malice and impatience that will be incorporated by Yeats in his image of the rough beast. A French noble at Agincourt describes, in prospect, the vulturous hovering of crows waiting to attack the corpses of the English who will have died in battle. Eager for their expected feast on English carrion, "their executors, the knavish crows, / Fly o'er them, all impatient for their hour." We know that the rough beast has been, like the crows, "all impatient for [his] hour," because, once loosed on the world, he knows that his appointed hour, long craved by him, has come "at last." Yeats had been alluding to Jesus' words about the appointed hour ever since 1896: in his youthful poem "The Secret Rose," a benign apocalypse is ushered in by the idealized romance symbol of the rose. He even remembered — writing in 1919 — his original inscription of the longing word "Surely" in the envisaged victory of the Secret Rose:

> Surely thine hour has come, thy great wind blows,
> Far-off, most secret, and inviolate Rose?

"Surely thine hour has come;" "Surely a revelation is at hand": apocalyptic symbols thread their way through Yeats' life-work. In the same volume as "The Secret Rose," we find a contrastively violent version of the End Times, drawing on the sinister Irish legend of a battle in "The Valley of the Black Pig" ushering in what Yeats called "an Armageddon which shall quench all things in the Ancestral Darkness again." Just as the brave warrior Cuchulain — in Yeats' deathbed poem, "Cuchulain Comforted" — must be reincarnated as a coward to complete his knowledge of life, so the serene beauty of the Secret Rose must, to be complete, coexist with a twin, a wildness of apprehension. Maud Gonne, whom Yeats loved in frustration all his life, incarnated for him the conjunction of wildness and beauty:

> But even at the starting post, all sleek and new,
> I saw the wildness in her and I thought
> A vision of terror that it must live through
> Had shattered her soul.

Maud had already appeared in 1904 as the paradoxical "wild Quiet," "eating her wild heart" (an image of wild love borrowed from the opening sonnet of Dante's *La Vita Nuova*). She is the female companion to another apocalyptic creature, the Sagittarius of the zodiac; he is a Great Archer poised, his bow drawn, in the woods of Lady Gregory's estate. He, like Shakespeare's predatory birds, "but awaits his hour" to loose arrows upon a degenerate Ireland, where English archaeologists are sacrilegiously excavating sacred Tara and the ignorant Dublin masses are actually celebrating the coronation in England of Edward VII:

> I am contented for I know that Quiet
> Wanders laughing and eating her wild heart
> Among pigeons and bees, while that Great Archer,
> Who but awaits His hour to shoot, still hangs
> A cloudy quiver over Pairc-na-lee.

By 1919, in "The Second Coming," the Yeatsian apocalyptic symbol has shed its early romance component of the idealized Rose, has lost the starry constellation of the vengeful zodiacal Archer, and, in the hour of its Second Coming, has become "a vision of terror" like the one Yeats saw in the young Maud's soul. Yeats had thought of calling his poem "The Second Birth," but by renaming it "The Second Coming," he ensured that in spite of the rocking cradle, all his recurrences of "Mine hour is not yet come" recall the self-manifestation of Jesus not as a child, but as the adult of Cana, the miracle-worker who will return to the world at the end of time.

"The Second Coming" is in fact a thicket of allusions. A hybrid one pointing to Spenser's *Faerie Queene* and Milton's *Paradise Lost* adds an opaque quality to the mythical dimension of the rough beast: he cannot be accurately described. Yeats presents him vaguely as "a shape," borrowing from Spenser the concept of Death's resistance to visual representation and from Milton the shapeless word "shape." In Spenser's first Mutability Canto, after a procession of months representing the passage of time, Death, symbol of the end of time, appears both seen and unseeable, "Unbodièd, unsouled, unheard, unseen":

> And after all came Life, and lastly Death;
> Death with most grim and griesly visage seene,
> Yet is he nought but parting of the breath;
> Ne ought to see, but like a shade to weene,
> Vnbodièd, vnsoul'd, vnheard, vnseene.

Imitating his master, the "sage and serious poet, Spenser," Milton has his Satan meet Death, equally indescribable except by the word "shape" and its successive ever-less-visible negations (Milton substitutes "shadow" for Spenser's Hades-issued "shade.") Death confounds even Satan:

> The other shape,
> If shape it might be call'd that shape had none

Distinguishable in member, joynt, or limb,
Or substance might be call'd that shadow seem'd,
For each seem'd either; black it stood as Night,
Fierce as ten Furies, terrible as Hell,
And shook a dreadful Dart; what seem'd his head
The likeness of a Kingly Crown had on.

Retaining the word "shape" but changing the concept of the shapeless shadowy "shape" inherited from his predecessors, Yeats attempts to describe in disarticulated images the nameless figure of his own chimerical "vast image" with a "lion body and head of a man,": he adds a description of its gaze "blank and pitiless as the sun," sexualizing it by the "slow thighs" unattached to any completed bodily description, and debasing it by its "slouching" motion, its lurching advance as it gradually reactivates its stony limbs. So grotesque is the figure, so unnameable by any visual word, that Yeats rejects even his own impotent efforts at specialized description, tethering his final question to the vague words "rough beast," offering nothing but its genus. It is a generalized "beast" rather than a recognized species, let alone an individual creature.

137

There are, then, four evolving motions successively representing Yeats' mind and emotions in "The Second Coming." We see first an impersonal set of prophetic declamations; these are replaced by a first-person narration of the appearance of the troubling "vast image" coming to replace the Christian past; this, disappearing, is replaced by a "factual" account of the obsolescence of Christianity ("Now I *know*"); but after this flat declaration of secure knowledge, Yeats can muster no further direct object of what he "knows." Instead, he launches a final speculative query ("And *what* rough beast"). These four feeling-states — impersonal omniscience; a first-person boast of a private "revelation"; a "true" historical judgment as to the nightmarish dissolution of the Christian era; and a blurred query uttered in fear — mimic the poet's changes of response as he attempts to write down an accurate poem of this life-moment. A desire for authentically human speech has made him turn away from his initial confident (and baseless) soothsaying to a personal, transitory, (and therefore uncertain) private "revelation." He tries finally to attain to truth in judging the end of the Christian era.

But what truth can he declare of what is to come? He acknowledges — in a move wholly unforeseen in the strong and quotable opening octave — how limited his "knowledge" actually is. The "darkness" of fear cannot be resoundingly swept away by a transitory image from an unknowable source: opacity drops again. By the end, Yeats must forsake his proposed prophetic and visionary and historical styles and resort to a frustrated human voice that confesses the helplessness of the human intellect and the humiliation of admitting incomplete knowledge. At the inexorable approach of an unknowable, shapeless, coarse, and destructive era, "the darkness drops again."

It is not mistaken, however, to think of the resounding opening summary list as "Yeats' views" as he begins the poem. He even quotes himself in a letter of 1936 to his friend Ethel Mannin, anticipating the next war: "Every nerve trembles with horror at what is happening in Europe, 'the ceremony of innocence is drowned.'" The sentiments are genuine, but in a poem something more has to happen than the static observation of a moment in time. A credible artifact has to be

138

constructed, the "sweet sounds" have to be articulated, and a persuasive structure has to be conceived. Since Yeats had lost faith in both Blakean denunciation and Shelleyan optimism by the time he wrote "The Second Coming," he had gained the humility to confess, at the end of the poem, the limits of human knowledge and human vision. Though his diction is still grand in his closing, he is no longer boasting his seer-like knowledge, no longer claiming a unique private vision, no longer able to assuage the nightmare of the End Times of Christianity. To admit Yeats' final acknowledgment of human incapacity is essential to perceiving his overreaching in his earlier claims to prophetic power and visionary insight.

Painful as it is to see the truncated opening lines — however memorable — become all that is left of the poem, and of Yeats' character, in popular understanding, it is more painful to see the disappearance of the human drama of the poem in itself as it evolves, in its desire for authentically human speech and an authentic estimation of human powers — better and truer things than arrogant and stentorian utterances of omniscience. In repudiating his first octave of omniscience, making a break, and then having to write a different "sonnet" to attain a more accurate account of himself and his time, Yeats repeats, by remaking his form, his disavowal of the vain human temptation to prophecy. "Attempting to become more than Man, we become less," said Blake, in what could serve as an epigraph to Yeats' intricate and terrifying and regularly misread poem.

SEAN WILENTZ

Abolition and American Origins

The turbulent politics of the present moment have reached far back into American history. Although not for the first time, the very character of the ideals expressed in the Declaration of Independence and the Constitution have been thrown into question by the hideous reality of slavery, long before and then during the founding era and for eighty years thereafter; and then by slavery's legacy. In this accounting, slavery appears not as an institution central to American history but as that history's essence, the system of white supremacy and economic oligarchy upon which everything else in this country has been built, right down to the inequalities and injustices of today.

More than forty years ago, when a similar bleak pessimism was in the air, the pioneering African American historian Benjamin Quarles remarked on that pessimism's distortions. The history of American slavery could never be properly grasped, Quarles wrote, "without careful attention to a concomitant development and influence — the crusade against it," a crusade, he made clear, that commenced before the American Revolution. Quarles understood that examining slavery's oppression without also examining the anti-slavery movement's resistance to it simplifies and coarsens our history, which in turn coarsens our own politics and culture. "The anti-slavery leaders and their organizations tell us much about slavery," he insisted — and, no less importantly, "they tell us something about our character as a nation."

If we are to speak about the nation's origins, we must get the origins right. As we continue to wrestle with the brutal, and soul-destroying power of racism in our society, it is essential that we recognize the mixed and mottled history upon which our sense of our country must rest. In judging a society, how do we responsibly assess its struggle against evil alongside the evil against which it struggles? With what combination of outrage and pride, alienation and honor, should we define our feelings about America?

On November 5, 1819, Elias Boudinot, the former president of the Continental Congress, ex-U.S. Congressman, and past director of the U.S. Mint, wrote to former President James Madison, enclosing a copy of the proceedings of a meeting held a week earlier in Trenton, New Jersey, opposing the admission of Missouri to the Union as a slave state. The crisis over Missouri — which would lead to the famous Missouri Compromise the following year — had begun in the House of Representatives in February, but Congress had been out of session for months with virtually no sign of popular concern. In late summer, Boudinot, who was 79 and crippled by gout, mustered the strength to help organize a modest protest gathering in his hometown of Burlington, long a center of anti-slavery. The far larger follow-up meeting in Trenton was truly impressive, a "great Assemblage of persons" that included the governor of New Jersey and most of the state legislature. The main speaker, the Pennsylvania Congressman Joseph Hopkinson, who was also a member of the Pennsylvania Abolition Society, had backed the House amendment that touched off the crisis, and his speech in Trenton, according to one report, "rivetted the attention of every auditor." Boudinot, too ill to travel to the state capital, agreed nevertheless to chair a committee of correspondence that wrote to dozens of prominent men, including ex-President Madison, seeking their support.

If Madison ever responded to Boudinot's entreaty, the letter has not survived, but no matter: Madison's correspondence with another anti-slavery advocate made clear that he was not about to support checking the future of slavery in Missouri. Boudinot's and the committee's efforts did, however, meet with approval from antislavery notables such as John Jay. It also galvanized a multitude of anti-Missouri meetings all across the northern states, pressuring Congress to hold fast on restricting slavery's spread. "It seems to have run like a flaming fire through our middle States and causes great anxiety," Boudinot wrote to his nephew at the end of November. The proslavery St. Louis *Enquirer* complained two months later that the agitation begun in Burlington had reached "every dog-hole town and blacksmith's village in the northern states." The protests, the largest outpouring of mass antislavery opinion to that point in American history, were effective: by December, according to the New Hampshire political leader William Plumer, it had become "political suicide" for any free-state officeholder "to tolerate slavery beyond its present limits."

Apart from indicating the scope and the fervor of popular antislavery opinion well before the rise of William Lloyd Garrison, two elements in this story connect in important ways to the larger history of the antislavery movement in the United States, one element looking forward from 1819, the other looking backward. Of continuing future importance was the breadth of the movement's abolitionist politics, as announced in the circular of the Trenton mass meeting. Although it aimed, in this battle, simply to halt the extension of slavery, the anti-Missouri movement's true aim, the circular announced, was nothing less than the complete destruction of slavery in the United States. "The abolition of slavery in this country," it proclaimed, was one of "the anxious and ardent desires of the just and humane citizens of the United States." It was not just a matter of requiring that Missouri enter as a free state: by blocking human bondage from "every other new state that may hereafter be admitted into the Union," it would be only a matter of time before American slavery was eradicated. Just as important, the abolitionists took pains to explain that restricting slavery in this way fell within the ambit of Congress' powers, "in full accordance with the principles of the Constitution." Here lay the elements of the antislavery constitutionalism — asserting congressional authority over slavery in places under its jurisdiction — that would evolve, over the ensuing thirty-five years, into the Republican Party's program to place slavery, as Abraham Lincoln put it, "in the

143

course of ultimate extinction."

The second connection, looking backward, was embodied by Elias Boudinot. Some historians have linked Boudinot's antislavery enthusiasm in 1819 to his Federalist politics; more persuasive accounts see it as a natural outgrowth of a deeply religious humanitarianism that had led him, after his retirement from politics and government, to help found the American Bible Society and become a champion of American Indians. The most recent comprehensive study of the Missouri crisis depicts him as something of a throwback, "the quintessential antiegalitarian patrician Federalist" with a pious humanitarian streak who had lingered long enough to play a part in the commencement of the nation's crisis over slavery.

In fact, Boudinot had already had a long career not only as an antislavery advocate but also as an antislavery politician. He first threw himself seriously into antislavery politics in 1774 when, as a member of the colonial assembly, he worked closely with his Quaker colleague and abolitionist leader Samuel Allinson in ultimately unsuccessful efforts to hasten total abolition in New Jersey. In 1786, Boudinot joined with another antislavery politician, Joseph Bloomfield, in founding the New Jersey Society for Promoting the Abolition of Slavery; and after several years of indifferent activity, the Society presented a gradual emancipation plan that Bloomfield, elected New Jersey's governor in 1803, signed into law the following year. Boudinot, meanwhile, was elected to the first U.S. Congress in 1789, where he denounced slavery as an offence against the Declaration of Independence and "the uniform tenor of the Gospel." In all, if the antislavery arguments of the 1850s dated back to the Missouri crisis, then the antislavery politics that brought about that crisis dated back to the Revolutionary era.

These two connections — the history of the antislavery

constitutionalism that surfaced in the Missouri crisis and the history of antislavery politics dating back to the Revolution — deserve an important place in our account of our origins. I have argued, in a recent book, that by refusing to recognize the legitimacy of property in man in national law, the Federal Convention in 1787 left open ground upon which antislavery politics later developed at the national as well as the state level. Those politics emerged, to be sure, out of the local struggles that dated back before the American Revolution. But the ratification of the Constitution, even with that document's notorious compromises over slavery, left room for the rise of antislavery politics on the national level. And the origins of those politics, as I wish to make clear here, lay in the efforts by antislavery agitators and their allies in Congress, beginning in the very first Congress, to find in the Constitution the authority whereby the national government could abolish slavery or, at the very least, hasten slavery's abolition.

These national antislavery politics, it needs emphasizing, developed by fits and starts, and only began to gather lasting strength in the 1840s. The abolitionists enjoyed just a few significant successes at the national level during the twenty years following the Constitution's ratification, and they endured some important defeats. These were some of the leanest years in the history of antislavery politics. But that the abolitionists won anything at all, let alone anything significant, contradicts the conventional view that southern slaveholders thoroughly dominated national politics in the early republic. The abolitionists did occasionally prevail; and just as important, in doing so they discovered and began to refine the principles and stratagems of antislavery constitutionalism that would guide antislavery politics through to the Missouri crisis and then, further refined, to the Civil War.

Abolition and American Origins

Reviewing the early history of these abolitionist politics — running from the birth of the federal government in 1789 until the abolition of American involvement in the Atlantic slave trade in 1807 — is part of a broader re-evaluation currently underway of what Manisha Sinha has called "the first wave" of abolitionist activity that lasted from the Revolutionary era through the 1820s. Scholarship by a rising generation of historians, including Sarah Gronningsater, Paul J. Polgar, and Nicholas P. Wood, as well as Manisha Sinha, have begun to revise completely the history of antislavery in this period. They have more or less demolished, for example, the once dominant view of northern emancipation as a grudging and even conservative undertaking, led by polite gentlemen unwilling to take their antislavery too far. When completed, the work of these scholars and others will, I am confident, become the basis for a new narrative for the history not just of antislavery but of American politics from the Revolution to the Civil War. But there is a lot of work left to do.

Prior to the 1750s, there was very little in the way of antislavery activity among white Americans, with the exception of the Quakers, and it took even the Quakers several decades of struggle among themselves before they turned misgivings about slavery into formal instructions to abandon the institution. Amid an extraordinary moral rupture at mid-century, wider antislavery activity began in earnest. Initially, these efforts emphasized limited public efforts to change private behavior, relying on moral suasion to hasten manumissions, but soon enough some antislavery reformers turned to politics in more forceful ways. In 1766 and 1767, Boston instructed its represen-

tatives in the colonial assembly to push for the total eradica-
tion of slavery. In 1773, a Quaker-led campaign against the slave
trade, captained by Anthony Benezet, the greatest antislavery
agitator of the time, swept through the middle colonies and
touched New England; and in that same year several Massachu-
setts towns petitioned the assembly to abolish the slave trade
and initiate gradual emancipation. Black abolitionists, includ-
ing Felix Holbrook and Prince Hall in Massachusetts, initi-
ated their own petition drives, supplementing the freedom
suits that would kill slavery in Massachusetts outright in
the mid-1780s. Bills for the gradual abolition of slavery were
debated in New Jersey in 1775 and in Connecticut in 1777;
Vermonters approved the first written constitution ever to ban
adult slavery in 1777; and by 1780 ascendant radical reformers
in Pennsylvania led by George Bryan prepared to enact the first
gradual emancipation law of its kind in history.

By then, political abolitionists had begun organizing their
own institutions. On April 14, 1775 — five days before the
battles of Lexington and Concord — a group consisting chiefly
of Quakers formed the Society for the "Relief for Free Negroes
Unlawfully Held in Bondage," the first society with antislavery
aims anywhere in the world. Although the Revolution soon
disrupted the group, it reorganized in 1784 as the Pennsylvania
Society for the Promotion of the Abolition of Slavery; three
years later, the society named Benjamin Franklin — conspicu-
ously a non-Quaker — as its president. In 1785, the New-York
Manumission Society appeared, dedicated to the same basic
goals. By 1790, two more states, Rhode Island and Connecticut,
had approved gradual emancipation. Slavery was ended in
Massachusetts by judicial decree in 1783, had crumbled in New
Hampshire; and at least six more abolitionist societies had
formed from Rhode Island as far south as Virginia (where, in

147

1785, an abolition law was debated to supplement a widened manumission law enacted in 1782). In 1794, the state societies confederated as the American Convention for Promoting the Abolition of Slavery and Improving the Condition of the African Race.

Abolitionist politics at the national level would await the framing and ratification of the Federal Constitution in 1787-1788. Since the Articles of Confederation had afforded the national government no authority over national commerce, let alone either slavery or the Atlantic slave trade, national abolitionist politics barely existed. The one exceptional effort came in 1783, when a small Quaker delegation from the Philadelphia Yearly Meeting delivered to the Confederation Congress, then sitting in temporary exile in Princeton, a petition signed by some five hundred Quakers, asking in vain for a prohibition of the Atlantic trade. With the calling of the Federal Convention in 1787, though, both of the then-existing abolitionist societies, in Philadelphia and New York, mobilized to send petitions. Benjamin Franklin, a delegate to the convention as well as president of the Pennsylvania Abolition Society decided on tactical grounds against presenting his group's forceful memorial opposing the Atlantic slave trade, while the New-York Manumission Society failed to complete its broader antislavery draft before learning that slavery as such would not be debated at the convention.

To comprehend the national abolitionist politics that followed these developments requires a closer look at the Constitution's paradoxes and contradictions concerning slavery. None of the framers' compromises over slavery that many historians cite as the heart of the supposedly proslavery Constitution were nearly as powerful in protecting slavery as an assumption that was there from the start: that whatever else it could do, the federal government would be powerless to interfere with slavery in the states where it existed — a doctrine that became known as the federal consensus. This assumption, far more than the three-fifths clause or the Atlantic slave trade clause or the fugitive slave clause or anything else, was the basis of the slaveholders' confidence that the Constitution had enshrined human bondage. But if the federal government could not abolish slavery outright, then how might it be done, short of hoping that the slaveholders of South Carolina and Georgia would suddenly see the light — a prospect that the South Carolinians and Georgians made clear was not in the offing anytime soon? Once the abolitionists had launched the campaign for emancipation in the North, this would be their great conundrum — but they seized upon it immediately, with actions as bold as their demands. In doing so, they fostered a convergence of radical agitation and congressional politics that would have enduring if as yet unforeseen repercussions.

Far from discouraging abolitionist activity, the ratification of the Constitution, even with its notorious compromises over slavery, bolstered it. Above all, the framers' granting to the new national government, over furious southern objections, the authority to abolish the nation's Atlantic slave trade, even with a twenty-year delay, struck many and probably most abolitionists and their political allies as a major blow for freedom. This should not be surprising: as historians note too rarely, it was the first serious blow against the international slave trade undertaken anywhere in the Atlantic world in the name of a national government; indeed, the American example, preceded by the truly inspiring anti-slave agitation led by Anthony Benezet, encouraged the rise of the British movement to end the Atlantic trade, formally organized in 1787. Some leading American abolitionists described the Constitution as nothing less than, in the words of the framer James Wilson, "the foundation for banishing slavery out of this country." Ending the trade had long been considered the vital first step toward eradicating slavery itself; and it seemed at the least highly probably that, as soon as 1808 arrived, Congress would do so. More immediately, though, members of the Pennsylvania Abolition Society wanted to see if Congress would entertain extending its constitutional authority beyond the slave trade provision.

The first great confrontation over slavery in national politics was a famous but still largely misunderstood conflict in the House of Representatives during the First Congress' second session in New York, the nation's temporary capital, in 1790. Through a friendly congressman, the Pennsylvania Abolition Society presented a petition to the House of Representatives, above the signature of its aging president Franklin, bidding the representatives to "step to the very verge of the powers vested in you" and to abolish slavery itself, not simply the Atlantic slave trade. (At the request of John Pemberton of the PAS, two groups of Quakers had already sent milder petitions referring only to the trade.) Paying no attention to the federal consensus, the PAS petition specifically cited the preamble of the Constitution that empowered the new government to "promote the general Welfare and secure the blessings of Liberty to ourselves and our Posterity," which they contended authorized far-reaching if unspecified congressional action against slavery. Without telling Congress exactly what to do, the petitioners bid the representatives to look beyond the federal consensus to find ways they could attack slavery — to the extent, quite possibly, of disregarding the federal consensus entirely.

A fierce on-and-off debate over the next three months ended with Congress affirming the federal consensus as well as the ban on congressional abolition of the Atlantic trade until 1808. The outcome is often portrayed fatalistically as a crushing defeat for the abolitionists, sealing the immunity of slavery in the new republic while calling into question the rights of abolitionists even to petition the Congress — an effort undertaken, in one historian's estimation, by naïve and "psychologically vulnerable" reformers, unprepared "for the secular interest politics of a modern nation."

In fact, although the petition (along with the two others from regional Quaker meetings) did not gain the sweeping reforms it sought, it was decidedly not a failure. For one thing, the mobilization behind it, far from weak-kneed, was the first auspicious political protest of any kind to be directed at the new national government. Strikingly modern in its strategy and its tactics, the abolitionists blended insider maneuvering and hard-headed direct appeals to members of Congress with popular propagandizing and political theater of a kind associated with the protest movements of much later decades. The campaign was spearheaded by a delegation of eleven Quaker lobbyists from Philadelphia, including John Pemberton and Warner Mifflin, who were certainly the opposite of naïve and vulnerable. As a consequence, the congressional deliberations over the petitions took a surprisingly radical turn, and in the end the effort secured important political as well as practical gains.

Lower South slaveholders reacted with predictable fury as

151

soon as congressmen friendly to the abolitionists introduced the petitions on the floor of the House. The slaveholders' diatribes asserted that the constitutional ban on congressional abolition of the Atlantic slave trade until 1808 meant that the Constitution barred any federal interference with slavery whatsoever. Given the federal consensus, meanwhile, the slaveholders called the petitions unconstitutional on their face and demanded they be rejected without further debate. But despite the inflation of their numbers in the House by the three-fifths clause, the proslavery forces were badly outnumbered. ("Alass — how weak a resistance against the whole house," one resigned South Carolina congressman wrote.) By a vote of 43 to 11, the House approved sending the radical petitions to a special committee for consideration.

Working hand-in-hand with members of the special committee, the abolitionists immediately supplied them with a small library of abolitionist writings, while they arranged, through the Speaker of the House, an ally, to distribute additional abolitionist propaganda to the rest of the chamber. The Quaker lobbyists then advised the committee on its report behind the scenes, sharing drafts and submitting their own suggestions while backing up the PAS petition's claim that the "General Welfare" section of the Constitution's preamble gave Congress some unspecified powers over slavery. The committee narrowly turned aside that suggestion — by a single vote, John Pemberton reported — and agreed that the Congress could not ban the Atlantic slave trade before 1808. Yet it also asserted, contrary to lower South protests, that the federal government could regulate the trade as it saw fit at any time. More portentously, the members included wording that the Constitution empowered Congress to abolish slavery outright after 1808 — making the special committee's report perhaps the most radical official document on slavery approved by any congressional entity before the Civil War.

When the report reached the House, the abolitionists swung into action as both agitators and what today we would call lobbyists. Quakers crowded the House gallery to witness the debate, their presence in Quaker gray suits and broad-brimmed black hats inciting and unnerving the southerners. Outside the hall, the abolitionists pursued individual congressmen right down to their lodging houses and taverns and eating places to make their case. Mifflin began a letter-writing campaign, addressed both to individual congressmen and to the House at large. The abolitionists also arranged with allies in the New-York Manumission Society to have a full record of the House debates printed along with antislavery articles in the New York *Daily Advertiser*, as well as to distribute pamphlets vividly describing the horrors of the slave trade.

Finally the House affirmed Congress' powerlessness over slavery where it existed and over the Atlantic trade before 1808, and a revised report removed the select committee's language about abolishing slavery itself after 1808. Yet the outcome was hardly a one-sided triumph for the proslavery southerners. The lower South failed utterly in its initial effort to dismiss the petitions without debate. Evidently, contrary to the slaveholders, Congress might well have some authority over slavery worth debating. In the course of arguing that point, moreover, several House members had affirmed that, short of abolishing slavery outright, Congress might restrict slavery in various ways quite apart from the slave trade, including, James Madison remarked, banning slavery from the national territories, where, he declared, "Congress have certainly the power to regulate slavery." And over howls

153

from lower South slaveholders, the final report affirmed that Congress could legislate over specific matters connected to the Atlantic trade before 1808 — issues that, as we shall see, the abolitionists would agitate successfully. In all, the federal consensus stood, but at the same time the House majority repulsed the proslavery forces and backed the abolitionists on whether slavery was immune from federal authority.

Over the ensuing decade, the abolitionists, far from discouraged, redoubled their national efforts, despite some serious setbacks. The Southwest Territory — what would become the state of Tennessee — was admitted to the Union with slavery in 1790, with little debate. A coterie of antislavery congressmen could not stave off passage of the Fugitive Slave Act of 1793. Five years later, a spirited antislavery effort to bar slavery from Mississippi Territory was defeated by a wide margin.

And yet the abolitionists had reason to remain optimistic. At the state level, the New York legislature, under intense abolitionist pressure, finally passed a gradual emancipation law in 1799 and New Jersey followed five years later, completing the northern "first emancipation." In part as a response to the Fugitive Slave Act, the American Convention of Abolition Societies was up and running in 1794. There were various signs, from a proliferation of freedom suits in Virginia to the spread of antislavery opinion in Kentucky and Tennessee, that the upper South was seriously questioning slavery. In national politics, antislavery congressmen, numbering about a dozen and led by a few northerners who worked closely with the abolitionists, made good in 1794 on the victory wrung from the abolitionist petition debates four years earlier, passing a law that outlawed the use of any American port or shipyard for constructing or outfitting any ship to be used for the importing of slaves.

Five years later the Reverend Absalom Jones, a prominent abolitionist and mainstay of Philadelphia's free black community, helped lead an even more propitious effort. Late in 1799, a group of seventy free men of color in Philadelphia, headed by Jones, sent yet another petition to the House of Representatives. The drafters of the petition, as Nicholas Wood has shown, were John Drinker and John Parrish, prominent local Quaker abolitionists who had long worked closely with Jones and other black abolitionists; the signers included members of various black congregations, including Jones' St. Thomas African Episcopal Church, the majority of them unable to sign their names.

The petitioners asked for revisions of the laws governing the Atlantic slave trade as well as the Fugitive Slave Law of 1793. But they also went further, as far as the PAS petitioners had in 1790, pressing for — as the abolitionist congressman Nicholas Waln observed when he introduced the petition to the House — "the adoption of such measures as shall in due course emancipate the whole of their brethren from their present situation." Stating that they "cannot but address you as Guardians of our Civil Rights, and Patrons of equal and National Liberty," the petitioners expressed hope that the House members

will view the subject in an impartial, unprejudiced light. — We do not ask for the immediate emancipation of all, knowing that the degraded State of many and their want of education, would greatly disqualify for such a change; yet humbly desire you may exert every means in your power to undo the heavy burdens, and prepare the way for the oppressed to go free, that every yoke may be broken.

As if brushing aside the House's decision in 1790, the abolitionists, citing once again the Constitution's preamble, wanted Congress to probe once more the document's antislavery potential. The idea that Congress had untapped antislavery powers was emerging as a core abolitionist argument. And, though the sources are silent, this portion of the petition may have also had tactical purposes. In 1790, the defeat of grand claims about emancipation proved the prelude to the House affirming Congress' authority over more specific issues connected to slavery. Roughly the same thing would happen this time.

Southern slaveholders and their New England allies reacted with predictable wrath. John Rutledge, Jr. of South Carolina thanked God that Africans were held in slavery, then railed against the "new-fangled French philosophy of liberty and equality" — he was talking about Thomas Jefferson and his supporters — that was abroad in the land. Rutledge's fellow Federalist, the notorious Atlantic slave trader John Brown of Rhode Island, attacked the petition's effort to restrain American participation in the trade, while another New England Federalist, Harrison Gray Otis, sneered that most of the petitioners were illiterate and thus unable to understand what they had endorsed, and that receiving their memorial would mischievously "teach them the art of assembling together, debating, and the like."

The next day, the House considered a resolution condemning those portions of the petition "which invite Congress to legislate upon subjects from which the General Government is precluded by the Constitution." The resolution passed 85 to 1, a crushing repudiation of the idea that Congress possessed implied powers to interfere directly with slavery where it already existed. Even the abolitionist congressman who presented the free blacks' petition ended up voting with the majority.

But that was only part of the story. The core of antislavery Northerners fiercely rebutted the proslavery outbursts. George Thacher, a Massachusetts Federalist and longtime antislavery champion in the House, repudiated the racist attacks on the petitioners, upheld the right of constituents to a redress of grievances regardless of their color, and condemned racial slavery as "a cancer of immense magnitude, that would some time destroy the body politic, except a proper legislation should prevent the evil." Moreover, once the condemnation resolution predictably passed — Thacher's was the sole vote in opposition — the House was free to act on the petitioners' more specific demands, which it swiftly did, sending the petition to committee — thereby, among other things, affirming the right of free blacks to petition Congress.

The committee assigned to consider the petition sympathized with its section on the fugitive slave law — free blacks, its report contended, were "entitled to freedom & Protection" — but the slaveholders and their allies prevailed on that issue on jurisdictional grounds. On the slave trade, however, Congress took action. After a heated debate, the House, with the concurrence of the Senate, approved by a wide margin the Slave Trade Act of 1800, banning even indirect involvement by Americans with the shipping of Africans for sale in any foreign country while also authorizing naval vessels to seize ships that were in violation. While it expanded enforcement of the restrictive law enacted six years earlier, the new law reinforced expectations that the Atlantic slave trade to the United States would be entirely abolished at the earliest possible date in 1808.

The scale of this antislavery victory should not be exaggerated — indeed, three years later South Carolina would re-open its own slave trade with a vengeance — but neither should it be scanted. Most immediately, within a year, under the new law's provisions, the man-of-war *U.S.S. Ganges* seized two illegal slave schooners off the coast of Cuba and discovered more than one hundred and thirty African captives, men, women, and children, in chains, starving and naked; once freed, the Africans obtained apprenticeships and indentures from the Pennsylvania Abolition Society. The free black petition debate also marked a highpoint in the efforts by the antislavery congressmen, first to restrict and regulate the Atlantic slave trade prior to its abolition, and then to reform and restrict the Fugitive Slave Law.

More broadly, that same small but resolute group took up new antislavery battles and established an antislavery presence that from time to time became an antislavery majority. This was not just the agitation of an elite. It must be emphasized that the congressmen acted in coordination with dense interregional as well as interracial networks of antislavery activists, organized in state abolition societies, churches and church committees, mutual aid societies, fraternal groups, and more. With such popular backing, year after year, antislavery congressmen voiced defiantly antiracist as well as antislavery sentiments on the floor of the House, exploring the Constitution in search of antislavery meanings, trying to find in it whatever powers they could whereby the federal government could limit slavery's expansion leading to its eventual eradication. Some of their successes were defensive, as when they defeated efforts to augment the Fugitive Slave Act, to otherwise restrict the rights of free blacks, and to repeal the Northwest Ordinance's ban on slavery in Illinois and Indiana. But the antislavery forces in Congress could be aggressive as well.

In 1804, once again bidden by abolitionist petitions, the Senate approved a provision that would have effectively shut the domestic slave trade out of the entire Louisiana Territory, obtained from France a year before, while the House, stunningly, passed a bill that banned outright further introduction of slavery into the territory. The House provision failed to gain approval from the Senate, and the efforts to keep slavery out of Louisiana proved futile, but the passing success was a signal that the antislavery presence in Congress had grown since 1790. Fittingly, the effort in the House was led by a sharp-witted and acid-tongued member from New Jersey named James Sloan, a Jeffersonian Republican who had cut his political teeth as a member of the New Jersey Abolition Society and as its delegate to the American Convention. A permanent goad to the southern slaveholders, including those in his own party, Sloan would cause an uproar in the House in 1805 by proposing a plan for gradual emancipation in the District of Columbia — yet another effort to find places in the Constitution giving the federal government the authority to attack slavery.

Finally, in 1807, at the earliest date stipulated by the Constitution, Congress approved the abolition of the Atlantic slave trade to the United States. With the bill supported by most of the large Virginia delegation, whose slaveholders stood benefit, the outcome was a foregone conclusion, but the antislavery members had to beat back several efforts to soften the law, including one proposal by the states-rights dogmatist John Randolph which in effect would have recognized slaves as property in national law. "Hail! Hail, glorious day," the New

York black abolitionist minister Peter Williams, Jr., an ally of the New-York Manumission Society, exclaimed at the city's celebration.

This high point in the politics of early American abolitionism would also prove a turning point. Although national agitation continued, there was a noticeable decline in enthusiasm in the ranks, at least outside Pennsylvania, once New York and New Jersey had completed their emancipation laws. A powerful racist backlash instigated by the Haitian Revolution and then by reactions to northern emancipation jolted the existing abolitionist societies and paved the way for the emergence of the American Colonization Society. Just as their British counterparts perfected the massive petition campaigns required to shake Parliament into abolishing Britain's Atlantic slave trade, also achieved in 1807, the American movement began to falter. Above all, the dramatic shift in the Southern economy that came with the introduction of the cotton gin in 1793 and the consequent renaissance of plantation slavery dramatically changed the terms of antislavery politics, dispelling forever the original abolitionist hope that the closing of the Atlantic trade would doom American slavery.

Northern antislavery opinion did rebound after 1815 and reached a political flashpoint during the Missouri crisis of 1819-1820. But the abolitionist organizations, including the American Convention, although still alive and active, were becoming less of a factor in guiding events in Congress than they had been at the end of the eighteenth century. By now, with the expansion of mass mainstream party politics, popular mobilizations in the form of an impromptu Free Missouri movement did more to embolden antislavery congressmen than did the abolitionist's continued memorials, petitions, and lobbying efforts. And then, in the wake of the Missouri crisis, shaken mainstream politicians sealed what amounted to a bipartisan consensus to prevent slavery from ever again entering into national political debates. With national politics seemingly closed to antislavery agitation, the old Quaker abolitionist strategy of working directly with sympathetic officeholders and political leaders began to look feeble.

But the fight had been irreversibly joined. The established abolitionist movement's strategies left an important legacy on which later antislavery political movements would build. Even as the early abolitionist movement sputtered out, it played a part in shaping abolitionism's future. In forming as sophisticated a political movement as they did, the early abolitionists created a practical model for organized political agitation in the new republic, antedating the political parties that arose thereafter. Although the effectiveness of that model declined after 1800 or so, it never disappeared; and elements of it would remain essential to later abolitionist politics, including the transformation of abolitionist petitioning into monster popular campaigns, along the lines that British abolitionists had pioneered after 1787.

The legacy was even more important with respect to antislavery ideology and strategy. If the initial impetus of the early abolitionists, dating back to 1775, had been to politicize antislavery sentiment, in order to make direct claims on government, so the abolitionists of the early republic perpetuated the idea that politics was the only sure means to achieve slavery's eradication. In national politics, after the ratification of the Constitution, that meant, above all, advancing antislavery interpretations of the framers' work. Although the most expansive ideas about Congress' authority over slavery met with ever firmer resistance, the idea that Congress possessed numerous implicit or indirect powers to hasten slavery's demise remained.

Consider again the petition from the free men of color of Philadelphia in 1799. In addition to asking Congress to find the authority to abolish slavery, the petition included its own innovative antislavery interpretation of the Constitution to demonstrate that the Fugitive Slave Law was unconstitutional: as "no mention is made of Black people or Slaves" in the Constitution, the document observed, it followed that "if the Bill of Rights or the declaration of Congress are of any validity," then all men "may partake of the Liberties and unalienable Rights therein held forth." The assertion got nowhere, but it had been made, and as long as abolitionists kindled a basic optimism about the Constitution's antislavery potential, they would sustain their belief that political efforts, and not moral suasion alone, would bring the complete abolition of American slavery.

This optimism peaked again during the Missouri crisis, when abolitionists seized upon federal control of the territories and the admission of new states as an instrument to commence slavery's abolition. The optimism persisted through the 1820s, even as the colonization movement flourished and even as mainstream political leaders built a new system of national politics based on two opposed intersectional national parties — a party system deliberately designed to keep antislavery agitation at the margins. In 1821, a sometime colonizationist, the pioneering abolitionist editor Benjamin Lundy, offered a comprehensive seven-point plan to abolish slavery under the Constitution that began with banning slavery in the national territories and abolishing the domestic slavery trade. Four years later, Lundy joined with the abolitionist and political economist Daniel Raymond in trying to establish an antislavery political party in Maryland. After that failed, Lundy persuaded the American Convention to pick up the dropped thread of James Sloan's earlier agitation in the House and pressure Congress to use its authority to abolish slavery and the slave trade in the District of Columbia. He then had the idea of mounting a mass petition campaign to support the demand; and in 1828, working in coordination with a Pennsylvania Abolition Society member, congressman Charles Miner, who had announced his intention to work for abolition in the district, he forced the issue to the floor of the House. Younger PAS members warmed to the campaign and kept it going; so would, somewhat ironically in retrospect, the young editor whom Lundy later picked up as his assistant and brought into the abolitionist cause, none other than William Lloyd Garrison.

The optimism would be badly battered in the 1830s and 1840s. Some members of a new generation of radical abolition-ists, led by Garrison, would conclude that there was no hope of achieving abolition and equality in a political system attached to a proslavery U.S. Constitution — a "covenant with death" and "agreement with hell," in Garrison's famous condem-nation. Only moral suasion backed with militant protest, Garrison declared, would advance the cause; moral purifica-tion would have to precede political action. Taking the long view, this represented as much a regression as an advance, back to the anti-political stance of the more pious of the Quaker abolitionists in the 1750s and 1760s. Garrison's absolutist high-mindedness forthrightly but perversely lifted the cause above the grimy necessities of actual politics.

Yet for all of Garrison's fiery and intrepid polemics, he

163

and his followers were a minority inside the abolitionist movement, increasingly so after 1840. The abolitionist majority never relinquished the idea, passed on from the first-wave abolitionists, that Congress, by acting wherever it could against slavery, would hasten slavery's destruction. Inside Congress, meanwhile, a luminary with antislavery convictions but no previous antislavery record, John Quincy Adams, led a small group of colleagues in a guerilla war against the gag rule and finally prevailed in 1844. Adams, the ex-president turned congressman, was a singular figure in American politics, unlike any before or since; and the 1840s were not the 1820s or the 1790s. But Adams, who came to work closely with abolitionists, in his way reprised the roles of George Thacher, James Sloan, and Charles Miner, becoming the face of antislavery inside the Capitol — "the acutest, the astutest, the archest enemy of slavery that ever existed," in the view of his fiercely proslavery Virginia rival Henry A. Wise.

By the time he collapsed and died on the floor of the House in 1848, opposing the American war with Mexico, Adams had also helped turn antislavery politics back toward issues concerning federal power over slavery in the territories — the very issues that, within a decade, led to the formation of the Republican Party. The abolitionists search for the constitutional means to attack slavery, begun in 1790, culminated in the agitation over Kansas, the convulsions that followed the Dred Scott decision in 1857, and everything else that led to the Civil War. All of which is a vast and complicated story, making the final connection between the antislavery politics of Anthony Benezet and Benjamin Franklin with those of Frederick Douglass and Abraham Lincoln. The important point, in the consideration of American origins, is that the early American abolitionists, audacious in their own time, formulated the essentials of a political abolitionism that, however beleaguered and often outdone, announced its presence, won some victories, and made its mark in the national as well as state politics of the early republic. It was not least owing to this constitutive achievement of American democracy that in the relatively brief span of fifty years, some of them very violent, slavery would be brought to its knees.

Which brings us back to Benjamin Quarles' observations, about the concomitant development of American slavery and American antislavery. The struggle for justice is always contemporaneous with injustice, quite obviously, and the power of injustice to provoke a hostile response is one of the edifying lessons of human life. Once joined, that struggle forever shapes both sides: there is no understanding the growth of pro-slavery politics, leading to the treason of secession, without reference to the growth of anti-slavery politics, just as anti-slavery politics makes no sense absent pro-slavery politics. But the history of anti-slavery in America, even during its most difficult periods, is not merely a matter of edification. It is also a practical necessity, a foundation for political action. It presents contemporary anti-racism with a tradition from which it can draw its ideas and its tools. It is a barrier against despair, and a refreshment of our sense of American possibility. The struggle against slavery was hard and long, and it was won. The struggle against racism is harder and longer, and it has not yet been won. But as our history shows, it has certainly not been lost.

CELESTE MARCUS

The Sludge

*I was never more hated than when I tried to be honest....
I've never been more loved and appreciated than when I tried
to "justify" and affirm someone's mistaken beliefs; or when
I tried to give my friends the incorrect, absurd answers they
wished to hear. In my presence they could talk and agree with
themselves, the world was nailed down, and they loved it.
They received a feeling of security.*

RALPH ELLISON, *INVISIBLE MAN*

One Friday afternoon, in a carpeted alcove off the main sanctuary of my school, a Jewish school in the suburbs of Philadelphia, my class collected in a circle as we did every week. A young, liberally perfumed Israeli woman in a tight turtleneck sweater read to us from a textbook about the exodus from Egypt. I asked her why our ancestors had been enslaved to begin with, and then wondered aloud whether it was because only former slaves can appreciate freedom. I remember the feeling of the idea forming in my very young mind, and the struggle to articulate it. Clumsily, with a child's vocabulary, I suggested to my teacher that Jewish political life began with emancipation, and that this origin ensured that gratitude to God would be the foundation of our national identity. Could that have been God's motivation? I don't remember her answer, only her mild bemusement, and my impression that she did not have the philosophical tools or the inclination to engage with the question. I was left to wonder on my own about the nature of slavery, the distant memories that undergird identity, and God's will; without a teacher, without a framework. I was by myself with these questions.

Of course, we were not gathered in that schoolchildren's circle to study philosophy. We were studying the Biblical tale not in order to theorize about the nature of slavery and freedom, or to acquire a larger sense of Jewish history, but because it was expected of us, and every other grade in the school, this and every week since the school's founding, to study the weekly portion of the Torah, because that is what Jewish students in a Jewish school of that denomination do. I had mistaken a social activity for an intellectual one. The norms of a community demanded this conversation of us, because otherwise the community would be suspect. People would whisper that graduates of our school lacked

The Sludge

the capacity for full belonging within their particular Jewish group, because we had failed to receive the proper training in membership. The overarching objective of our education was initiation. The prayers that we were taught to say before and after eating, and upon waking up in the morning, and going to the bathroom, and seeing a rainbow, and on myriad other quotidian occasions, served the same purpose. These were not theological practices; we were not taught to consider the might and creative power of the God whom we were thanking — the meanings of what we recited, the ideas that lay beneath the words. We uttered all those sanctifying words because it was what our school's permutation of the Jewish tradition taught Jews to do. We were performing, not pondering.

Divine commandments were the sources and accoutrements of our liturgies and rituals. But we lingered much longer over the choreography than over the divinity. The substance of our identity was rules, which included the recitation of certain formulas for certain concepts and customs. And our knowledge of the rules, how or whether we obeyed them, would signal what sort of Jews we were. The primary purpose of this system was to provide talismans that we could use to signal membership. In the context of my religious education, the meaning of the symbols was less important than how I presented them. Badges were more central than beliefs. The content of the badges — the symbols and all the concomitant intellectual complications — was left alone. Marinating within that culture inculcated in me an almost mystical reverence for my religion and for its God because it placed them in a realm outside of reason. I could not interrogate them: holiness is incommensurate with reason. Without the indelible experience of that schooling in anti-intellectualism, the beauties and intoxicants of tradition would be inaccessible to me. Even now, when I witness expressions of fine religious faith, I am capable of recognizing and honoring them because of that early training.

The anti-intellectualism had another unwitting effect: the indifference of my community to the cerebral and non-communal dimensions of the way we lived meant that I could develop my own relationship with them. Since they were unconcerned with the aspects of religious life to which I most kindled, I was free to discover them independently. They didn't care what I thought, so I set out to think. In this manner I began to acquaint myself with fundamental human questions, to feel my way around and develop the rudiments of ideas about morality, slavery, love, and forgiveness. My academic syllabi were rife with references to these themes, but they were rarely discussed directly. They were like so many paintings on the wall: we would walk by them a hundred times a day and never stop and look. As children we became comfortable in their presence, but we did not exactly study them together, so I studied them alone, without the commentaries that would harden them into a catechism.

In a certain ironic sense, I was lucky. When someone is taught to think about fundamental human questions within a group, her conception of those themes will be shaped by the group. The goal of that sort of group study, perhaps not overtly articulated but always at work, would be to initiate her into a particular system of particular people, to provide her with a ready-made attitude and a handy worldview, to train her to think and speak in the jargon of that worldview, and to signal membership within the company of those who espouse it.

The Sludge

If language is a condition of our thoughts, it is also a source of their corruption. Thinking outside a language may be impossible, but thought may take place in a variety of vocabularies, and the unexamined vocabularies, the ones that we receive in tidy and dogmatic packages, pose a great danger to clear and critical thinking. My good fortune was that I was not socialized philosophically. My religious tradition was not presented to me as a philosophical tradition. I was not inducted into a full and finished vernacular that would dictate or manipulate how I would think. And I was young enough not to have become so sensitive to political or cultural etiquettes that they would inhibit or mitigate independent reflection and study. The space in my head into which I retreated to think was built and outfitted mainly by me, or so it felt; and there, in that detached and unassisted space, I became accustomed to the looming awareness that these themes were too complicated for me to really understand (an awareness which provoked an ineradicable distrust for communal ideological certainties). Yet this did not diminish my desire to spend time there. My relationship with my burgeoning ideas felt privileged, the way a child feels playing with plundered high heels or lipstick without the context to understand the social significations that those instruments may one day carry. If I misunderstood them, if they baffled me, there was no reason to be embarrassed. My sense of possibility was large and exciting, because it was unburdened by the adult awareness that convictions have social consequences by which they may then be judged.

My limited field of human experience — the people I knew, the fictional and historical figures to which I had been introduced — comprised all the materials with which I could conduct my solitary musings. I studied the rhythms and tendencies of human interactions. I watched the way that other people responded to each other, the way they held themselves when they were alone or in society. This stock of knowledge informed how I thought people in general do and ought to behave. (My theory of slavery and emancipation was a product of this discipline: for example, I noted that I got anxious for recess when in school but bored by endless freedom on the weekend or vacation. We appreciate freedom when we are enslaved: is that what Scripture wanted me to understand? Well, that was consistent with my experience.) My inquiries were catalyzed and sustained by pure curiosity about human beings and in retrospect they seem to have been relatively untainted by my community's biases. Perhaps I am idealizing my beginnings, but I really do have the memory of an open mind and a pretty level playing field. Like the adolescent heroines in Rohmer's films, I genuinely wanted to know how people are so I could figure out how I should be.

The effects of this solitary and informal mental life were permanent. Having developed the space in my head independent of a received blueprint, my intellectual methods would always be fundamentally unsocialized. Despite the external pressures, I have never successfully unlearned these attitudes. I don't doubt that there were many influences from my surroundings, from my community and my culture, that I was absorbing without recognizing them, but still I felt significantly on my own and, as I say, lucky. But I was also quite lonely. The loneliness intensified as I got older and my family became more religious. The high school that I attended was much more traditional than my earlier schools had been. There were more rules, endless esoteric rituals and cultural habits that I had to learn in order to convince myself and others that I was one of them, that I belonged there. I failed often. There was so much that I didn't know, and, more to the point, there

The Sludge

was something about the weather around me that perpetually exposed my difference. No matter how hard I tried to remake myself into a member, to dismantle and rebuild the space in my head, everyone could sense that the indoctrination was not taking. I recited the script with a foreign accent.

In a flagrant, chronic, and no doubt annoying manifestation of otherness, I would badger my teachers and peers for reasons and explanations. *Why* were we — I was a "we" now - obeying all these rules? I was not in open revolt: I sensed that our tradition was rich and I was eager to plumb the treasures that I had been bequeathed. But it seemed a gross dereliction to obey the laws without considering their purpose. My intentions were innocent, perhaps even virtuous, but my questions were discomfiting anyway. Even now I often recall a particularly representative afternoon. A group of girls in my grade were discussing the practice called *shmirat negiah*, the strict observance of physical distance between the sexes, which prohibits men and women who are not related from touching one another. I wondered: Why had the rule been written to begin with? When did Jews begin to enforce it? What kind of male-female dynamic did it seek to cultivate? Did such emphatic chasteness in preparation for marriage help or harm that union? These were reasonable questions, except that in a context of orthodoxy they could be received as subversive. A girl I admired — a paragon of membership — complained that the practice made her awkward and scared of men, and that she could not understand why her mother enforced it. "Why don't you just ask your mother why she thinks you ought to do it?" I finally asked. "Because," she sighed, "she'll just tell me that I have to because that is what Jews do." My mind recoiled. Why on earth would a mother shirk the opportunity (and the responsibility) to help her child grapple with such an important question? Why wouldn't she consider the law itself a catalyst for conversations about such primary themes? Yet even as I asked myself these questions, I knew the answer. Membership mattered more than meaning.

But surely that attitude did not govern all human communities. This could not be all there was. Somewhere, I assumed, there were institutions in which people directly addressed the ideas I wondered about on my own. Somewhere there were groups in which the exploration of meaning was an essential feature of membership. In the secular world, which I naively called "the real world," I imagined intellectual camaraderie would be easier to find. Surely secular people, when they talk about justice, sex, mercy, and virtue, must be interested in seriously engaging those themes. In the real world, surely, there would be no orthodoxies, and people would have no reason to incessantly analyze one another's behaviors in order to grant or deny them legitimacy. They would not spread petty rumors about neighbors failing to uphold the code or refuse to eat at the tables of those who were not exactly like them, as the worst members of my origin bubble did. They would not, forgive me, cancel each other.

Of course I was wrong. As it turns out, the secular world also has liturgies, dogmas, ostracisms, and bans. It, too, hallows conformity. It has heretics, and it even has gods: they just don't call them that. In college I discovered the temples of the progressives, the liberals, the conservatives, and more. Each has a vernacular of its own, comprised of dialects and rituals which serve to establish membership, welcome members, and turn away outsiders. In this realm of proud secularity, my religious

The Sludge

upbringing proved unexpectedly useful. It had prepared me to identify the mechanisms of group power, and the cruel drama of deviance and its consequences. (What is cancellation, if not excommunication?) It turned out that all too often in the real world, the open world, the democratic world, the enlightened world, when people talk about fundamental human questions they are far more interested in signaling membership and allegiance than in developing honest answers to them.

It is true that many of these questions are hard to answer. The intensity with which people hold convictions belies their complexity. Independent and critical reasoning is not for the faint of heart, and the length and difficulty of the search may eventually make skeptics or cynics of them. It is much simpler to memorize a script, and to establish a quasi-mystical allegiance to ones politics. Holiness is incommensurate with reason, remember. Still, the demands of a nuanced politics are not, I think, why people are reluctant to wrestle with ideas on their own. There are advantages to wholesale worldviews and closed systems. They provide something even more alluring than conviction: solidarity. They are a cure not only for perplexity but also for loneliness. A group with which to rehearse shared dogma, and to style oneself in accordance with the aesthetic that those dogma evoke: this is not a small thing. Thus the answer to a philosophical or moral question becomes…community. We choose our philosophy on the basis of our sociology. This is a category mistake — and the rule by which we live.

In a different world, most people would readily admit ignorance or doubt about political or cultural subjects the same way that my young peer would have had no reason to refrain from hugging friends of the opposite gender if Jewish custom did not forbid it. If their group ignored the subject, so would they. Most would not be ashamed of their confusion because intellectual confusion is not a common fear. But isolation is. We dread marginality more than we dread error. After all, the social costs of idiosyncrasy or independence are high. We fear finding ourselves at our screens, watching others retweet or like or share one another's posts without a cohort of our own in which to do the same. Who does not wish to be a part of a whole? (Identity politics is the current name for this cozy mode of discourse.) In my experience, when most people talk about politics, they are largely motivated by this concern, which compromises the integrity of these conversations. They disguise a social discourse as an intellectual discourse.

I call this phony discourse the sludge. The sludge is intellectual and political kitsch. It is a shared mental condition in which all the work of thinking has already been done for us. It redirects attention away from fundamentals by converting them into accessories, into proofs of identity, into certificates of membership.

In a sludge-infected world, in our world, if someone were to say, "that fascist presides over a hegemonic patriarchy," her primary purpose would be to communicate to her interlocutor that she is woke, trustworthy, an insider, an adept, a spokesperson, an agent of a particular ideology, proficient in its jargon. She would also be indicating the denomination of progressivism to which she subscribes, thus erecting the ideological boundaries for the conversation. If someone else were to say, of the same person, that he is a "cosmopolitan" or a "globalist" or a "snowflake" she would be doing the same thing in a different vernacular. (They would both use the terms "liberal" and "neoliberal" as slurs, probably without a firm sense of what either one means.) In the context of these two conversations, whether or not the individual in question is a snowflake or a fascist is as good as irrelevant. The subject of the conversation is just an occasion for manifesting group solidarity. Righteousness is an accoutrement of the code. In fact, asking either person to justify the assumptions inherent in her statement would be as irregular as asking me to justify my faith in God after witnessing me thank Him for the apple I am about to eat. She would answer with her equivalent of "that's just what Jews do." In both these cases, belonging is prior to belief.

The effect of sludge-infected language is that quite often the focal point of debates about politics or philosophy is not at all the literal subject at hand. Members are conditioned to *present* as if they care about the substance of a particular ideology. Learning to present as if you care about something is very different from learning to actually care about something. Caring is difficult, it is a complicated and time-consuming capacity which requires discipline, openness, and analysis. This is not a trivial point. Imagine a sludge-infected romantic relationship (or just look around you) — if, instead of taking a close and patient interest in her lover's needs, a woman simply asked herself, "What are the kinds of things that people who are in love do?," and having done those things, considered herself well acquitted of these duties and therefore in love. She may tell him that she loves him, and she may be loving or supportive in a generic kind of way, but she will not really know him. Details about his inner life, about his insecurities and his demons, will not interest her. Romantic success, for her, would be to appear from the outside as if they have created a successful partnership. She will have treated love programmatically, in accordance with the expectations of her social context. Who her lover is when he is not playing the role she has assigned to him will remain mysterious. When tragedy strikes, they will be forced to recognize that they do not know or trust each other.

Sludge-infected politics are similarly behavioral and unsettling. Practitioners exploit opportunities for genuine expressions of devotion as occasions to signal membership. Consider the effect of the sludge on antiracism. Suppose we were taught to present as antiracists rather than to seriously consider the imperatives of antiracism (or, again, just look around you). Antiracism (like feminism, like Zionism, like socialism, like isms generally) is difficult to cultivate and strengthen. It requires work and must be consciously developed. It is the result of many individual experiences and sacrifices, highs and lows, of sustained and thoughtful interest and introspection. If we consider ourselves acquitted of our responsibility to antiracism merely by posting #handsupdontshoot at regular intervals on social media, perhaps garnering a host of likes and followers, the duties of an honest and reflective antiracism will remain unacknowledged (and the sentiment to which that slogan refers will be cheapened). Our antiracism would be not internal but external, not philosophical but stylistic.

If a person is a dedicated antiracist, over the years she will come to better appreciate the enormity of the battle against racism. She will develop the minute concerns and sensitivities of a veteran. She will realize that the world is not made up only of friends and enemies. She will know that sometimes, in order to do good, one must work alongside unlikely allies, and that purists are incapable of effecting sustainable change. The very language she uses to discuss her mission will be informed

177

by this knowledge. Indeed, it would strike her as shabby and disloyal to regurgitate common slogans when speaking about the specific, discomfiting realities of which she has intimate knowledge and which she is serious about mitigating. She will choose more precise and shaded words, her own words, careful words. The novice will listen to her and think, "I would never have thought about it that way." If, by contrast, a person is motivated by the pressure to appear as a loyal soldier, she will never gain this wisdom. Her concerns will be only about the rituals, the liturgies, and the catechisms of a particular politics, however just the cause. Outsiders will recognize her language from Twitter or Facebook or other digitized watering holes, and of course they will ratify it, but she will have gained all that she ever really sought: admiration and affirmation.

In this manner, movements that purport to exist in service to certain values may perpetuate a status quo in which those values, demanding and taxing, are named but never seriously treated. We ignore them, and pretend — together, as a community — that we are not ignoring them. Every time a self-proclaimed "n-ist" presents as an "n-ist," every time a tweet or a post racks up a hundred likes in service to that presentation, she can tell herself she has fulfilled the responsibilities of her "n-ism" and so she will not feel further pressure to do so.

Consider two examples. First, a college student with two thousand followers on Instagram who attends every Black Lives Matter protest armed with placards, and who posts regularly about white privilege and the guilty conscience of white America. Suppose this woman's antiracism manifests itself primarily as a crippling guilt in the face of systemic inequity from which she benefits: her service to antiracism is not nonexistent, or merely "performative," since she does force her followers to think about uncomfortable subjects (though it is quite likely that her followers already agree with her, but never mind), and she does contribute to the increasing awareness that these injustices must be named and reckoned with *now*.

It is good that our college student marched. But compare her to a white septuagenarian who has moved into an increasingly gentrifying neighborhood, who is well off and even a member of the American elite, who has the cell phone numbers of more than a few important people. She has never once felt guilty for having been born into power and privilege. She is not a marcher. Now imagine that this woman, out of mere decency, involves herself in the everyday lives of her black neighbors (something which most people like her fail to do). She is who they turn to when forced to confront a system which she can manipulate for them, which they cannot navigate without her. She is the one they call when, say, one of their sons is unjustly arrested (again), or when the school board threatens to cut the district's budget (again), because they trust that she will work tirelessly on their behalf. She learns over time, through direct experience, about the blisters and lacerations of racism, and about how to preempt and treat them. Owing to her skin color and her tax bracket, she, like our college student, profits from systemic inequity, but, unlike our college student, she takes regular and concrete actions to help the disadvantaged. Her actions are moral but not ideological. She is not a tourist in the cause and the cause is not a flex of her identity. Yet she is regularly in the trenches and she is alleviating hardship.

Which of these women has more ardently and effectively fought against racism? I have no objection to activism, quite the contrary, but it must be constantly vigilant against declining into the sludge. (Of course neither the good neighbor nor the tweeting marcher are engaged, strictly

The Sludge

speaking, in politics; at the very least they both must also vote.) Sludge-like discourse is not a new phenomenon, of course — prior to the mass revulsion at the murder of George Floyd there was the convulsion known as #MeToo, which exposed some terrible abuses and established some necessary adjustments but was mired in the sludge and the culture of holy rage. And there is another historical revolution to consider: in all the centuries of thought distorted by community, there has never been a greater ally and amplifier of this phenomenon than the new technology. It is uncannily ideal for such shallowness and such conformism, and the best place to go to prove your purity. Owing to it, the sludge has become unprecedentedly manic and unprecedentedly ubiquitous. For all its reputation as an engine for loneliness and isolation, the internet is in fact the perfect technology of the herd. Consider Twitter, the infinitely metastazing home of the memberships and the mobs. For demagogues and bigots and liars and inciters it has solved once and for all the old problem of the transmission and distribution of opinion. The echo-chambers of the righteous progressives and the righteous reactionaries exist side by side in splendid defiance of one another, drunk on themselves, on their likes, retweets, shares, and followers (the latter a disarmingly candid appellation). All these echo chambers — these braying threads — are structurally identical. Authority is granted to those with the highest numbers. The xenophobic "influencer" with the most followers is granted power for precisely the same reason, and according to the same authority, as the justice warrior with the most followers. And followers are won according to the same laws in all realms: those who are proficient in the vernacular, who can convince others that they are full members, that they understand the code and its implications best, they are the ones to whom the like-minded flock. The priests of one temple wrathfully say, "You are sexist" and those of another wrathfully say "You are un-American" in the same way members of my old community would wrathfully say, "You are a sinner." It all means the same thing: get out.

The sludge does not govern all discourse in America, but a horrifying amount of our "national conversation" is canned. And instead of discussing actual injustices we have endless conversations about how to discuss such things. What can be said and what cannot be said? Why talk about slavery when you can talk about the 1619 Project? Why talk about the nuances and ambiguities endemic to any sexual encounter when you can talk about #MeToo? Why complicate the question for yourself when you can join the gang? Every time we choose one of these options over the other, we demonstrate what kind of knowledge matters to us most.

And one of the most pernicious effects of this degradation of our discourse occurs in our private lives — in personal relationships. Increasingly in conversations with friends I recognize a thickening boundary, a forcefield that repels us from the highly charged subject of our discussion. We bump up against it and decide not to *go there*, where integrity and trust would take us. At the point of impact, when honesty collides with membership and shrinks away, I sometimes feel as if I am being pushed back not just from the subject matter but also from the friend herself. She begins to speak in a pastiche of platitudes borrowed from the newsletters clogging her (and my) inbox. I don't seem to be talking to her anymore, I can't get through to her own thoughts, to her own perspective — which, I stubbornly insist, lies somewhere beneath the slogans and the shorthands. All too often I find myself following suit. Neither one of us is willing to express our respective curiosities and anxieties on matters related to politics. We just bat the keywords around and pretend we are really in dialogue with each other. He declares that the world will end if Biden is elected, she declares that the world will end if Trump is elected, and I am expected not to ask "Why?" Instead I am being invited to join him or to join her, and the more hysterically, the better.

Once this parameter, this border wall, has been erected, taking it down would require a troublesome break from social convention. One of us would have to be disruptive, even impolite, to pull us out of the sludge-slinging which prohibits intellectual and verbal independence. And so usually we carry on within those boundaries, interacting as representatives of a cohort or a movement, not as intellectually diligent citizens with a sense of our own ignorance and an appetite for what the other thinks. We become paranoid about discursive limits. Ever present in our conversation is the danger that if one of us deviates from the etiquette, the other will accuse her of being offensive, or worse. The wages of candor are now very high. We have made our discourse too brutal because we are too delicate.

So we obey the rules in which we have trained ourselves, and look for safety in numbers. We invoke the authority of dogma, hearsay, and cliche. We substitute popularity for truth. We quote statistics like gospel, without the faintest sense of their veracity, as if numbers can settle moral questions. We denounce the character of people we have not met simply because others — in a book group, a twitter thread, a newspaper column, or a mob — say they are no good. The actual interpretation of concepts such as climate change or race or interventionism is less significant than the affiliations that they denote. And when the conversation is over, we are where we were when it began, left to shibboleths and confirmed, as Lionel Trilling once complained about an earlier debasement, in our sense of our own righteousness. But this must not be the purpose of conversation, public or private. It is disgraceful to treat intellectual equals as if they cannot be trusted with our doubts. It is wrong to celebrate freedom of thought and freedom of speech and then think and speak unfreely. "Polarization" is just another name for this heated charade. In an open society, in American society, one should not be made to feel like a dissident for speaking one's own mind.

The Sludge

ADAM ZAGAJEWSKI

Mahler's Heaven and Mahler's Earth

Gustav Mahler: the face of a man wearing glasses. The face attracts the attention of the viewer: there is something very expressive about it. It is a strong and open face, we are willing to trust it right away. Nothing theatrical about it, nothing presumptuous. This man wears no silks. He is not someone who tells us: I am a genius, be careful with me. There is something energetic, vivid, and "modern" about the man. He gives an impression of alacrity: he could enter the room any second. Many portraits from the same period display men, Germanic and not only Germanic men, politicians, professors, and writers, whose faces disappear stodgily into the thicket of a huge voluptuous beard, as if hiding in it, disallowing any close inspection. But the composer's visage is naked, transparent, immediate. It is there to speak to us, to sing, to tell us something.

I bought my first recording of Gustav Mahler many decades ago. At the time his name was almost unknown to me. I only had a vague idea of what it represented. The recording I settled on was produced by a Soviet company called *Melodiya* — a large state-owned (of course) company which sometimes produced great recordings. There was no trade in the Soviet Union and yet the trademark *Melodya* did exist. It was the Fifth Symphony, I think — I've lost the vinyl disc in my many voyages and moves — and the conductor was Yevgeny Svetlanov. For some reason the cover was displayed in the store window for a long time; it was a modest store in Gliwice, in Silesia. Why the display of Mahler's name in this provincial city which generally cared little for music?

It took me several days before I decided to buy the record. And then, very soon, when I heard the first movement, the trumpet and the march, which was at the same time immensely tragic and a bit joyful too, or at least potentially joyful, I knew from this unexpected conjunction of emotions that something very important had happened: a new chapter in my musical life had opened, and in my inner life as well. New sounds entered my imagination. At the same time I understood — or only intuited — that I would always have a problem distinguishing between "sad" and "joyful," both in music and in poetry. Some sadnesses would be so delicious, and would make me so happy, that I would forget for a while the difference between the two realms. Perhaps there is no frontier between them, as in the Schengen sector of contemporary Europe.

Mahler's Heaven and Mahler's Earth

The Fifth Symphony was my gateway to Mahler's music. Many years after my first acquaintance with it, a British conductor told me that this particular symphony was deemed by those deeply initiated in Mahler's symphonies and Mahler's songs as maybe a bit too popular, too accessible, too easy. "That trumpet, you know." "And, you know, then came Visconti," who did not exactly economize on the Adagietto from the same symphony in the slow, very slow shots in *Death in Venice,* where this music, torn away from its sisters and brothers, the other movements, came to serve a mass-mystical, mass-hysterical cultish enthusiasm, floating on the cushions of movie theaters chairs. Nothing for serious musicians, nothing for scholars and sages.... But I do not agree. For me the Fifth Symphony remains one of the living centers of Gustav Mahler's music and no movie will demote it, no popularity will diminish it, no easily manipulated melancholy in a distended Adagietto will make me skeptical about its force, its freshness, its depth.

As for that trumpet: the trumpet that I heard for the first time so many years ago had nothing to do with the noble and terrifying noises of the Apocalypse. It was nothing more than an echo of a military bugle — which, the biographers tell us, young Gustav must have heard almost every week in his small Moravian town of Jihlava, or Iglau in German, which was the language of the Habsburg empire, where local troops in their slightly comic blue uniforms would march in the not very tidy streets to the sounds of a brass orchestra. Yet there was nothing trivial or farcical about this almost-a-bugle trumpet. It told me right away that in Mahler's music I would be exposed to a deep ambivalence, a new complication — that the provincial, the din of Hapsburgian mass-culture, will forever pervade his symphonies. This vernacular, this down-to-earth (down to the cobblestones of Jihlava's streets) brass racket, always shadows Mahler's most sublime adagios.

The biographical explanation is interesting and important, but it is not sufficient. An artist of Mahler's stature does not automatically or reflexively rely on early experiences for his material. He uses them, and transposes them, only when they fit into a larger scheme having to do with his aesthetic convictions and longings. The strings in the adagios seem to come from a different world: the violins and the cellos in the adagios sound like they are being played by poets. But then in the rough scherzo-like movements we hear the impudent brass. From the clouds to the cobblestones: Mahler may be a mystical composer, but his mysticism is tinged with an acute awareness of the ordinary, often trite environment of all the higher aspirations.

His aesthetic convictions and longings: what are they? Judging from the music, one thing seems to be certain: this composer is looking for the high, maybe for the highest that can be achieved, for the religious, for the metaphysical — and yet he cannot help hearing also the common laughter of the low streets, the unsophisticated noise of military brass instruments. His search for the sublime never takes place in the abstract void of an inspiration cleansed of the demotic world which is his habitat. Mahler confronts the predicament well known to many artists and writers living within the walls of modernity but not quite happy with it, because they have in their souls a deep yearning for a spiritual event, for revelation. They are like someone walking in the dusk toward a light, like a wanderer who does not know whether the sun is rising or setting. They have to decide how to relate to everything that is not light, to the vast continent of the half trivial, half necessary arrangements of which the quotidian consists. Should they ignore it, or attempt to secede from it? But then what they have to say will be rejected as nothing more than lofty rhetoric, as something artificial, as unworldly in the sense of unreal. They will be labeled "reactionary" or, even worse, boring. Anyway, aren't they to some degree made from the same dross that they are trying to overcome, to transcend?

And yet if they attach too much importance to it, if they become mesmerized by what is given, by the empirical, then the sheer weight of the banality of existing conditions might crush them, flatten them to nothingness. The dross, right. But let us be fair about modernity: it has plenty of good things as well. It has given us, among other things, democracy and electricity (to paraphrase Lenin). Any honest attitude toward modernity must be extremely complex. Modernity, for better and worse, is the air we breathe. What is problematic for some artists and thinkers is modernity's anti-metaphysical stance, its claim that we live in a post-post-religious world. Yet there are also artists and thinkers who applaud modernity precisely for its secularism and materialism, like the well-known French poet who visited Krakow and during a public discussion of the respective situations of French poetry and Polish poetry said this: "I admire many things in present- day Polish poetry, but there is one thing that makes me uneasy — you Polish poets still struggle with God, whereas we decided a long time ago that all that is totally childish."

To be sure, they — the anti-moderns, as Antoine Compagnon calls them — may also become too bitter and angry, so that their critique of the modern world can go too far and turn into an empty gesture of rejection. In his afterword to a collection of essays by Gerhard Nebel — the German conservative thinker, an outsider, once a social-democrat, always an anti-Nazi, after World War II a marginal figure in the intellectual landscape of the Bundesrepublik, a connoisseur of ancient Greek literature, someone who saw dealing with *die Archaik* as one of the remedies against the grayness of the modern world — Sebastian Kleinschmidt presents such a case. He admires the many merits of Nebel's writing, his vivid emotions, his intolerance of any routine, of any *Banausentum* or life lived far away from the appeal of the Muses, his passionate search for the real as opposed to the merely actual — but he is skeptical of Nebel's overall dismissal of modern civilization, since it is too sweeping to be persuasive, too lacking in nuances and distinctions. Perhaps we can put the problem this way: there is no negotiation involved, no exchange, no spiritual diplomacy.

When coping with modernity, with those aspects of it which insist on curbing or denying our metaphysical hunger, we must be not only as brave as Hector but also as cunning as Ulysses. We have to negotiate. We need to borrow from modernity a lot: since we encounter it every day, how could we avoid being fed and even shaped by it? The very verb "to negotiate" is a good example of the complexity of the situation. It comes from from *neg* — *otium*, from the negation of *otium*. *Otium* is the Latin word for leisure, but for contemplation too. Thus the verb *to negotiate* denotes a worldly activity that tacitly presupposes the primacy of unworldly activities (because the negation comes second, after the affirmation).

In French, *le négoce* means commerce, business. We can add to it all the noise of the market and the parliament. When we negotiate, we have no *otium*. But it is also possible to negotiate in order to save some of the *otium*. We can negate *otium* for a while but only in order to return to it a bit later, once it has

189

been saved from destruction. As I say, we must be cunning. By the way, the notion of *otium* that gave birth to the verb "to negotiate" is not a marginal category, something that belongs only to the annals of academia, to books covered by dust. For the Ancients it was a central notion and a central activity, the beginning and the end of wisdom. And even now it plays an important role in a debate in which the values of modernity are being pondered: those who have problems with the new shape of our civilization accuse it of having killed *otium*, of having produced an infinity of new noises and activities which contribute to the end of leisure, to the extermination of contemplation.

But can we discuss Mahler's music along with poetic texts by, say, Yeats and Eliot, along with the other manifestoes of modernism? Talking about music in a way that makes it seem like philosophy or a philosophical novel, a kind of *Zauberberg* for piano and violin, is certainly flawed. Questions are methodically articulated in philosophy and, though never fully answered, they wander from one generation to another, from the Greeks to our contemporaries. Does art need such questions? Does music need them? The first impulse is to say no, art has nothing to do with this sort of intellectual inquiry. Isn't pure contemplation, separated from any rational discourse, the unique element of art, both painting and music, and perhaps poetry as well?

But maybe pure contemplation does not need to be so pure. We do not know exactly how it works (another question!), but we do know that art always takes on some coloring from its historic time, from the epoch in which it is created. Art obviously has a social history, and earthly circumstances. And yet impure contemplation is still contemplation. Let us listen for a minute to the words of a famous painter, an experienced practitioner — to Balthus in his conversations with Alain Vircondelet, which were conducted in the last years of the painter's life:

> Modern painting hasn't really understood that painting's sublime, ultimate purpose — if it has one — is to be the tool or passageway to answering the world's most daunting questions that haven't been fathomed. The Great Book of the Universe remains impenetrable and painting is one of its possible keys. That's why it is indubitably religious, and therefore spiritual. Through painting, I revisit the course of time and history, at an unknown time, original in the true sense of the word. That is, something newly born. Working allows me to be present on the first day, in an extreme, solitary adventure laden with all of past history.

How fascinating: a great painter tells us that in his work he used not only his eye and his hand but also his reason, his philosophical mind; that when he painted he felt the presence of great questions. Even more: he tells us that the pressure of these questions was not inconsequential, that it led him to spirituality. We know that Mahler, in a letter to Bruno Walter, also mentioned the presence of great questions and described his state of mind while being in contact with the element of music in this way: "When I hear music, even when I am conducting, I often hear a clear answer to all my questions — I experience clarity and certainty."

Certainly, the questions that sit around a painter or a

191

composer like pensive cats are very different from those which besiege a philosopher. Do they require a response? Here is one more authority: in a note serving as a preface to the publication of four of his letters about Nietzsche, Valéry remarked that "Nietzsche stirred up the combativeness of my mind and the intoxicating pleasure of quick answers which I have always savored a little too much." The irony of it: "the intoxicating pleasure of quick answers" in a thinker who, as we know, was so proud of his philosophizing with a hammer. Of course, this one sentence comprises in a nutshell the entire judgment that mature Valéry passed on Nietzsche — the early temptation and the later rejection of such a degree of "the combativeness of the spirit." And it confirms our intuition: the questions that accompany art, painting, music, and poetry cannot be answered in a way similar to debates in philosophy seminars, and yet they are an invisible and inaudible part of every major artistic exertion.

In a way, Mahler's doubleness of approach seems completely obvious; the brass and the strings attend each other, and need each other, in the complex patterns of his symphonies. I have read that in his time he was accused by many critics of triviality in his music. They claimed that his symphonies lacked the dignity of Beethoven's symphonies, the depth of great German music. What they ferociously attacked as trivial is probably the thing that I admire so much in Mahler's music — the presence of the other side of our world, the inclusion of its commonness and its coarseness, of the urban peripheries, of village fairs, of the brass — the quotation of provincial life, of public parades and military marches, almost like in Nino Rota's scores for Fellini. Very few among Mahler's contemporaries were able to see the virtue of it.

The charge of triviality also had anti-Semitic undertones

and followed in the footsteps of Wagner's accusation, in his "Judaism in Music," that Jewish composers were not able to develop a deep connection with the soul of the people, and were limited to the world of the city only, gliding slickly on the surface. Jewish composers apparently could not hear the song of the earth, argued such critics. How wonderful, then, that Mahler triumphed in his own Song of the Earth! Jewish composers were accused — among the many sins of which they were accused — of introducing modern elements into their music. Never mind that one of the principal modernizers of Western music was Wagner himself.

I have yet to understand why Mahler has for so long, from the very beginning, been so overwhelmingly important for me, so utterly central to the evolution of my soul. Once, in speaking with some American friends, I asked them who "made" them, in the sense of a master, a teacher, *un maître à penser*, and the reason was I wanted to tell them that Gustav Mahler made me. It was an exaggeration, I know, and a bit precious. I had other masters as well. And yet my statement was not false. Did it have to do only with the sonorities of his symphonies, with the newness of his music, the unexpected contrasts and astonishing passages swinging between the lyric to the sardonic? Was it the formal side uniquely? For many years I resisted the temptation to translate my deep emotional bond to his music — the deep consonance between Mahler's work and my own search in the domain of poetry — into intellectual terms, maybe fearing that too much light shed on it would diminish its grip on my imagination. I still hold this superstitious view, but I also suspect that there may be some larger intellectual benefit to be gained from an exploration of my obsession.

For everyone who has a passionate interest in art and in

ideas, sooner or later a problem arises. When we look for truth and try to be honest, when we try as a matter of principle to avoid dogmatism and any sort of petrification, any blind commitment to this or that worldview, we are, it seems, necessarily condemned to deal with shards, with fragments, with pieces that do not constitute any whole — even if, consciously or not, we strive for the impossible "whole." But then if we also harbor a love for art — and it is not at all unusual to have these two passions combined in a single individual — a strange tension appears: in art we deal with forms which, by definition, cannot be totally fragmentary. To be sure, at least since the Romantic moment we have been exposed to fragments, and accustomed to fracture, in all kinds of artistic enterprises, from music and poetry to painting — but even these fragments tend to acquire a shape. If we juxtapose them with the "truth fragments," with Wittgensteinian scraps of philosophical results, an integrated pattern is created by virtue of some little embellishment, by a sleight of hand; a magician is at work who tends to forget the search for truth because the possibility of a form, a more or less perfect form, suddenly attracts him more strongly than the shapelessness of a purely intellectual assessment.

These two dissimilar but related hunts, one for truth, one for form, are not unlike husky dogs pulling a sled in two slightly different directions: they are sometimes able to achieve an almost-harmony. The sled fitfully moves forward, but at other times the competing pressures threaten to endanger the entire expedition. So, too, are our mental hunts and journeys, forever hesitating between a form that will allow us to forget the rather uncomfortable sharpness of truth and a gesturing for truth that may make us forget the thrill of beauty and the urge to create, at least for the time being.

This brings us back to Mahler. The doubleness in his music that I have described may be understood as reflecting the ambiguity of the double search for truth and form. Mahler was a God-seeker who recognized the ambivalence of such a quest in art. He was torn between the search for the voluptuousness of beauty and the search for the exactness of truth.

Hartmut Lange, a German writer living in Berlin, a master of short prose, told me once that Mahler's *Song of the Earth*, which he listens to all the time and adores in a radical way, "is God." I was taken aback. The deification of this almost-symphony, which I also ardently admire, made me feel uneasy. But I find it more than interesting that this great music can be associated with, and even called, God. This suggests a quasi-religious aspect of the music, and even a sober secularist cannot escape at times placing the work within the circle nearing the sacred.

Among the many approaches to the sacred we may distinguish two: one which consists in searching, in a quest, and is conducted in a climate of uncertainty and even doubt, and another which proclaims a kind of sureness, a positive certainty, a eureka-like feeling that what was sought has been found. In our tormented and skeptical time it is not easy to find examples of such a positive and even arrogant attitude, at least not within serious culture. Among the great modern poets and writers only few were blessed by certainty. Even the great Pascal had his doubts, and so much earlier. Gustav Mahler belongs to the seekers, not the finders. The quest is his element, and doubt is always near.

It is true for both poetry and music: whenever one approaches an important work, one is much more outspoken when it comes to discussing the elements within it that will yield to the intellectual or even dialectical categories that the reader or listener cherishes. The other ingredients, especially those that represent pure lyricism and thus are at the very heart of the work in question, are hardly graspable, at least in words. What can we say? It is beautiful, it pierces my soul, or some other platitude of the sort. Or we can just sigh to signal our delight. Sighing, though, is not enough; it is too inarticulate, and in print it evaporates altogether. This is the misery of writing about art: the very center of it remains almost totally ineffable, and what can be rationally described is rather a frame than the substance itself.

A frame that enters into dialogue with its period, with its cultural and historical environment, can be much better described than the substance of a symphony or a painting. The nucleus of a work, or of an artist's output, is less historical, less marked by the sediments of time, and therefore mysterious. It is also more personal, more private. This is certainly the case with Mahler's music, whose very core constitute those lyric movements, those endless *ostinati* that we find everywhere, first in his songs, in *Lieder eines fahrenden Gesellen* and the other *lieder*, then in his symphonies, and supremely in their adagios, and then finally in the unsurpassable *Lied von der Erde*. And the *Ninth Symphony*! I don't have in mind only the final *Adagio* but also the first movement, the *Andante comodo*, which displays an incredible vivacity and, at the same time, creates an unprecedentedly rich musical idiom — a masterful musical portrayal of what it means to be alive, with all the quick changes and stubborn dramas, the resentments and the raptures, that constitute the exquisite and weary workshop of the mind and the heart.

But let us not forget, when we celebrate the lyric sections, the sometimes simple melodies, and the long *ostinati*, let us not forget all the intoxicating marches, the half sardonic, half triumphant marches that originated in a small Moravian town but then crossed the equator and reached the antipodes. These marches give Mahler's music its rhythm, its vigor, its muscle. There is nothing wan in Mahler's compositions, nothing pale on the order of, say, Puvis de Chavannes; instead they display, even in their most tender and aching passages, an irreversible vitality. The marches propel the music and give it its movement, its strolls and dances and strides. The "vulgar" marches convey the mood of a constant progression, maybe even of a "pilgrim's progress." Nothing ever stagnates in Mahler compositions, they are on the move all the time.

It's unbecoming to disagree with someone who was a great Mahler connoisseur and also contributed enormously to the propagation of his work, but it is hard to accept Leonard Bernstein's observation that the funeral marches in Mahler's symphonies are a musical image of grief for the Jewish God whom the composer abandoned. The problem is not only that there is scant biographical evidence for such an interpretation. More importantly, the marches are more than Bernstein says they are. They represent no single emotion. Instead they oscillate between mourning and bliss and thus stand (or walk or dance) high above any firm monocausal meaning.

In the *Song of the Earth,* it is the sixth and last movement, *der Abschied*, the Farewell, that crowns Mahler's entire work. Musicologists tell us that its beauty consists mainly in the combination of a lyrical melodic line with the rich chromaticism of the orchestra. But obviously such an observation can barely render justice to the unforgettable charm of this sensual music which unwillingly bids farewell to the earth; we hear in this work the tired yet ecstatic voice of the composer who knew how little life was left to him. Perhaps only in Rilke's *Duino Elegies* can we find an example of a similar seriousness in embracing our fate, an instance of a great artist finally abolishing any clear distinction between sadness and joy.

There is a fine poem written in the early 1980s by the Swedish poet and novelist Lars Gustafsson. It is called "The Stillness of the World Before Bach" and it caught the attention of many readers. Here is part of it:

> There must have been a world before
> the Trio Sonata in D, a world before the A minor partita,
> but what kind of a world?
> A Europe of vast empty spaces, unresounding,
> everywhere unawakened instruments,
> where the Musical Offering, the Well-Tempered Clavier
> never passed across the keys.
> Isolated churches
> where the soprano line of the Passion
> never in helpless love twined round
> the gentler movements of the flute [...]
> > [translated into English by Philip Martin]

Of course there were many voices and many composers before Bach, and not at all "a Europe of vast empty spaces." What would Palestrina, Gabrielli, and Monteverdi say? What would the monks say who created and developed Gregorian chant? Still, in Gustafsson's poem we immediately recognize some deeper truth. I imagine that in a similar poem in which Gustav Mahler would replace Johann Sebastian Bach, the poet would describe not "a Europe of vast empty spaces" but rather a Europe of cities, great and small ones, of empty Sunday streets, of empty parks, of waiting rooms.

The Mahler gesture resembles in some respect the Bach achievement, but it is very different too. Bach was a genius of synthesis, who appeared after centuries of the development of Western art and on this fertile soil built a great edifice of music. There is less synthetic energy in Mahler's creation; the significance of his work seems to reside in its spiritual implication. Mahler, more than any of his contemporaries, tries to graft onto this lay world of ours a religious striving, to convey a higher meaning to a largely meaningless environment without ever forgetting or concealing the obvious features of a secular age.

Mahler's Heaven and Mahler's Earth

Night Thoughts

Long ago I was born.
There is no one alive anymore
who remembers me as a baby.
Was I a good baby? A
bad? Except in my head
that debate is now
silenced forever.
What constitutes
a bad baby, I wondered. Colic,
my mother said, which meant
it cried a lot.
What harm could there be
in that? How hard it was
to be alive, no wonder
they all died. And how small
I must have been, suspended
in my mother, being patted by her
approvingly.
What a shame I became
verbal, with no connection
to that memory. My mother's love!
All too soon I emerged
my true self,
robust but sour,
like an alarm clock.

LOUISE GLÜCK

A Memory

A sickness came over me
whose origins were never determined
though it became more and more difficult
to sustain the pretense of normalcy,
of good health or joy in existence —
Gradually I wanted only to be with those like myself;
I sought them out as best I could
which was no easy matter
since they were all disguised or in hiding.
But eventually I did find some companions
and in that period I would sometimes walk
with one or another by the side of the river,
speaking again with a frankness I had nearly forgotten —
and yet, more often we were silent, preferring
the river over anything we could say —
on either bank, the tall marsh grass blew
calmly, continuously, in the autumn wind.
And it seemed to me I remembered this place
from my childhood, though
there was no river in my childhood,
only houses and lawns. So perhaps
I was going back to that time
before my childhood, to oblivion, maybe
it was that river I remembered.

JAMES WOLCOTT

Futilitarianism, or To the York Street Station

Wednesday, April 8th...a date etched in black for socialists and progressives, marking the end of a beautiful fantasy. It was on that doleful day that Senator Bernie Sanders — acknowledging the inevitable, having depleted his pocketful of dreams — announced the suspension of his presidential campaign. It was the sagging anticlimax to an electoral saga that came in like a lion and went out with a wheeze. For months the pieces had been falling into place for Sanders to secure the Democratic nomination, only to fall apart in rapid slow motion on successive Super Tuesdays, a reversal of fortune that left political savants even more dumbstruck than usual. Taking to social

media, some of Sanders' most fervent and stalwart support-
ers in journalism, punditry, and podcasting responded to the
news of his withdrawal with the stoical grace we've come to
expect from these scarlet ninja. Shuja Haider, a high-profile
leftist polemicist who's appeared in the *Guardian, The Believer,*
and the *New York Times,* tweeted: "Well the democratic party
just officially lost the support and participation of an entire
generation. Congratulations assholes." (On Twitter, commas
and capital letters are considered optional, even a trifle fussy.)
Will Menaker, a fur-bearing alpha member of the ever popular
Chapo Trap House podcast (the audio clubhouse of the
self-proclaimed "dirtbag left"), declared that with Bernie out of
the race, Joe Biden, "has his work cut out for him when it comes
to winning the votes of a restive Left that distrusts and dislikes
him. It's not impossible if he starts now by sucking my dick."
Others were equally pithy.

It fell upon *Jacobin,* the neo-Marxist quarterly and church
of the one true faith, to lend a touch of class to the valedic-
tory outpourings. Political admiration mingled with personal
affection as it paid homage to the man who had taken them
so far, but not far enough. On its website (the print edition
is published quarterly) it uncorked a choral suite of tributes, 203
elegies, and inspirational messages urging supporters to keep
their chins up, their eyes on the horizon, their gunpowder
dry, a song in their hearts: "Bernie Supporters, Don't Give
Up," "We Lost the Battle, but We'll Win the War," "Bernie
Lost. But His Legacy Will Only Grow." In this spirit, the
magazine's editor and founder, Bhaksara Sunkara, author
of *The Socialist Manifesto: The Case for Radical Politics in an Era
of Extreme Inequality,* conducted a postmortem requiem on
YouTube with his Jacobin comrades processing their grief
and commiserating over their disappointment. Near the end

of the ceremony, Sunkara declared that Bernie's legacy would be as a moral hero akin to Martin Luther King, Mother Jones, and Eugene V. Debs. Which offered a measure of bittersweet consolation, but was not what Sunkara had originally, thirstily desired. "I wanted him to be fucking Lenin. I wanted him to take power and institute change." But the Bernie train never reached the Finland Station, leaving the Jacobins cooling their heels on the platform and craning their necks in vain.

Politically and emotionally they had banked everything on him. "Socialism is the name of our desire," Irving Howe and Lewis Coser had famously written, and for long fallow seasons that desire lay slumbrous on the lips until awakened by Bernie Sanders, the son of Jewish immigrants from Poland, the former mayor of Burlington, Vermont, the junior senator of that state, and lifelong champion of the underdog. Where so many longtime Washington figures had been led astray by sinecures, Aspen conferences, and unlimited canapes, Sanders had been fighting the good fight for decades without being co-opted by Georgetown insiders and neoliberal think tanks, like a protest singer who had never gone electric. He might not be a profound thinker or a sonorously eloquent orator (on a tired day he can sound like a hoarse seagull), and his legislative achievement may be a bit scanty, but his tireless ability to keep pounding the same nails appealed to youthful activists that had come to distrust or even detest the lofty cadences of Barack Obama now that he was gone from office and appeared to halo into Oprah-hood. Eight years of beguilement and what had it materially gotten them? grumbled millennials slumped under student debt and toiling in unpaid internships. What Bernie lacked in movie-poster charisma could be furnished by *Jacobin,* which emblazoned him as a lion in winter.

So confident was *Jacobin* that the next great moment in history was within its grasp that in the winter of 2019 it devoted a special issue to the presidency of Bernie Sanders, whose cover, adorned with an oval portrait of Sanders gazing skyward, proclaimed: "I, President of the United States and How I Ended Poverty: A True Story of The Future." Subheads emphasized that this was not just an issue of a magazine, a mere collation of ink and paper, it was the beginning of a crusade — a twenty-year plan to remake America. Avengers, assemble! At the public launch of the "I, President" issue, Sunkara rhetorically asked, "Is there a point in spending all day trying to explain, like, the Marxist theory of exploitation to some 18-year-old? Yes! Because that kid might be the next Bernie Sanders."

Alas, *Jacobin* made the mistake of counting their red berets before they were hatched, and now the issue is fated to become a collector's item, a poignant keepsake of what might have been. Had Sanders remained in the race and won the presidency, *Jacobin* would have been as credited, identified, and intimately associated with the country's first socialist administration as William F. Buckley, Jr.'s *National Review* was with Ronald Reagan's. *Jacobin* could have functioned as its ad hoc brain trust, or at least its nagging conscience. From that carousel of possibilities the magazine instead finds itself reckoning with the divorce of its socialist platform from its standard bearer, facing the prospect of being just another journal of opinion jousting for attention. No longer ramped up as a Bernie launch vehicle, *Jacobin* must tend to the churning ardor for grand-scale structural change and keep its large flock of followers from straying off into the bushes, which is not easy to do after any loss, no matter how noble. "In America, politics, like everything else, tends to be all or nothing," Irving

Howe observed in *Socialism and America*. And after working so hard on Bernie's behalf, it's hard to walk away with bupkis.

Jacobin possesses a strong set of jaws, however. It will not be letting go of its hold in the marketplace of ideas anytime soon. For better or ill, it will continue to set the tone and tempo on the left even in the absence of its sainted gran'pop. Since initiating publication in 2010, *Jacobin* has established itself as an entrepreneurial success, a publishing sensation, and an ideological mothership. It has built up its own storehouse of intellectual capital, an identifiable brand. Taking its name and sabre'd bravado from the group founded by Maximilien Robespierre that conducted the French Revolution's Reign of Terror (an early issue featured an IKEA-like guillotine on the cover, presumably for those fancying to stage their own backyard beheadings — "assembly required," the caption read), *Jacobin* located a large slumbering discontent in the post-Occupy Wall Street/Great Recession stagnancy among the educated underemployed and gave it a drumbeat rhythm and direction.

From the outset the magazine exuded undefeatable confidence, the impression that history with a capital H was at its back. Its confidence in itself proved not misplaced. Where even before the coronavirus most print magazines were on IV drips, barely sustainable and in the throes of a personality crisis, *Jacobin's* circulation has grown to 40,000 plus (more than three times that of Partisan Review in its imperious prime); it has sired and inspired a rebirth of socialist polemic (*Why Women Have Better Sex Under Socialism, The ABCs of Socialism, Why You Should Be a Socialist, and the forthcoming In Defense of Looting*), and helped recruit a young army of activists to bring throbbing life to

Democratic Socialists of America, whose membership rolls as of late 2019 topped 56,000, with local chapters popping up like fever blisters.

The editorial innovation of Sunkara's *Jacobin* was that it tapped into animal spirits to promote its indictments and remedies, animal spirits normally being the province of sports fans, day traders, and bachelorette parties but not of redistributionists, egalitarians, and social upheavers. Even its subscription form is cheeky: "The more years you select, the better we can construct our master plan to seize state power." Although the ground game of socialism was traditionally understood as a conscientious slog — meetings upon meetings, caucusing until the cows come home, microscopic hair-splitting of doctrinal points — *Jacobin* lit up the scoreboard with rhetoric and visuals that evoked the heroic romanticism of revolution, history aflush with a red-rose ardor. The articles can be dense and hoarse with exhortations ("we must build...," "we must insist..." we must, we must), the writing unspiced by wit, irony, and allusion (anything that smacks of mandarin refinement), and the infographics more finicky than instructive, but the overall package has a jack-in-the-box *boing!*, a kinetic aesthetic that can be credited to its creative director, Remeike Forbes. Not since the radical *Ramparts* of the 1960s, designed by Dugald Stermer, has any leftist magazine captured lightning in a bottle with such flair.

Effervescence is what sets *Jacobin* apart from senior enterprises on the left such as *The Nation, Dissent, New Left Review,* and that perennial underdog *Monthly Review,* its closest cousin being *Teen Vogue,* Conde Nast's revolutionary student council fan mag — the Tiger Beat of glossy wokeness. When not extolling celebrity styling ("Kylie Jenner's New Rainbow Manicure Is Perfect for Spring"), *Teen Vogue* posts junior

Jacobin tutorials on Rosa Luxemburg and Karl Marx, whose "writings have inspired social movements in Soviet Russia, China, Cuba, Argentina, Ghana, Burkina Faso, and more..." (most of those movements didn't pan out so well, but they left no impact on Kylie's manicure).

Jacobin recognized that hedonics are vital for the morale and engagement of the troops, who can't be expected to keep chipping away forever at the fundament of the late-capitalist, post-industrial, Eye of Sauron hegemon. No longer would socialists be associated with aging lefties in leaky basements cranking the mimeograph machine and handing out leaflets on the Upper West Side — socialism now had a hip new home in Brooklyn where the hormones were hopping and bopping pre-corona. "'Everybody looks fuckin' sexy as hell,'" shouted [Bianca] Cunningham, NYC-DSA's co-chair. 'This is amazing to have everybody here looking beautiful in the same room, spreading the message of socialism.'" So recorded Simon van Zuylen-Wood in "Pinkos Have More Fun," his urban safari into the dating-mating, party-hearty socialist scene *for New York* magazine.

In the middle of the dance floor I ran into Nicole Carty, a DSA-curious professional organizer I also hadn't seen since college, who made a name for herself doing tenant work after Occupy Wall Street. (DSA can feel like a never-ending Brown University reunion.) "Movements are, yeah, about causes and about progress and beliefs and feelings, but the strength of movements comes from social ties and peer pressure and relationships," Carty said. "People are craving this. Your social world intersecting with your politics. A world of our own."

Jacobin's closest companion and competitor in the romancing of the young and the restless is *The Baffler*, founded in 1988, at the height of the Reagan imperium, allowed to lapse in 2006, revived from cryogenic slumber in 2010, and going strong ever since. Both quarterlies publish extensive and densely granulated reporting and analytical pieces on corporate greed, treadmill education, factory farming, and America's prison archipelago, though *The Baffler* slants more essayistic and art-conscious, a Weimar journal for our time. The chief difference, however, is one of temperament and morale. Where *Jacobin*, surveying the wreckage and pillage, holds out the promise that the cavalry is assembling, preparing to ride, *The Baffler* often affects a weary-sneery, everything-sucks, post-grad-school vape lounge cynicism, as if the battle for a better future is a futile quest — the game is rigged, the outcome preordained. "Forget it, Jake, it's Chinatown."

The Baffler's bullpen of highly evolved futilitarians leans hard on the words "hell" and "shit" to register their scorn and disgust at the degradation of politics and culture in our benighted age by rapacious capital with the complicity of champagne-flute elitists and the good old dumb-ox American booboisie. It's Menckenesque misanthropy (minus Mencken's thunder rolls of genius) meets *Bladerunner* dystopia with a dab of Terry Southern nihilism, and it's not entirely a warped perspective — the world is being gouged on all sides by kleptocratic plunder. But *The Baffler* offers mostly confirmation of the system's machinations, the latest horrors executed in fine needlepoint, no exit from the miasma. Each issue arrives as an invitation to brittle despair.

Jacobin, by contrast, acts as more of an agent of transmutation, a mojo enhancer for the socialist mission. This is from "Are You Reading Propaganda Right Now?" by Liza Featherstone, which appeared in its winter 2020 issue:

> One of the legacies of the Cold War is that Americans assume propaganda is bad. While the term "propaganda" has often implied that creators were taking a manipulative or deceptive approach to their message — or glossing over something horrific, like World War I, the Third Reich, or Stalin's purges — the word hasn't always carried that baggage. Lenin viewed propaganda as critical to building the socialist movement. In his 1902 pamphlet *What Is to Be Done?*, it's clear that his ideal propaganda is an informative, well-reasoned argument, drawing on expertise and information that the working-class might not already have. That's what we try to do at *Jacobin*.

It is worth asking how much these excitable Leninists actually know about their Bolshie role model. Did they notice Bernie's response to Michael Bloomberg's use of the word "communist" to describe him at one of the debates? He called it "a cheap shot." Say what you will about Sanders, but he recoiled at the charge. He, at least, is familiar with Lenin's work.

Jacobin's mistake was to think it could play kingmaker too. In *It Didn't Happen Here: Why Socialism Failed in the United States,* Seymour Martin Lipset and Gary Marks delineated the unpatchable differences between "building a social movement and establishing a political party," or, in this case, taking over an existing one. (As Irving Howe cautioned, "You cannot opt for the rhythms of a democratic politics and still expect it to yield

the pathos and excitement of revolutionary movements.")
Political parties represent varied coalitions and competing
interests, requiring expediency, horse trading, and tedious,
exhausting staff work to achieve legislative ends. Lipset and
Marks: "Social movements, by contrast, invoke moralistic
passions that differentiate them sharply from other contend-
ers. Emphasis on the intrinsic justice of a cause often leads to a
rigid us-them, friend-foe orientation."

The friend-foe antipathy becomes heightened and
sharpened all the more in the Fight Club of social media,
where the battle of ideas is waged with head butts and low
blows. In print and online, *Jacobin* wasn't just Sanders' heraldic
evangelist, message machine, and ringside announcer ("After
Bernie's Win in Iowa, the Democratic Party Is Shitting Its
Pants" — actual headline), it doubled as the campaign's
primary enforcer, methodically maligning and elbowing aside
any false messiah obstructing the road to the White House,
ably assisted by the bully brigade of "Bernie Bros" and other
nogoodniks who left their cleat marks all across Twitter.
Excoriation was lavished upon pretenders who had entered
the race out of relative obscurity and momentarily snagged
the media's besotted attention, such as Texas' lean and toothy
Beto O'Rourke, whose campaign peaked when he appeared
as *Vanity Fair's* cover boy and petered out from there ("Beto's
Fifteen Minutes Are Over. And Not a Moment Too Soon,"
wrote *Jacobin's* Luke Savage, signing the campaign's death
certificate).

Pete Buttigieg received a more brutal hazing, ad
hominemized from every angle. *Jacobin* despised him from
the moment his Eddie Haskell head peeped over the parapet
— that this Rhodes scholar, military veteran who served in
Afghanistan, and current mayor of South Bend, Indiana had

211

written a tribute to Bernie Sanders when he was in high school only made him seem more fishily Machiavellian in their minds. A sympathetic, personally informed profile by James T. Kloppenberg in the Catholic monthly *Commonweal* portrayed Buttigieg as a serious, driven omnivore of self-improvement, but in *Jacobin* he barely registered as a human being, derided as "an objectively creepy figure" by Connor Kilpatrick ("That he is so disliked by the American public while Sanders is so beloved...should hearten us all"), and roasted by Liza Feather-stone for being so conceited about his smarts, an inveterate showoff unlike you-know-who: "Bernie Sanders, instead of showing off his University of Chicago education, touts the power of the masses: 'Not Me, Us.' The cult of the Smart Dude leads us into just the opposite place, which is probably why some liberals like it so much."

There was no accomplishment of Buttigieg's that *Jacobin* couldn't deride. Buttigieg's learning Norwegian (he speaks eight languages) to read the novelist Erlend Loe would impress most civilians, but to *Jacobin* it was more feather-preening, and un-self-aware besides: "Pete Buttigieg's Favorite Author Despises People Like Him," asserted Ellen Engelstad with serene assurance in one of the magazine's few stabs at lit crit. Even Buttigieg's father — the renowned Joseph Buttigieg, a professor of literature at Notre Dame who translated Antonio Gramsci and founded The International Gramsci Society — might have washed his hands of this upstart twerp, according to *Jacobin*. By embracing mainstream Democratic politics, "Pete Buttigieg Just Dealt a Blow to His Father's Legacy," Joshua Manson editorialized. The American people, Norwegian novelists, the other kids in the cafeteria, Hamlet's ghost — the message was clear: nobody likes you, Pete! Take your salad fork and go home!

Buttigieg may have betrayed his Gramscian legacy but it was small beans compared to the treachery of which another Sanders rival was capable. In "How the Cool Kids of the Left Turned on Elizabeth Warren," *Politico* reporter Ruairi Arrieta-Kenna chronicled *Jacobin*'s spiky pivot against Elizabeth Warren, that conniving vixen. Arrieta-Kenna: "It wasn't so long ago that you could read an article in *Jacobin* that argued, 'If Bernie Sanders weren't running, an Elizabeth Warren presidency would probably be the best-case scenario.' In April, another *Jacobin* article conceded that Warren is 'no socialist' but added that 'she's a tough-minded liberal who makes the right kind of enemies,' and her policy proposals 'would make this country a better place.'" Her platform and Sanders' shared many of the same planks, after all.

Planks, schmanks, the dame was becoming a problem to the *Jacobin* project, cutting into Bernie's constituency and being annoyingly indefatigable, waving her arms around like a baton twirler. Warren needed to be sandbagged to open a clear lane for Bernie. Hence, "in the pages of *Jacobin*," Arrieta-Kenna wrote, "Warren has gone from seeming like a close second to Sanders to being a member of the neoliberal opposition, perhaps made even worse by her desire to claim the mantle of the party's left." The J-squad proceeded to work her over with a battery of negative stories headlined "Elizabeth Warren's Head Tax Is Indefensible," "Elizabeth Warren's Plan to Finance Medicare for All Is a Disaster," and "Elizabeth Warren Is Jeopardizing Our Fight for Medicare for All," and warned, quoting Arrieta-Kenna again, "that a vote for Warren would be 'an unconditional surrender to class dealignment.'" When Warren claimed that Sanders had told her privately that a woman couldn't defeat Donald Trump and declined to shake Bernie's hand after the January 14 Democratic debate, she completed

213

the arc from valorous ally to squishy opportunist to Hillary-ish villainess. Little green snake emojis slithered from every cranny of Twitter at the mention of Warren's name, often accompanied by the hashtag #WarrenIsASnake, just in case the emojis were too subtle. Compounding her trespasses, Warren declined to endorse Sanders after she withdrew from the race, blowing her one shot at semi-redemption and a remission of sins. Near the end of *Jacobin's* YouTube postmortem, Sunkara expressed sentiments that seemed to be universal in his cenacle: "Fuck Elizabeth Warren," he explained, "and her whole crew."

Once Buttigieg and Warren dropped out of serious contention, the sole remaining obstacle was Joe Biden, whom *Jacobin* considered a paper-mache relic in a dark suit loaned out from the prop department and seemingly incapable of formulating a complete sentence, much less a coherent set of policies — an entirely plausible caricature, as caricatures go. Occasionally goofy and even surreal in his off-the-cuff remarks, Biden doesn't suggest deep reserves of fortitude and gravitas. In February 2020, Verso published *Yesterday's Man: The Case Against Joe Biden* by *Jacobin* staff writer Branko Marcetic, its cover photograph showing an ashen Biden looking downcast and abject, as if bowing his weary head to the chopping block of posterity. But on the first Super Tuesday, the Biden candidacy, buoyed by the endorsement by the formidable James Clyburn and the resultant victory in South Carolina, rose from the dusty hallows and knocked Sanders' sideways. It was the revenge of the mummy, palpable proof that socialism may have been in vogue with the media and the millennials but rank and file Democrats, especially those of color, weren't interested

214

in lacing up their marching boots. For them, the overriding imperative was not Medicare for All or the Green New Deal but denying Donald Trump a second term and the opportunity to reap four more years of havoc and disfigurement. In lieu of Eliot Ness, Joe Biden was deemed the guy who had the best shot of taking down Trump and his carious crew.

For a publication so enthralled to the Will of the People and the workers in their hard-won wisdom, it's remarkable how badly *Jacobin* misread the mood of Democratic voters and projected its own revolutionary ferment on to it — a misreading rooted in a basic lack of respect for the Democratic Party, its values, its history, its heroes (apart from FDR, since Sanders often cited him), its institutional culture, its coalitional permutations — all this intensified with an ingrained loathing for liberalism itself. From its inception, *Jacobin*, like so many of its brethren on the Left, has displayed far more contempt and loathing for liberals, liberalism, and the useless cogs it labels "centrists" than for the conservatives and reactionaries and neo-fascists intent on turning the country into a garrison state with ample parking. It has a softer spot for hucksters, too. It greeted libertarian blowhard podcaster Joe Rogan's endorsement of Sanders as a positive augury — "It's Good Joe Rogan Endorsed Bernie. Now We Organize" — and published a sympathetic profile of the odious Fox News host Tucker Carlson. This has been its modus operandi all along. In a plucky takedown of the magazine in 2017 called "*Jacobin* Is for Posers," Christopher England noted, "It can claim two issues with titles like 'Liberalism is Dead,' and none, henceforth, that have shined such a harsh light on conservatism." For *Jacobin*, liberalism may be dead or playing possum but it keeps having to be dug up and killed again, not only for the exercise but because, England writes, "conservatism, as its contributors consistently note, can only be defeated if liberalism is brought low." Remove the flab and torpor of tired liberalism and let the taut sinews of the true change-maker spring into jaguar action.

Which might make for some jungle excitement, but certainly goes against historical precedent. "In the United States, socialist movements have usually thrived during times of liberal upswing," Irving Howe wrote in *Socialism and America*, cautioning, "They have hastened their own destruction whenever they have pitted themselves head-on against liberalism." Tell that to *Jacobin*, which either didn't learn that lesson or considered it démodé, irrelevant in the current theater of conflict. With the Democratic Party so plodding and set in its ways, a rheumy dinosaur that wouldn't do the dignified thing and flop dead, the next best thing was to occupy and replenish the host body with fresh recruits drawn from young voters, new voters, disaffected independents, blue-collar remnants, and pink-collar workers. Tap into this vast reservoir of idealism and frustration to unleash bottoms-up change and topple the status quo, writing *fini* to politics as usual. Based on 2016 and how strongly Sanders ran above expectations, this wasn't a reefer dream.

The slogan for this campaign was "Not Me. Us," and it turned out there were a lot fewer "us" this time around. "Mr. Sanders failed to deliver the voters he promised," wrote John Hudak, a deputy director and senior fellow at the Brookings Institution, analyzing the 2020 shortfall. "Namely, he argued that liberal voters, new voters, and young voters would dominate the political landscape and propel him and his ideas to the nomination. However, in nearly every primary through early March, those voters composed significantly smaller percentages of the Democratic electorate than they did in 2016." It wasn't simply a matter of Sanders competing in a more crowded field this time, Hudak reported. In the nine primaries after Warren's withdrawal, when it became a two-person race, "Mr. Sanders underperformed his 2016 totals by an average of 16.0%, including losing three states that he won in 2016 (Idaho, Michigan, and Washington)." How did *Jacobin* miss the Incredible Sanders Shrinkage of 2020?

It became encoiled in its own feedback loop, hopped up on its own hype. "Twitter — a medium that structurally encourages moral grandstanding, savage infighting, and collective action — is where young socialism lives," van Zuylen-Wood had observed in "Pinkos Have More Fun," and Twitter, to state the obvious, is not the real world, but a freakhouse simulacrum abounding with trolls, bots, shut-ins, and soreheads. *Jacobin* and its allies so dominated online discourse that they didn't comprehend the limits of that dominance until it hit them between the mule ears. They fell victim to what has come to be known as Cuomo's Law, which takes its name from the New York gubernatorial contest in 2018 between Andrew Cuomo and challenger Cynthia Nixon, a former cast member of *Sex and the City* and avowed democratic socialist. On Twitter, Nixon had appeared the overwhelming popular favorite, Cuomo the saturnine droner that no one had the slightest passion for. But Cuomo handily defeated Nixon, demonstrating the disconnect between online swarming and actual turnout: ergo, Cuomo's Law.

Confirming Cuomo's Law, Joe Biden probably had less Twitter presence and support than any of the other major candidates, barely registering on the radar compared to Sanders, and yet he coasted to the top of the delegate count until the coronavirus hit the pause button on the primary season. Sanders' endorsement of Biden in a joint livestream video on April 13th not only conceded the inevitable but delivered a genuine moment of reconciliation that caught many off-guard, steeped in the residual rancor of 2016. Whatever his personal disappointment, Sanders seems to have made peace with defeat and with accepting a useful supporting role in 2020; he refuses to dwell in acrimony. The same can't be said about many of the defiant dead-enders associated with *Jacobin*, who, when not rumor-mongering about Biden's purported crumbling health, cognitive decline, incipient dementia, and basement mold, attempted to kite Tara Reade's tenuous charges of sexual harassment and assault at the hands of Biden into a full-scale Harvey Weinstein horror show, hoping the resultant furor would dislodge Biden from the top of the ticket and rectify the wrong done by benighted primary voters. For so *Jacobin* had written and so it was said: "If Joe Biden Drops Out, Bernie Sanders Must Be the Democratic Nominee."

Like Norman Thomas, the longtime leader of the Socialist Party in America, Bernie Sanders bestowed a paternal beneficence upon the left that has given it a semblance of unity and personal identity. He is the rare politician one might picture holding a shepherd's crook. The problem is that identification with a singular leader is an unsteady thing for a movement to lean on. Long before Thomas died in 1968, having run for the presidency six times, the socialist movement had receded into gray twilight, upstaged by the revolutionary tumult on campuses and in cities. *Jacobin* is determined to make sure history doesn't reprise itself once Sanders enters his On Golden Pond years. Preparing the post-Bernie stage of the socialist movement, a pair of *Jacobin* authors, Meagan Day and Micah Uetricht, collaborated on *Bigger Than Bernie: How We Go from the Sanders Campaign to Democratic Socialism* (Verso), a combination instruction manual and inspirational hymnal.

The duo doesn't lack for reasons to optimize the upside

for the ardent young socialists looking to Alexandria Ocasio-Cortez as their new scoutmaster. The coronavirus crisis has laid bare rickety infrastructure, the lack of preparedness, near-sociopathic incompetence, and widespread financial insecurity that turned a manageable crisis into a marauding catastrophe, making massive expansion of health coverage, universal basic income, and debt relief far more feasible propositions. The roiling convulsions following the death of George Floyd once again exposed the brutal racism and paramilitarization of our police forces. A better, more humane future has never cried out more for the taking. But there is a catch: it can be seized only in partnership with liberal and moderate Democrats, no matter how clammy the clasping hands might be, no matter how mushy the joint resolutions, and this will be galling for *Jacobin's* pride and vocation, making it harder for them to roll out the tumbrils with the same gusto henceforth. The magazine, after conducting introspective postmortems ("Why the Left Keeps Losing — and How We Can Win") and intraparty etiquette lessons ("How to Argue with Your Comrades"), finds itself feeling its way forward, with the occasional fumble. When Bhaskar Sunkara announced on Twitter that he intends to cast his presidential vote for Green Party candidate Howie Hawkins (who he?), one of those showy public gestures that leaves no trace, he received pushback from fellow comrades in *The Nation* ("WTF Is *Jacobin's* Editor Thinking in Voting Green?") and elsewhere. Clarifying his position in *The New York Times,* where clarifications learn to stand up tall and straight, Sunkara assured the quivering jellies who read the opinion pages that "contrary to stereotypes, we are not pushing a third candidate or eager to see Mr. Trump's re-election. Instead we are campaigning for core demands like Medicare for All, saving the U.S. Postal

Futilitarianism, or To the York Street Station

Service from bipartisan destruction, organizing essential workers to fight for better pay and conditions throughout the coronavirus crisis and backing down-ballot candidates, mostly running on the Democratic ballot line... Far from unhinged sectarianism, this is a pragmatic strategy."

Jacobin pragmatism? This is a historical novelty. By November we will know if they are able to make it to the altar without killing each other. It's hard to settle once you've had a taste of Lenin.

ANDREA MARCOLONGO

Ancient Family Lexicon, or Words and Loneliness

"Whoever knows the nature of the name... knows the nature of the thing itself, " Plato observed in his *Cratylus*. *To know* is a complex verb, difficult but rich. According to the dictionary, it means "to have news of a thing," "to know that it exists or what it is." In classical languages, the concept of *knowing* was linked with *being born*. Thus by coming into the world others have "news" about us: their recognition of us is part of our birth.

Knowing the roots of the words at the basis of human relationships permits us to revive a world in which individuals existed as men and women or boys and girls with no middle ground. I will explain what that means. The ancestors of these appellations (woman, girl, man, boy) denoted a particular way of being that subsequent cultures have lost. As the meaning of the words changed, the beings themselves changed. Back then, before these semantic developments, it was understood that the condition of boyhood was synonymous with immaturity, and the divide between childhood and adulthood had to be put to the test of life. Moreover, youth and old age were not personal categories but attitudes of soul and mind. What follows is a sort of Indo-European family lexicon, and a portrait of a lost world.

Mother
The word comes from the Indo-European *mater*, formed by the characteristically childish elementary root *ma-* and the suffix of kinship *-ter*. In Greek it is *mētēr*, in Latin *mater*, in Sanskrit *mātar*, in Armenian *mayr*, in Russian *mat*, in German *Mutter*, in English *mother*, in French *mère*, in Italian, Spanish and Portuguese *madre*, in Irish *máthair*, in Bosnian *majika*.

Father
The word comes from the Indo-European *pater*, formed by the elementary root *pa-* and the suffix of kinship *-ter*. In Greek it is *patèr*, in Latin *pater*, in Sanskrit *pitar*, in ancient Persian *pita*, in Spanish, Italian and Portuguese *padre*, in French *père*, in German *Vater*, in English *father*.

These terms are so ancient, so primordial that they have survived the history of languages and the geography of peoples. Since they were first uttered, these words have consistently been among the first spoken by human beings. They are solid words, like a brick house, like a mountain. It is our fathers and our mothers who teach us first to name things. It is natural that a child should first articulate *ma-* or *pa-*. There is no child who does not seek to be loved and held, who is not in need of care and protection from a mother and father. And we never forget these words; we hold them inside ourselves all the way to the end. Studies on Alzheimer's and senile dementia patients who have spoken a second language throughout their lives, a language different from that of their country of origin, show that they refer to dear ones using their original language. Native language. Mother-tongue.

Human

The classical etymology of the word *man* — meaning a human being — comes from the Latin *homo*, which dates back to the Indo-European root of *humus*, "earth," a result of a primordial juxtaposition, perhaps even opposition, between mortal creatures and the gods of heaven. In the Bible, the Creator infuses earth with soul, creating the human compound. In French the term became *homme*, in Spanish *hombre*, a root that disappears in the Germanic languages, where we have *man* in English and *Mann* in German. The usage may now seem archaic, but it contains a universal idea.

The Greek *ánthrōpos* has a disputed etymology. According to some, it is linked to the words *anō*, "up," *athréo*, "look," and *óps*, "eye," a very fine combination of roots that indicates the puniness of men faced with the immensity of the divine and bound to raise their eyes to heaven from the ground. According to others, it is a descendent of the term *anèr*, "male," "husband," corresponding to the Latin *vir*. In both cases, the condition of "adult man" is colored by the concepts of strength, energy, ardor — of overcoming childhood through tests of courage, which reverberate in the Latin and Greek words *vis* and *andreia*.

Thus we have the universal concept of a human being

223

Ancient Family Lexicon, or Words and Loneliness

who is small, humble, tied to the earth on which she has her feet firmly planted until the day of her death but not entirely material, puny but bent towards heaven - and also strong, therefore heroic, because she has succeeded in enlarging herself. In order to transition from girlhood to womanhood and from boyhood to manhood, one must pass a test. Through this test — or tests: the trials of a human life — girls and boys prove the measures of their strength, tenacity, and courage and in so doing become adults. Once the test is past, their nature itself is forever altered as their name is changed — no middle ground from girl to woman, from boy to man.

Son, Daughter
"Son" is connected with the Latin *filius*, "suckling," linked to the root *fe-*, "sucking," an affective and infantile term typical of the Indo-European -*dhe*, "to suckle," which is found today in some Germanic languages as in the English word *daughter* or in the Bosnian one *dijete*, "boy."

The further we move away from the linguistic essence, from the primeval universality of the Indo-European roots, the more complicated things become, and the more the words grow apart and differ from Romance languages to Germanic ones. The notion of "boy" or "girl" as adolescents still unprepared for adult life does not surface until the fourteenth century. This concept is a foreign loan that dates back to the late Middle Ages and derives from the Arabic *raqqās*, meaning "gallop," or "courier," or more specifically "boy who carries letters," a term of Maghrebian origin probably spread from Sicily through port exchanges in the Mediterranean, which was so rich in Arabisms. (We may note that this etymology has been made irrelevant by the conditions of modern work, in which many adults are treated as boys who carry letters, that is, are employed in infantilizing jobs that do not make full use of their adult skills.)

Young, Old

"Young" is a very pure and powerful word, and an imprecise one, not tied to a registry concept, in the same way that "old" is not. It clearly comes from the Indo-European root *yeun-*, from which the Sanskrit *yuvā*, the Avestan *yavan-*, the French *jeune*, the English *young*, the Latin *iuvenis*, the Spanish *joven*, the Portuguese *jovem*, the Romanian *juve*, the Russian *junyj*, the Lithuanian *jánuas*, the German *jung*. "Young" is the calf or foal tenaciously striving to balance on thin and trembling legs, trying and trying again, falling ruinously to the ground until it stands up, bleeding and covered with straw — but ready to go, to walk, to wander. Youth is strength, a drive, an arrow already fired.

At the opposite extreme of the life cycle is the old, the elderly, which means worn out, weary, weak, too tired to move, to go further — like a car worn down by too many roads, a car that suddenly stops, the engine melted. Elderly is the worn sole of a shoe that has walked too far. It is the hands of the elderly, like cobwebs that have caught too much wind in life. This idea comes from the Latin *vetulus*, a diminutive of *vetus*, which means "used," "worn out," "old." In French it is called *vieil*, in Spanish *viejo*, in Portuguese *velho*, in Romanian *vechi*. Old age is an attitude and not an age, it means stopping, even surrender. The string of the bow collapsed, the quiver empty.

Love

Love is a pledge, as the etymology shows. The notion of betrothal, the ideas of bride and bridegroom, derive from

225

the Latin *sponsum* and *sponsam*, from the past participle of the verb *spondeo*, which means "to promise," corresponding to the Greek *spèndō*. In French it is called *époux* and *épouse*, in Spanish and Portuguese *esposo, esposa*. The original meaning of those words lay in the idea of the indissolubility of the promise of love. Once made, it cannot be revoked. The trust and the faith expressed in the promise were so sacred that they were celebrated by the couple with a libation to the gods.

In the Romance languages, however, the meaning of that promise has slipped into the future, to the rite that has yet to happen, in the word *fiancé*, which derives from *fides* in Latin, which means "faith." It is this faith in the promise of love, in its futurity, that gives strength to lovers such as Renzo and Lucia, made immortal by Alessandro Manzoni in *I promessi sposi,* who did everything possible to fulfill that promise of love contained, primordially, in the definition of "betrothed."

Mom.

As I mentioned, the word comes from the Indo-European root *ma-*, a universal utterance of affection, which has as its basis in the elementary sequence *ma-ma*. This childish word has identical counterparts in all Indo-European languages, a sound of affection that extends beyond borders in the welter of different languages around the world.

Memory is often full of italicized passages, experiences that remain fresh despite the passage of time, but sometimes deletions overshadow the italics. For a long time I had forgotten the sound of the word *mom*. I could not say it anymore because I had not said it out loud for over fifteen years. I had even stopped thinking it.

Stabat mater, "the mother stood" next to the son, reads a thirteenth-century religious poem attributed to Jacopone da Todi, which later became universal in the Christian liturgy to indicate the presence of the sad mother next to the suffering son. Once, beside me, the daughter, there stood my mother. We celebrated our birthday on the same day, she and I: born premature, I was, as long as we both lived, her birthday present. When I was a child we always had a double party for the "women," as my father called us. Since she died, every birthday of mine has been cut in half. And since then I have never been sure of exactly how old I am.

Every January I get closer and closer to the age my mother was when she died. Meanwhile, like the turtle in the paradox of Zeno, I move further and further away from that lost, skinny, lonely girl who was between the third and the fourth year of high school when her mother died of a cancer as swift as a summer: she fell ill in June and passed in September, on the first day of school. For years I never told anyone of my early loss, it was one of my surgical choices. The silence gave me relief from the empty words of the others: *poor girl, so young.* I discovered a new space inside me, a sorrow that I did not know before and could now explore, unseen, unheard. I was an orphan.

It seems impossible to admit it now, like all the admissions of the "imperfect present perfect" that we are, but there was a long period in which I practically stopped talking. *I am fine* was the only sentence in my stunted girlish vocabulary. Not until I was seventeen did I begin to understand the value that the ancients attributed to words — and I began to respect them in silence with an uncompromising loyalty, learning to say little and to keep almost everything quiet.

After high school I moved to Milan, enrolled at the university, and started a new life, which I call my second one. For years I never said anything to the people I met, to my friends, to my boyfriends, about my mother's death. As a daughter I was mute. Anyway, almost nobody ever asked me. My silence was unchallenged. And then, with the publication of my first book, in which I shared my passion for ancient Greek, my third life began — my linguistic life, the era of saying — the advent of the words that I use to make everything real, especially death.

I remember the exact moment that my verbal mission, my reckoning with mortality through language, started. I was presenting my book to the students in a high school in Ostuni when, at question time, a sixteen-year-old boy asked me, with the frankness of those who believe that I must know the most intimate things in the world because I wrote a book on Greek grammar, "Why in Greek is a human being also called *brotòs*, or destined to die?" "Because death is part of life," I said, almost without thinking about it. I was disconcerted by the rapidity of my response: I already knew the answer, even if I had not read it in any book or treatise. I reminded myself that I had no need of a book to know this. She had died; I had lived it. And so on that day I reclaimed the first word that I uttered in my life, like so many of the women and men who have come and will come into the world and have gone and will go out of it. They gave it back to me, those high school boys. I started to say *mom* again.

My mother, mine, who went away a long time ago and whom I resemble so much, the one who taught me my first words.

The ancients believed that there was a perfect alignment between the signifier and the signified, between word and meaning, between name and reality, owing to the power of naming, to the descriptive force of a word to denote a thing.

The Greek adjective *etymos* means "true," "real," from which the word "etymology" was later derived. It was coined by the Stoic philosophers to define the practice of knowing the world through the origin of the words that we use — the words that makes us what we are. I fell in love with the strange study of etymology in high school, and never gave up trying to understand the world according to it, to squeeze what surrounds me out of the language that surrounds me — notwithstanding my friends' teasing that I cannot say anything without a reference to Greek or Latin.

Many centuries later, taking up a thought of Justinian, Dante remarked in the *Vita Nuova* that *nomina sunt consequentia rerum*, "names are consequences of things" — that is, words follow things, they are upon them, they adhere to them, they reveal reality. Reality's debt to language is very great. Words are the gates to what is. And to what is not: the opposite is also true, that if something has no name, or is not articulated in thought or speech, then it is not there. Silence about a thing does not mean that it is not real, but without a name and without words it is unrecognized and so, in a sense, not here, not present, now and now and now again, among us.

Much that cannot now be said was once certainly said, about things that were once here but are gone, about a reality that has been lost. Dust.

Ancient Family Lexicon, or Words and Loneliness

Two years ago I read an article in The *New York Times* that left me with such uneasiness that I was prompted to look more deeply inside myself and the people around me. The journalist declared that these first years of the new millennium are the "era of anxiety." "The United States of Xanax," he called the present era in his country's history, after the most famous pill among the anxiolytics, whose percentage of diffusion in the population, including children, is in the double digits, and whose cost at the local pharmacy is slightly higher than the price of an ice cream and slightly less than a lunch at McDonald's. Depression — that disease of the soul that until the twenties of the last century was considered as incurable, as inconsolable, as its name, *melancholia* — is today no longer fashionable, said the *Times*. It has been usurped. The years of bewilderment in the face of the abyss sung about by Nirvana — and which led to the suicide of Kurt Cobain — are over. Instead we suffer from a different kind of disease, an anxiety that makes us disperse ourselves busily, and scatter ourselves in the name of efficiency, so as not to waste time but instead to manage it frantically. And as we strive not to lose time, we lose ourselves.

The author of the article cited the case of Sarah, a 37-year-old woman from Brooklyn working as a social media consultant who, after having informed a friend in Oregon that she was going to visit her over the weekend, was seized by worry and fear when her friend did not reply immediately to her email. A common experience, perhaps: how many times do we fear that we have hurt a loved one without knowing exactly how? Is such worry a sincere concern about the other, or is it a narcissistic, self-focused guilt? How often are we out of breath as if we were running when in fact we are standing still?

But Sarah took her worry to an uncommon extreme.

Waiting for the answer that was slow to arrive and that presaged her worst fear, she turned to Twitter and her 16,000 followers, tweeting, "I don't hear from my friend for a day — my thought, they don't want to be my friend anymore," adding the hashtag "#ThisIsWhatAnxietyFeelsLike." Within a few hours, thousands of people all over the world followed her example, tweeting what it meant for them to live in a state of perpetual anxiety, prisoners of a magma of indistinct, inarticulate emotions. At the end of the day, Sarah received a response from her friend: she had simply been away from her house and had not read the email. She would be more than happy to meet her, she had been hoping to see her for so long. A few days later Sarah remarked without embarrassment to journalists who were intrigued by the viral phenomenon: "If you are a human being who lives in 2017 and you are not anxious, there is something wrong with you."

Is that really so? Must we surrender to this plague of anxiety? Are we supposed to forget what we know — that friendship is measured in presence and memory, and not in the rate of digital response or the speed of reply? Are we required to infect our most significant relationships with the spirit of highly efficient customer service? Is it a personal affront if a loved one or a friend allows herself half a day to live her life before attending to us? Have we so lost the art of patience that we must be constantly reassured that we have not been abandoned? Are we living out of time, out of our time, if we do not agree to be prisoners of anxiety? Must we conform and surrender and live incompletely, making others around us similarly incomplete?

I think not. It is perverse to regard anxiety as an integral and indispensable part of our life and our contemporaneity. It is difficult to admit, especially when we are unhappy, but we come into the world to try to be happy. And to try to make others happy.

Sarah may have suffered from an anxiety disorder, a serious illness that required appropriate treatment, or perhaps, as she later admitted, she simply felt guilty because, too busy with her work, she had not communicated with her friend for months and was now embarrassed about her absence, about suddenly making herself heard. When we abdicate the faculty of speech, we can only reconstruct the thoughts and feelings of others by means of clues. Often we interpret them incorrectly. Silence confuses us.

I was once like that. There was a time when anyone could read the words *senza parole* — "speechlessness" — on my wrist. It was the expression that I got tattooed on my skin when I lost my mother : *I can't say a word, I don't want to speak.* It was my first tattoo, an indelible warning whenever someone held out his hand to help me. I pushed away from everyone after my mother died, especially from myself. I even dyed my hair black so as not to see in the mirror a reflection which resembled the mother I no longer had.

But "speechlessness" is now the word I hate most, because I understood later, much later, that the words you need to say are always available to you, and you have to make the effort to find them. Just as Plato said, words have the power to create, to form reality — real words, which have equally real effects on our present. As Sarah's sad story reveals, the absence of words is the absence of reality. Without words there is no life, only anxiety, only malaise.

I covered up that tattoo in Sarajevo, a few days before my first book was published, because I had finally found my words. When people smile at the black ink stain that wraps my right wrist like a bracelet, I smile too, because only I know what is underneath, the error that was stamped on my flesh that I have now stamped out. How much life was born after the muzzle was destroyed!

Whatever production of ourselves we stage, there will always be a little detail — a precarious gesture, a forced laugh, an uncertainty, an imbalance — that exposes the inconsistency between what we are doing and what we really want to do.

We are not films, there is no post-production in life, and special effects lose their luster quickly. We are perpetually a first version, *opera prima*, drafts and sketches of the tragedy or comedy of ourselves, as in that moment at sunset in Syracuse or Taormina when the actors entered the scene to begin the show.

Today we all live entangled in a bizarre situation. We have the most immense repository of media in human history and we no longer know what or how or with whom to communicate. I am convinced that we have never before felt so alone. The reason is not that we are silent. Quite the contrary. We talk and talk and talk, until talking exhausts us. But the perpetual cacophony allows us to ignore that we communicate little of substance. We tend to say the bare minimum, to speak quickly and efficiently, to abbreviate, to signal, to hide, to be always easy and never complex. We seem, simultaneously, afraid of being misunderstood and afraid of being understood. The human act of saying has become synthetic, a constant pitch, a transactional practice borrowed from business in which we must persuade our interlocutors in just a few minutes to commit everything they have. Our speech is an advertisement, a performance. Joy is a performance, pain is a performance —

and a speedy one. If we do not translate our sentiments into slogans and cliches, graphics and "visualizations," if we do not express ourselves in the equivalents of summaries, slides, and abstracts, if our presentation of our feelings or our ideas exceed a commonly accepted time limit (reading time: three minutes), then we fear that nobody will have the patience to listen to us.

We have swapped the infinity of our thoughts for the stupid finitude of 280 characters. We send notices of our ideas and notifications of our feelings, rather like smoke signals. Is there anything more like a smoke signal than Instagram stories, which are similarly designed to disappear?

Brevity is now the very condition of our communication. We behave like vulgar epigrammatists, electronically deforming the ancient art of Callimachus and Catullus. We condense what we have to say into each of the many chats on which we try desperately to make ourselves heard by emoticons and phrases and acronyms shot like rubber bullets that bounce here and there as in an amusement park. We refuse subordinate clauses, the complicated verbal arrangement — appropriate for the complexity of actual ideas and feelings — known as hypotaxis, fleeing from going *hypò*, or "below" the surface, and preferring instead to remain *parà*, or "next," on the edge of the parataxis, the list of the things and people we love.

We refuse to know each other and in the meantime we all talk like oracles.

It is a fragile paradox, which should be acknowledged without irony (that hollow armor) and which demands love rather than bitter laughter: the less we say about ourselves, the more we reveal about ourselves. Only we do it in a skewed, precarious way. And we do it deceptively, even treasonously.

Our brevity is only a postponement of what sooner or later will be expressed, but in a twisted way. Surely others have observed the tiny breakdowns, the personal explosions that plague any person forced to live in a perpetual state of incompleteness. Have you never seen someone who, finding herself without words, ends up screaming and madly gesticulating? Everywhere we end up sabotaging the image of perfection that we impose on ourselves with small, miserable, inhuman actions. An unjustified fit of anger on a train: a wrong seat, a suitcase that doesn't fit, a crying baby, a dog, an insult at the traffic light, and suddenly we are hurling unrepeatable shrieks out the window before running away like thieves. Or perhaps you have observed another symptom of this unhealthy condition: anxious indecision — an unnerving slowness to order at the restaurant, *you choose, I don't know, I'm not sure, maybe yes, of course not*, in front of a bewildered waiter, while we collapse as if the course of our whole life depended on the choice of a pizza.

Once upon a time, revolutions were unleashed to obtain freedom from a master. Today the word "revolution" is thrown around in political discourse, but in our inner lives it makes us so afraid that we prefer to oppress ourselves, to renounce the treasures of language and the strengths they confer. And so silence has become our master, imprisoning us in loneliness. A noisy silence, a busy loneliness. The result is a generalized anxiety that, when it explodes, because it always explodes sooner or later, makes us ashamed of ourselves.

When we give our worst to innocent strangers, we would like immediately to vanish, to erase the honest image of ourselves unfiltered. We tell ourselves that is only what we did there — on the subway at rush hour when an old lady cluttered us with her shopping bags, or in the line at the

Ancient Family Lexicon, or Words and Loneliness

post office, annoyed because we lost our place while we were fiddling with the phone or with a post on Facebook in which we commented on something about which we do not care and about which we have nothing to say because there is nothing to say about it. That is not who we *really* are. It was a mistake. It was not representative — or so we tell ourselves.

If we are ashamed, if we want to disappear after these common eruptions, it is for all that we have not done, for all that we have not said, to these strangers and to others we have encountered before. By remaining silent, or by speaking only efficiently, before the spectacle of life, without calling anything or anyone by name, without relishing descriptions, not only do we not know things, as Plato warned, but we do not even know ourselves.

Who are we, thanks to our words?

ELI LAKE

America in the World: Sheltering in Place

I

On the third week of America's quarantine against the
pandemic, a new think tank in Washington had a message for
the Pentagon. "The national security state, created to keep us
safe and guard our freedoms, has failed," Andrew Bacevich,
the president of the Quincy Institute for Responsible State-
craft, told viewers on a Skype video from home, interspersed
with the sounds of sirens and images of emergency rooms.
While microbes from China were mutating and coming to
kill us, he preached, we were wasting our time hunting terror-
ists and projecting military power abroad. It was a sequitur in
search of a point — as if America ever faces only one danger at

a time. When the black plague struck Europe and Asia in the fourteenth century, it did not mean that Mongol hordes would no longer threaten their cities. Nor does the coronavirus mean that jihadists are not plotting terror or that Russia is not threatening its neighbors or that China is not devouring Hong Kong.

His casuistry aside, Bacevich was playing to the resentments of Americans who sincerely believe that American foreign policy is driven by an addiction to war. For the first two decades of post-cold war politics, this argument was relegated to the hallucinations of the fringe. But no more. A new national consensus had started to form before the plague of 2020: that there are almost no legitimate uses for American military power abroad, that our wars have been "endless wars," and that our "endless wars" must promptly be ended. On the subject of American interventionism, there is no polarization in this notoriously polarized country. There is a broad consensus, and it is that we should stay out and far away.

The concept of "endless wars" has its roots in the middle of the twentieth century. In 1984, most famously, George Orwell depicted a totalitarian state that invents its own history to justify perpetual war between the superpowers to keep its citizens in a state of nationalist fervor. In American political discourse, the concept of a war without end was baked into the influential notion of "the manufacture of consent," a notion manufactured by Noam Chomsky according to which the media teaches the American people to support or acquiesce in the nefarious activities of the military-industrial complex. But the "endless wars" that so many Americans wish to end today are not like the ones that Orwell imagined. Today Americans seek to end the war on terror, which in practice means beating back insurgencies and killing terrorist leaders in large swaths of the Islamic world. Orwell's wars were endless because none of the world's states possessed the power to win them. The war on terror, by contrast, endures because of a persistent threat to Western security and because weaker states would collapse if American forces left. The war on terror pits the American Gulliver against fanatical bands of Lilliputians. But the asymmetry of military power does not change the magnitude — or the reality — of the carnage that "stateless actors" can wreak.

To get a feel for the new consensus on American quietism, consider some of the pre-pandemic politics surrounding the war in Afghanistan. In a debate during the presidential primaries, Elizabeth Warren insisted that "the problems in Afghanistan are not problems that can be solved by a military." Her Democratic rivals on the stage agreed, including Joe Biden. This is also Donald Trump's position. As Warren was proclaiming the futility of fighting for Afghanistan's elected government, the Trump administration was negotiating that government's betrayal with the Taliban. (And the Taliban was ramping up its violence while we were negotiating with it.) Before the coronavirus crisis, the Trump administration was spending a lot of its political capital on trying to convince skeptical Republican hawks that the planned American withdrawal would not turn Afghanistan into a haven for terrorists again, which of course is nonsense.

The emerging unanimity about an escape from Afghanistan reflects a wider strategic and historical exhaustion. Despite the many profound differences between Trump and Obama, both presidents have tried to pivot away from the Middle East to focus on competition with China. (Obama never quite made the pivot.) Both presidents have also mused publicly about how NATO allies are "free riders" on America's strength. And both presidents have shown no patience with the use of American military force. In 2012, even as the world

239

was once again becoming a ferociously Hobbesian place, the Obama administration's national defense strategy dropped the longstanding post-cold war goal of being able to win two wars in different geographical regions at once. (The Obama Pentagon seemed to think that land wars are a thing of the past and that we can henceforth make do with drones and Seals.) Trump's first defense strategy in 2018 affirmed the Obama formulation.

Moreover, a majority of Americans agreed with their political leaders. A Pew Research poll in 2019 found that around sixty percent of all Americans did not believe it was worth fighting in Iraq, Syria, or Afghanistan. That percentage is even higher among military veterans. Indeed, Pew research polling since 2013 has found that more Americans than not believe that their country should stay out of world affairs. Hal Brands and Charles Edel, in their fine book *The Lessons of Tragedy*, point out that majorities of Americans still agreed in the late 2010s that America should possess the world's most powerful military, and supported alliances, and favored free trade, but they conclude that many Americans are now resistant to the "sacrifices and trade-offs necessary to preserve the country's post-war achievements."

All of that was before covid19 forced most of the country to "shelter in place." In truth, sheltering-in-place has been the goal of our foreign and national security policy for most of a decade. And it will be much harder to justify a continued American presence in the Middle East, west Asia, Africa and even the Pacific after Congress borrowed trillions of necessary dollars for paycheck protection and emergency small business loans. In addition to all of the older muddled arguments for retreat, there will now be a strong economic case that the republic can no longer afford its overseas commitments, as if foreign policy and national security are ultimately about money. In other words, there are strong indications that the republic is undergoing a profound revision of its role in leading and anchoring the international order that it erected after World War II. The days of value-driven foreign policy, of military intervention on humanitarian grounds, and even of grand strategy, may be over. Should every terror haven, every failed state, every aggression against weak states, and every genocide be America's responsibility to prevent? Of course not. But should none of them be? America increasingly seems to think so. We are witnessing the birth of American unexceptionalism, otherwise known as "responsible statecraft."

II

At the end of the cold war, the spread of liberal democracy seemed inevitable. The Soviet Union had collapsed, and with it the communist governments of the Eastern European countries it dominated. China had momentously made room for a market in its communist system, a strange state-sponsored capitalism that brought hundreds of millions of people out of subsistence poverty. In the West, juntas and strongmen toppled and elected governments replaced them. In every region except for the Middle East and much of Africa, the open society was on the march.

One of the first attempts to describe the thrilling new moment was a famous, and now infamous, essay by Francis Fukuyama. In 1989, in "The End of History?," he surveyed a generation that saw the collapse of pro-American strongmen from Spain to Chile along with the convulsions behind the Iron Curtain and concluded that the triumph of liberalism was inevitable. (He has since revised his view, which is just as well.) His ideas provided the intellectual motifs for a new

241

era of American hegemony. "The triumph of the West, and the Western idea, is evident first of all in the total exhaustion of viable systematic alternatives to western liberalism," Fukuyama wrote. What he meant, in his arch Hegelian way, was that the age of ideological conflict between states was over. History was teleological and it had attained its telos. Fukuyama envisioned a new era in which great power wars would be obsolete. He did not predict the end to all war, but he did predict that big wars over competing ideologies would be replaced by a more mundane and halcyon kind of competition. The principled struggles of history, he taught, "will be replaced by economic calculation, the endless solving of technical problems, environmental concerns, and the satisfaction of sophisticated consumer demands."

Fukuyama's predictions were exhilarating in 1989 because the consensus among most intellectuals during the Cold War had been that the Soviet Union was here to stay. Early theorists of totalitarianism such as Hannah Arendt and Carl Friedrich had portrayed the Soviet state as an unprecedented and impermeable juggernaut that was terrifyingly strong and durable. The hero of Orwell's dystopia, the dissident Emmanuel Goldstein, resisted Big Brother but was never a real threat to the state. In the Brezhnev era, analysts of the Soviet Union began to notice that the juggernaut was crumbling from within and had lost the ideological allegiance of its citizens, even as its military and diplomatic adventures beyond its borders continued. Building on this increasingly realistic understanding of the failures of the communist state, Fukuyama observed that totalitarian systems were overstretched and brittle. The West could exhale.

Not everyone agreed. Samuel Huntington argued that conflict between great powers would remain because identity, not ideology, is what drives states to make war. While it was true that communism was weakening after the collapse of the Soviet Union, other illiberal forces such as religious fundamentalism and nationalism remained a threat to the American-led liberal world order. The hope that China or Iran could be persuaded to open their societies by appealing to prosperity and peace ignored that most nations were motivated not by ideals, but by a shared sense of history and culture. Leon Wieseltier similarly objected that the end of the Soviet Union and its empire would release ethnic and religious and tribal savageries, old animosities that were falsely regarded as antiquated. He also observed that the concept of an "end of history" was borrowed from the very sort of totalitarian mentality whose days Fukuyama believed were over. The worst fiends of the twentieth century justified their atrocities through appeals to history's final phase; the zeal required for their enormous barbarities relied in part on a faith that these crimes are advancing the inevitable march of history. For Wieseltier, there is no final phase and no inevitable march, and the liberal struggle is endless. "To believe in the end of history," he wrote, "you must believe in the end of human nature, or at least of its gift for evil."

243

As international relations theories go, "The End of History" was like a medical study that found that ice cream reduced the risk of cancer. Fukayama's optimistic historicism instructed that the easiest choice for Western leaders was also the wisest. Why devise a strategy to contain or confront Russia if it was on a glide path to democratic reform? Why resist American industrial flight to China if that investment would ultimately tame the communist regime and tempt it to embrace liberalism?

Every president until Trump believed that it was possible

to lure China and Russia into the liberal international order and attempted to do so. Instead of preparing for a great power rivalry, American foreign policy sought to integrate China and Russia into global institutions that would restrain them. Bill Clinton and George W. Bush expanded NATO, but they also invited Russia into the Group of 7 industrialized nations. Clinton, Bush, and Obama — the latter liked to invoke "the rules of the road" — encouraged Chinese-American economic interdependence. Until Obama's second term, the United States did next to nothing to stop China's massive theft of intellectual property. Until June 2020, Chinese corporations could trade freely on U.S. stock exchanges without submitting to the basic accounting rules required of American companies. The assumption behind these Panglossian views of China and Russia was that democratic capitalism was irresistible and the end of communism marked the beginning of a new era of good feelings. (Communism never ended in China, of course.) And it was certainly true that trade with China benefitted both economies: Chinese and American corporations prospered and American consumers enjoyed cheaper consumer goods.

This is not to say that there were no bouts of dissent. In his presidential campaign in 1992, Bill Clinton attacked George H. W. Bush for his capitulation to China after the uprising at Tiananmen Square. And even though Clinton did not alter the elder Bush's approach to China during his presidency, there was a lively debate about China's human rights abuses in the 1990s. Clinton expanded NATO, something the elder Bush opposed, but he and later George W. Bush and Barack Obama did little to push back against Russia's own regional adventures and aggressive behavior. Consider that no serious U.S. war plan for Europe was developed between the end of the Cold War and 2014, the same year that Russia invaded Ukraine and eventually annexed

Crimea, and five years after Russia invaded and occupied the Georgian provinces of South Ossetia and Abkhazia. We preferred to look away from Russia's forward movements — with his cravenness about Syria, Obama actually opened the vacuum that Russia was happy to fill — just as we preferred to look away from the growing evidence of China's strategic ambitions and human-rights outrages. We were reluctant to lose those good feelings so soon after we acquired them.

None of this meant that American presidents would not use force or wage war after the collapse of the Soviet Union. They did. But they did not engage in great power wars. The first Bush saved Kuwait from Saddam Hussein and saved Panama from the lesser threat of Manuel Noriega. Clinton intervened in the Balkans to stop a genocide and launched limited air strikes in the Middle East and Afghanistan. In the aftermath of September 11, George W. Bush waged a war on terror and toppled the tyrannies that held Iraq and Afghanistan captive. Obama intervened reluctantly and modestly and ineffectively in Libya; he withdrew troops from Iraq only to send some of them back; and he presided over a "surge" in Afghanistan, even though its announcement was accompanied by a timetable for withdrawal. Trump has launched no new wars, but he has killed Iran's most important general and the architect of its campaign for regional hegemony, and he has launched strikes on Syrian regime targets in response to its use of chemical weapons, though his strikes have not added up to a consistent policy. But even as optimism about world order has become less easy to maintain, even as the world grows more perilous in old and new ways, the American mood of retirement, the inclination

245

to withdrawal, has persisted. Fukuyama, who acknowledged that the threat of terrorism would have to be met with force, has remarked that our task is not "to answer exhaustively the challenges to liberalism promoted by every crackpot messiah around the world." But what about the genocides perpetrated by a crackpot messiah (or a rational autocrat)? And what about answering great power rivals? At the time, to be sure, we had no great power rivals. We were living in the fool's paradise of a "unipolar" world.

Bill Clinton came to the presidency from Little Rock without a clear disposition on the use of military force. He was at times wary of it. He pulled American forces out of Somalia after a militia downed an American helicopter. In his first term he dithered on the Balkan wars and their atrocities, favoring a negotiation with Serbia's strongman Slobodan Milosevic. He did nothing to stop Rwanda's Hutu majority from slaughtering nearly a million Tutsis for three months in the spring and summer of 1994. He was more focused than any of his predecessors or successors on brokering a peace between Israelis and Palestinians. Over time, of course, he evolved, but how the world suffers for the learning curve of American presidents! Clinton punished Saddam Hussein's defiance of U.N. weapons inspectors. He bombed suspected al Qaeda targets in Sudan and Afghanistan after the bombings of American embassies in Africa in 1998. He prevented Milosevic from cleansing Kosovo of Albanians and helped push back Serb forces from Bosnia.

Clinton was a reluctant sheriff, to borrow Richard Haass' phrase. In his first term he was unsure about using American force abroad. By the end of his second term, he had come to terms with the responsibilities of American power. "The question we must ask is, what are the consequences to our

246

security of letting conflicts fester and spread?," Clinton asked in a speech in 1999. "We cannot, indeed, we should not, do everything or be everywhere. But where our values and our interests are at stake, and where we can make a difference, we must be prepared to do so." He was talking about transnational threats and rogue states. In his second term, Clinton took a keen interest in biological weapons and pandemics. This meant using military power to prevent the proliferation of weapons of mass destruction and deter terrorists. As Madeleine Albright, Clinton's second secretary of state, memorably put it, America was the world's "indispensable nation."

Yet Clinton's activism did not extend to Russia or China. He helped to expand the NATO alliance, but also secured debt forgiveness for the Russian federation and used his personal relationship with Russian president Boris Yeltsin to reassure him that NATO's expansion was no threat to Moscow. Clinton also reversed his campaign promise on China and granted it most favored nation status as a trading partner, paving the way for the economic interdependence that Trump may be in the process of unraveling today. At the time, Clinton explained that "this decision offers us the best opportunity to lay the basis for long-term sustainable progress on human rights and for the advancement of our other interests with China." This reflected the optimism of 1989-1991. What other model did China have to emulate, but our own? Allow it to prosper and over time it will reform.

When Clinton left office, the consensus among his party's elites was that his foreign policy mistakes were errors of inaction and restraint. Clinton did nothing to prevent the genocide in Rwanda. He waited too long to intervene in the Balkans. It seemed that Americans had gotten over their inordinate fear of interventions. Why had it taken Clinton so long?

There was an activist mood in Washington before the attacks of September 11. And after hijacked commercial planes were turned into precision missiles and the towers fell, the sense that America needed to do more with its power intensified.

In the Bush years, American foreign policy fell first into the hands of neoconservatives. For their critics, they were a cabal of swaggering interlopers who twisted intelligence products and deceived a dim president into launching a disastrous war. In fact they were a group of liberals who migrated to the right and brought with them an intellectual framework and appreciation for social science that was absent from the modern conservative movement. In foreign policy they dreaded signs of American weakness or retreat, and in 1972 supported Scoop Jackson against George McGovern in the Democratic primaries. As that decade progressed, the wary and disenchanted liberals migrated to the former Democrat Ronald Reagan. In Reagan, they found a president who despised Soviet communism as much as they did.

In the 1990s, a new generation of neocons wanted to seize the opportunity of American primacy in the world after the Soviet Union's collapse. As Irving Kristol observed, "With power come responsibilities, whether sought or not, whether welcome or not. And it is a fact that if you have the kind of power we now have, either you will find opportunities to use it, or the world will discover them for you." In that spirit, the neoconservatives of the 1990s advocated an activist foreign policy. They argued that the United States should help to destabilize tyrannies and support democratic opposition movements. They were not content with letting history take its course; they wanted to push it along in the direction of freedom. Their enthusiasm for an American policy of democratization was based on both moral arguments and strategic arguments.

The focus in this period was Iraq. Neoconservatives had rallied around legislation known as the Iraq Liberation Act that would commit the American government to train and to equip a coalition of Iraqi opposition groups represented in the United States by Ahmad Chalabi, a wealthy Iraqi political figure who was trained as a mathematician in the United States. For the first half of the 1990s, the CIA funded Chalabi's Iraqi National Congress, but he had a falling out with the agency. The Iraq Liberation Act was a way to save the opposition group by replacing a once covert intelligence program with one debated openly in Congress. It should be noted that Chalabi's initial plan was not to convince America to invade Iraq, but to secure American training and equipment to build a rebel army comprised of Iraqis to topple Saddam Hussein. Clinton allowed the legislation to pass in 1997, but his government never fully implemented it.

George W. Bush ironically ran his campaign in 2000 with the promise of a humble foreign policy. Condoleezza Rice memorably declared at the Republican convention that America cannot be the world's 911. Not long afterward, 9/11 was the event that forced Bush to renege on his promise. Three days after that attack, Congress voted to authorize what we know today as the war on terror: the "endless wars" had begun. Over the last nineteen years, that authorization has justified a global war against a wide range of targets. Bush used it as the legal basis for strikes on terrorists in south Asia. Obama used it to justify his military campaign against the Islamic State, when it was a battlefield enemy of al Qaeda's Syrian branch. And while every few years some members of Congress have proposed changes to the authorization, these efforts have yet to succeed. Today many progressives believe the war on terror deformed America into an evil empire, patrolling the skies of the Muslim world with deadly drones, blowing up wedding parties in Afghanistan, torturing suspected terrorists and aligning with brutal thugs. Even Obama has not escaped this judgment. Some of these are fair criticisms. The war on terror was indeed a war. Innocent people died. At the same time, the other side of the ledger must be counted. Since 9/11, there have been no mass-casualty attacks by foreign terrorists inside our borders. On its own terms, from the rather significant standpoint of American security, this "endless war" has produced results.

In the first years of the war on terror, the pacifist left had little influence over the national debate. A better barometer of the country's mood was a column, published a month before the Iraq War, by Charles Krauthammer. He denounced what he said was Clinton's "vacation from history," and asked whether "the civilized part of humanity [will] disarm the barbarians who would use the ultimate knowledge for the ultimate destruction." Those words, and many others like them, helped to frame the rationale for the American invasion of Iraq. Note that Krauthammer did not write that Clinton's vacation from history was his failure to prepare for China's rise and Russia's decline. It was his failure to prevent the arming of smaller rogue states and terrorist groups. Krauthammer was still living in Fukuyama's world. And so was Bush. In his first term, Bush not only failed to challenge Russia or China, he sought to make them partners in his new global war. Bush famously remarked that he had looked into the eyes of Vladimir Putin and found a man he could trust. ("I was able to get a sense of his soul.") Bush's government would also designate a Uighur separatist organization as a terrorist group, giving cover to the persecution of that minority. The world learned in 2018 that China had erected a new Gulag in western China that now imprisons at least a million Uighurs.

China and Russia did not support Bush's Iraq war. Many Democrats did. In 2002, a slim majority of Democrats in the House opposed a resolution to authorize it, but in the Senate, 29 out of 50 Democrats voted for it. Most significant, every Democrat with presidential aspirations — from Hillary Clinton to Joe Biden — voted for the war, a vote for which they would later apologize. At the time of that vote, the ambitious Democrats who supported it did not know that opposition to that war would define their party for years to come. Neither did the establishment Democrats who opposed it. Al Gore, speaking at the Commonwealth Club of San Francisco, explained his opposition to the war: "If we go in there and dismantle them — and they deserve to be dismantled — but then we wash our hands of it and walk away and leave it in a situation of chaos, and say, 'That's for y'all to decide how to put things back together now,' that hurts us." Gore was not concerned that America may break Iraq, he was acknowledging that it was already broken. Nor was he worried about an "exit strategy." He worried that if America went to war in Iraq under a Republican president, the war may not be endless enough. America may leave too soon.

The Iraq war was also opposed by a group of international relations theorists who advocated for what is known as foreign policy realism. Unlike Fukuyama, the realists do not think it matters how a state chooses to organize itself. All states, according to the realists, pursue their own survival, or their national interest. Thirty-three prominent realists purchased an advertisement in the *New York Times* in 2002 urging Bush not to invade Iraq. They argued that the coming war would distract America from the campaign against al Qaeda and leave it in charge of a failed state with no good options to leave. It is worth noting that neither the pacifist left nor the foreign policy realists argued before the war that Saddam Hussein had no weapons of mass destruction, the liquidation of which was Bush's justification for the war. Both camps warned instead that an American invasion of Iraq could prompt the tyrant to use the chemical and biological weapons that everyone agreed he was concealing. As the professors wrote in their open letter, "The United States would win a war against Iraq, but Iraq has military options — chemical and biological weapons, urban combat — that might impose significant costs on the invading forces and neighboring states." The argument was that removing Saddam Hussein would further destabilize the Middle East.

Over the course of 2003, it became clear that the *casus belli* for Operation Iraqi Freedom — Saddam's refusal to come clean on his regime's weapons of mass destruction — was wrong. The teams of American weapons inspectors sent into the country could not find the stockpiles of chemical weapons or the mobile bio-weapons labs. The Bush administration sought to portray this error as an intelligence failure, which was largely correct. And so the war's unanticipated consequences, some of them the result of American error, eclipsed the fact that Iraqis had drafted a constitution and were voting for their leaders. In America, a great popular anger began to form, not only against the Iraq war but more generally against American interventionism. The Democrats became increasingly eager to take political advantage of it. Talk of American hubris proliferated. Progressives were growing wary of the institutions of national security, particularly the intelligence agencies.

Republicans under Bush were also divided between an embrace of the president's own idealism to make Iraq a democracy and the unsentimental realism of his vice president, who darkly warned after 9/11 that the war against terror would have to be fought in the shadows. Bush's own policies were inconsistent. Sometimes he pressured dictator allies to make democratic reforms, but he also empowered those same dictators to wage war against jihadists with no mercy. In Israel, Bush supported legislative elections that resulted in empowering Hamas in Gaza. (That was in 2006, the last time Palestinians voted for their leaders.) By the end of Bush's second term, however, great power competition had re-emerged. While America was preoccupied with the Muslim world, Russia invaded the former Soviet Republic of Georgia. Bush did what he could. He sent humanitarian supplies to Tbilisi packed on U.S. military aircraft. He tried to rally allies to support a partial ban on weapons sales to Moscow. But Russia had the good fortune of timing its aggression just as the world's financial markets collapsed. It was also lucky that the next American president would be Barack Obama.

Barack Obama had been a state senator in Illinois during the run up to the Iraq War, when his primary rival, Hillary Clinton, was a U.S. senator. She voted for the war. He gave a speech opposing it. At the time of the election, in a political party incensed by the Iraq war, Obama's speech in Chicago in 2002 functioned as a shield: he may have lacked Clinton's experience, but at least he did not support Bush's war. Back in 2002, though, Obama's speech was barely noticed. The *Chicago Tribune* news story led with Jesse Jackson's speech and made no mention of the ambitious state senator. When Obama was at the lectern, he had two distinct themes. First, he wanted the protestors to know that he, too, understood the evil of neoconservatism. "What I am opposed to is the cynical attempt by Richard Perle and Paul Wolfowitz and other armchair, weekend warriors in this administration to shove their own ideological agendas down our throats," he said. At the same time, Obama rejected the apologies for tyrants common on the hard left. Of Saddam, he said, "He is a brutal man. A ruthless man. A man who butchers his own people to secure his own power." But the young Obama did not think that Saddam threatened American interests. Echoing Fukuyama's optimism, he declared that "in concert with the international community he can be contained until, in the way of all petty dictators, he falls away into the dustbin of history."

Obama's patience with history, with its dustbins and its arcs, turned out to be, well, endless. His Chicago speech should have been a warning for the left wing of the Democratic Party that over time it would be disappointed by his presidency. As Obama said, he was not against war. (The tough-minded Niebuhrian speech that he delivered in Oslo when he accepted his ridiculous Nobel Prize underscored his awareness of evil in the world.) He was merely against dumb wars — or as he later put it, "stupid shit." He had come into office when the world was growing more dangerous, and he chose to respond to these dangers with careful and scholarly vacillations. He wanted the American people to know that he was thoughtful. The most salient characteristics of his foreign policy were timidity and incoherence, and a preference for language over action.

Thus, Obama withdrew American forces from Iraq in 2011, only to send special operators back to Iraq in 2014, after the

Islamic State captured the country's largest city. He "surged" forces in Afghanistan in his first term, but fired the general he chose to lead them, and spent most of his administration trying, and failing, to withdraw them. He spoke eloquently about the disgrace of Guantanamo, but never closed it. He declassified a series of Justice Department memos that made specious legal arguments to allow the CIA to torture detainees, but his Justice Department never prosecuted the officials responsible, as many in his base wanted. He sided with peaceful protestors in Egypt in 2011 at the dawn of the Arab Spring and urged Hosni Mubarak to step down, but after Egypt elected an Islamist president, the military toppled him in a coup thirteen months later and Obama declined to impose sanctions. He did manage to reach a narrow deal with Iran to diminish, but not demolish, its nuclear weapons program. By this time Iran was on a rampage in the Middle East, and the windfall that its economy received from the nuclear bargain would be reinvested in its own proxy wars in Syria, Iraq and Yemen. The deal alienated America's traditional allies in the Middle East and brought Israel closer to its Arab rivals.

The most spectacular failure of Obama's foreign policy, of course, was Syria. After the Arab Spring, Syrians demanded the same democratic freedoms that they saw blooming in Tunisia and briefly in Egypt. Obama supported them, at first. But the tyrant was watching: Bashar al-Assad had learned from what he considered the mistakes of Mubarak and Ben Ali. Assad was also fortunate that his patrons were Russia and Iran, who also lived in fear of popular uprisings. So began the Syrian civil war that to this day rages on. That war has flooded Europe and Turkey with refugees, with dire political consequences, and threatened for a few years in the middle of the 2010s to erase the borders established after World War I for the Middle East.

255

It is not the case that Obama did absolutely nothing to support the Syrian opposition. In 2012, he approved a covert program known as Timber Sycamore, in which the CIA endeavored to build up an army of "moderate rebels" against Assad. The plan was always flawed. Obama did not want American forces to fight inside Syria and risk an open clash with Iranian and Russian forces who were on the side of the Assad regime. (Obama was reluctant to offend the Russians and he was actively seeking détente with the Iranians.) America clung to its passivity as Syria's civil war and Iraq's embrace of Shiite majoritarian rule created the conditions for the emergence of the Islamic State. A few years later, Obama authorized a Pentagon program to arm and support a largely Kurdish army fighting the Islamic State. With the help of American air power, the Kurds and U.S. special forces eventually smashed the "caliphate" during Trump's first term in office.

Artlessly and in accord with his principles, Obama painted himself into a corner. He called on Assad to leave, but he never used American power to assist with that mission. Obama also warned of consequences if Assad used chemical weapons, which he called a "red line." In 2013, when Assad crossed this line, Obama threatened air strikes against Assad's regime. The moment of truth— about Syria, about American interventionism — had arrived. Obama punted. He gave a bizarre speech in which he asserted that he had the constitutional prerogative to strike Syria without a resolution from Congress but was asking Congress to authorize the attack anyway. In his swooning memoir of the Obama White House, Ben Rhodes recalls that the president told him, "The thing is, if we lose this vote it will drive a stake through the heart of neoconservatism — everyone will see they have no votes." Never mind the heart of Bashar al Assad! Rhodes continues: "I realized then that he was comfortable with either outcome. If we won authorization, he'd be in a strong position to act in Syria. If we didn't, then we would potentially end the cycle of American wars of regime change in the Middle East."

The episode broaches the early roots of the bipartisan consensus against "endless war." When the resolution came up for a vote, it barely got out of the Senate Foreign Relations Committee. As the Senate debated, Republican hardliners began to wobble. "Military action, taken simply to save face, is not a wise use of force," said Senator Rubio. "My advice is to either lay out a comprehensive plan using all of the tools at our disposable that stands a reasonable chance of allowing the moderate opposition to remove Assad and replace him with a stable secular government. Or, at this point, simply focus our resources on helping our allies in the region protect themselves from the threat they and we will increasingly face from an unstable Syria." In other words, Rubio would not support a modest air strike to impose some costs on a breach of an important international norm because it did not go far enough. The result of this twisted reasoning, and of the failure of the resolution, was the emboldening of Assad. Finally, at the last minute, Obama was saved by Assad's most important patron. Russian foreign minister Sergei Lavrov and Secretary of State John Kerry quickly patched together a plan whereby Syria, for the first time, would declare its chemical weapons stockpiles and allow international inspectors to get them out of the country. Over time, the deal proved worthless. Assad would gas his people again and again, eroding what was once a powerful prohibition on the use of chemical weapons in the twenty-first century. But if the deal did nothing to end the misery of Syria, it did a lot to end the misery of Obama. In 2013, Obama portrayed the bargain as a triumph of diplomacy, which it was — for Putin.

257

One of the first foreign policy priorities for Obama after his election was to mend relations with Moscow. This was called the "reset." Obama was most exercised by transnational threats: climate change, arms control, fighting terrorism, Ebola. He wanted Russia to be a partner. And Russia wanted recognition that it was still a great power.

After Obama folded on his "red line" in Syria, Putin made his move. Russian forces invaded Ukraine in 2014 to stop a democratic revolution and eventually annexed Crimea. Obama imposed a series of economic sanctions on Russian industries and senior officials, but he declined to arm Ukraine's government or consider any kind of military response. (He worried more about escalation than injustice.) His administration's advice to Kiev was to avoid escalation. The following year Obama did not challenge Russia when it established airbases inside Syria. He still needed the Russians for the Iran nuclear deal. By 2016, when the U.S. intelligence community was gathering evidence that Russians were hacking the Democratic National Committee and Hillary Clinton's campaign, Obama's White House waited until after the election to punish Moscow. Three weeks before the next

president would take the oath of office, Obama announced the expulsion of thirty-five spies and modest sanctions on Russia's intelligence services. It was a fine example of "responsible statecraft."

The thoughtful incoherence of Barack Obama was succeeded by the guttural anarchy of Donald Trump. It was nearly impossible to discern from Trump's campaign what his actual foreign policy would be if he won. His ignorance of international affairs was near total. He simultaneously pledged to pull America out of the Middle East and to bomb ISIS indiscriminately. He could sound like Michael Moore one minute, thundering that George W. Bush lied America into the Iraq War, and in the next minute like a Stephen Colbert imitation of a right-wing neanderthal, claiming that Mexico was deliberately sending its rapists into our country. And yet there was a theme in Trump's hectoring confusion. He hearkened back to a very old strain of American politics. One could see it in his slogan "America First," a throwback to the isolationism of Charles Lindbergh in the 1930s. When Trump asked mockingly what America was getting from its interventions in the Middle East or the protection its troops provided Europe through the NATO alliance, he was unknowingly channeling Senator Robert Taft and his opposition to the Marshall Plan. Past presidents, Republicans and Democrats, understood that the small upfront cost of stationing troops overseas in places such as Korea or Bahrain paid much greater dividends by deterring rivals and maintaining stability. Military and economic aid was a small price to pay for trade routes and open markets. But Trump rejected all of this.

As president, Trump's foreign policy has not been altogether catastrophic. (That is faint praise, I know.) He has used force in constructive flashes, such as the drone strike that killed Qassem Suleimani or the air strikes against Syrian landing strips after the regime gassed civilians. He never pulled America out of NATO as he said he would, though he declined to say publicly that America would honor the mutual defense commitments in the treaty's charter. He pulled out of Obama's nuclear deal with Iran, a deal whose merits were always a matter of controversy. He began to reverse the spending caps imposed during Obama's presidency on the Pentagon's budget. On China, the Trump administration has begun aggressively to target Beijing's thievery and espionage and takeover of international institutions.

Most consistently, Trump's foreign policy has been marked by an amoral transactionalism. Modern presidents of both parties have made bargains with tyrants, but they did so sheepishly, and often they appended talk of human rights to their strategic accommodations. Trump was different. He went out of his way to pay rhetorical tribute to despots and authoritarians who flattered him — Kim Jong Un, Vladimir Putin, Xi Jinping, Viktor Orban, Jair Bolsonaro. When Trump's presidency began, senior advisers such as General James Mattis and General H.R. McMaster tried to soften, and at times to undermine, his appetite to renounce American leadership in the world. McMaster made the president sit through a power-point presentation about life in Afghanistan before the Taliban to persuade him of the need for a small military surge there. After Trump abruptly announced the withdrawal of the small number of American forces in Syria, his advisers persuaded him that some should stay in order to protect the oil fields. And so it went until most of the first cabinet was pushed out in 2018 and 2019. The new team was more malleable to Trump's instincts. Trump's new secretary of state, Mike Pompeo, empowered an envoy to negotiate an American withdrawal from Afghanistan with the Taliban, without including the Afghan government, our ally, in the talks. Instead of undermining Trump's push to leave the Iran nuclear deal, as James Mattis and Rex Tillerson had done, the president's new team kept escalating sanctions.

Trump was erratic. Never has foreign policy been so confusing to anyone outside (and to some inside) the White House. Trump would impetuously agree with heads of state to major policy changes before the rest of his government could advise him of his options. Since Trump shares his internal monologue with the world on twitter, these lunges became policies, until he would later reverse them just as fitfully. To take one example: the sequence of tweets that announced Trump's deal in 2019 with Turkey to pull American support for its Kurdish allies in Syria had real consequences, even though Trump would later reverse himself. As the Turkish military prepared to enter an autonomous Kurdish region of Turkey, the Kurdish fighters who had bled to defeat ISIS were forced to seek protection from Russia, Iran, and Bashar al Assad.

During that crisis, Trump tweeted about one of his favorite themes: "The endless wars must end." For the first fifteen years of the post-9/11 era, that kind of talk would have been heresy for Republicans. Despite a few outliers inside the party like Ron Paul and Rand Paul, the party of Bush and Reagan supported what it called a "long war," a multi-generational campaign to build up allies so they could defeat terrorists without American support. Until very recently, Republicans understood that as frustrating as training local police in Afghanistan and counter-terrorism commandos in Iraq often can be, the alternative was far worse, both strategically and morally. The same was true of American deployments during the Cold War. To this day there are American troops in South Korea and Germany, in part because their very presence deterred adversaries from acting on their own aggressive or mischievous impulses. But Trump disagreed. And he echoed a growing consensus. "No more endless wars" is the new conventional wisdom.

III

The Quincy Institute for Responsible Statecraft was founded in 2019 as a convergence of opposites, with money from George Soros' Open Society Foundation and the Koch brothers. There was one thing about which the opposites agree, and that is the end of American primacy, and consequent activism, in the world. The new think tank hopes to mold the wide but inchoate opposition to "endless wars" into a coherent national strategy.

On the surface, the Quincy Institute presents itself in fairly platitudinous terms. "The United States should respect established international laws and norms, discourage irresponsible and destabilizing actions by others, and seek to coexist with competitors," its website says. "The United States need not seek military supremacy in all places, at all costs, for all time." That boilerplate sounds like the kind of thing one would hear in the 2000s from what were then known as the netroots: wars of choice are bad, international law is good. But there is an important distinction. The progressives who obsessed over the neoconservatives in the Bush years argued the ship of state had been hijacked. The Quincy Institute is arguing that the institutions it once sought to protect from those ideological interlopers were themselves in on the heist. The problem is not the distortion of our foreign policy by foreign interests. The problem is the system that created our foreign policy in the first place.

Consider this passage by Daniel Bessner on Quincy's website: "While there are national security think tanks that lean right and lean left, almost all of them share a bipartisan commitment to U.S. 'primacy' — the notion that world peace (or at least the fulfillment of the "national interest") depends on the United States asserting preponderant military, political, economic, and cultural power. Think tanks, in other words, have historically served as the handmaidens of empire." Bessner is echoing an idea from Stephen Walt, the Harvard professor who is also a fellow at the institute. At the end of *The Hell of Good Intentions*, which appeared in 2018, Walt called for a "fairer fight within the system," and recommended establishing a broader political movement and the creation of new institutions — a think tank? — to challenge what he perceives as the consensus among foreign policy elites to favor a strategy of liberal hegemony. American primacy in the world he deemed to be bad for America and bad for the world.

The Quincy Institute hired the perfect president for such a program. A retired Army colonel and military historian who lost his son in the Iraq War, Andrew Bacevich has emerged as a more literate and less sinister version of Smedley Butler. That name is largely forgotten today, but Butler was a prominent figure in the 1930s: a retired Major General who, after his service to the country, declared that "war is a racket" and that his career as a Marine amounted to being a "gangster for capitalism." Butler later admitted that he was approached by a cabal to lead a military coup against President Roosevelt, but he remains to this day a hero of the anti-war movement. In 2013, in *Breach of Trust,* Bacevich presented Butler as a kind of dissident: "He commits a kind of treason in the second degree, not by betraying his country but calling into question officially sanctioned truths." In this respect, Butler is the model for other retired military officers who dare to challenge official lies. Not surprisingly, *Breach of Trust* reads like the military history that Howard Zinn never wrote. It is a chronicle of atrocities, corruption, and government lies. Like Bacevich's other writings, it is a masterpiece of tendentiousness.

More recently, Bacevich has sought to recast the history of the movement to prevent Roosevelt from entering World War II, known as America First. He has acknowledged that America was correct to go to war against the Nazis, but still he believes that the America Firsters have gotten a bad rap. Until Donald Trump, the America First movement was seen as a cautionary

263

tale and a third rail. When Pat Buchanan tried to revive the term in the 1980s and 1990s, there was bipartisan outrage. After all, America First was led by Charles Lindbergh, an anti-Semite and an admirer of the Third Reich. Bacevich acknowledges this ugly provenance. And yet he chafes at Roosevelt's judgment that Lindbergh's movement was promoting fascism. "Roosevelt painted anti-interventionism as anti-American, and the smear stuck," Bacevich wrote in 2017 in an essay in *Foreign Affairs* charmingly called "Saving America First."

Bacevich imparts a grain of truth. The America First movement was largely a response to the unprecedented horrors of World War I, in which armies stupidly slaughtered each other and chemical weapons were used on a mass scale. And the war was sparked by miscalculations and secret alliances between empires and smaller states in Europe: it lacked the moral and strategic purpose of defeating the Nazis and the Japanese fascists. It is quite understandable that two decades after World War I ended, many Americans would be reluctant to fight its sequel. But Bacevich goes a bit further. In his *Foreign Affairs* essay, he instructed that "the America First Movement did not oppose Jews; it opposed wars that its members deemed needless, costly, and counterproductive. That was its purpose, which was an honorable one." But was it honorable? While it is true that in the 1930s major newspapers did a terrible job in covering the Third Reich's campaign against Jews and other minorities, those persecutions were hardly a secret. Nazi propaganda in the United States was openly anti-Semitic. The war weariness of post-World War I America does not confer nobility on America First's cause. In a recent interview Bacevich became testy when asked about that remark. "Come on now," he said. "I think that the anti-interventionist case was understandable given the outcome of the

First World War. They had reason to oppose U.S. intervention. And, again, let me emphasize, their calculation was wrong. It's good that they lost their argument. I do not wish to be put into a position where I'm going to make myself some kind of a defender for the people who didn't want to intervene against Nazi Germany." Good for him.

That exchange tells us a lot about the Quincy Institute. The think tank's foreign policy agenda and arguments echo the anti-interventionism of the 1930s. Most of its scholars are more worried about the exaggeration of threats posed by America's adversaries than the actual regimes doing the actual threatening. In May, for example, Rachel Esplin Odell, a Quincy fellow, complained that Senator Romney was overstating the threat of China's military expansion and unfairly blaming the state for the outbreak of the coronavirus: "The great irony of China's military modernization is that it was in large part a response to America's own grand strategy of military domination after the Cold War." In this, of course, it resembled most everything else.

The institute has hired staff that come out of the anti-neo-conservative movement of the 2000s. Here we come to a delicate matter. The anti-neoconservatives of that era flirted with and at times embraced an IR sort of anti-Semitism: the obsession with Israel and its influence on American statecraft. Like the America Firsters, the anti-neoconservatives worry about the power of a special interest — the Jewish one — dragging the country into another war. A few examples will suffice. In 2018, Eli Clifton, the director of Quincy's "democratizing foreign policy" program, wrote a post for the blog of Jim Lobe, the editor of the institute's journal *Responsible Statecraft*, that three Jewish billionaires — Sheldon Adelson, Bernard Marcus, and Paul Singer — "paved the way" for Trump's decision to withdraw from Obama's Iran nuclear deal through their generous political donations. It is certainly fair to report on the influence of money in politics, but given Trump's well-known contempt for the Iran deal, Clifton's formulation had an odor of something darker.

Then there is Trita Parsi, the institute's Swedish-Iranian vice president, who is best known as the founder of the National Iranian American Council, a group that purports to be a non-partisan advocacy group for Iranian-Americans but has largely focused on softening American policy towards Iran. In 2015, as the Obama administration was rushing to finish the nuclear deal with Iran, his organization took out an ad in the *New York Times* that asked, "Will Congress side with our president or a foreign leader?" a reference to an upcoming speech before Congress by the Israeli prime minister Benjamin Netanyahu. The National Iranian American Council's foray into the dual loyalty canard is ironic considering that Parsi himself has been a go-between for journalists and members of Congress who seek access to Mohammad Javad Zarif, Iran's foreign minister.

This obsession with Israeli influence in American foreign policy is a long-standing concern for a segment of foreign policy realists, who believe that states get into trouble when the national interest is distorted by domestic politics — an affliction that is particularly acute in democratic societies which respect the rights of citizens to make their arguments to the public and to petition the government and to form lobbies. The most controversial of the realists' scapegoating of the domestic determinants of foreign policy was an essay by Stephen Walt and John J. Mearsheimer (both Quincy fellows) that appeared in the *London Review of Books* in 2005. It argued that American foreign policy in the Middle East has been essentially captured by groups that seek to advance Israel's national interest at the expense of America's. "The thrust of US policy in the region derives almost entirely from domestic politics, and especially the activities of the 'Israel Lobby,'" they wrote. "Other special-interest groups have managed to skew foreign policy, but no lobby has managed to divert it as far from what the national interest would suggest, while simultaneously convincing Americans that US interests and those of the other country — in this case, Israel — are essentially identical."

Walt and Mearsheimer backed away from the most toxic elements of their essay in a subsequent book. The essay sought to explain the Iraq War as an outgrowth of the Israel lobby's distortion of American foreign policy. The book made a more modest claim about the role it plays in increasing the annual military subsidy to Israel and stoking American bellicosity to Israel's rivals like Iran. They also took pains to denounce anti-Semitism and acknowledge how Jewish Americans are particularly sensitive to arguments that present their organized political activity as undermining the national interest. Good for them. But the really important point is that events have discredited their claims. The all-powerful "Israel Lobby" was unable to wield its political influence to win the fight against Obama's Iran deal. It was not able to stop Obama's public pressuring of Israel to accept a settlement freeze. Decades earlier, it had not been able to thwart Reagan's sale of AWACs to the Saudis. Anyone who believes in an omnipotent AIPAC is looking for conspiracies.

Walt himself, and the Quincy Institute, now has a much more ambitious target: the entire foreign policy establishment. This is the central thesis of *The Hell of Good Intentions* — that the machinery of American foreign policy is rigged. It will always favor a more activist foreign policy, a more dominant military and liberal hegemony. All the pundits, generals, diplomats and think tank scholars in Washington are just too chummy with one another. A kind of groupthink sets in. (This never happens at the Quincy Institute.) The terms of foreign policy debate are narrowed. And analysts who seek an American retrenchment from the world are shunted aside.

To prove this point, Walt spends several pages observing how former government officials land jobs at prestigious think tanks and get invited to speak at fancy dinners. The result is that no one is ever held to account for their mistakes, while the courageous truth-tellers are ignored and isolated. (At times the book reads like a very long letter by a spurned friend asking why he never got an invitation to last month's retreat at Aspen.)

To illustrate this desperate problem, Walt turns to the annual conference for the World Affairs Councils of America. He ticks off speakers from past years—Susan Glasser, Vali Nasr, Paula Dobriansky — and observes, "These (and other) speakers are all dedicated internationalists, which is why they were invited." So whom does Walt want the World Affairs Councils of America to invite? "Experts with a more critical view of U.S. foreign policy, such as Andrew Bacevich, Peter Van Buren, Medea Benjamin, Glenn Greenwald, Jeremy Scahill, Patrick Buchanan, John Mueller, Jesselyn Radack, or anyone remotely like them."

There is so much to be said about all of these figures. Patrick Buchanan's ugly isolationist record is well known. But consider, at the other end of the ideological spectrum, Medea Benjamin. She is the founder of an organization called Code Pink, known mostly for disrupting public meetings, which last year briefly took control of the Venezuelan embassy in Georgetown to prevent representatives of the country's internationally recognized interim anti-Maduro government from taking over. A group of American anti-imperialists were defending the prerogatives of a dictator who had sold off his country's resources to China and Russia while his people starved. People like Benjamin are not dissidents. They are stooges.

In this way the hard-nosed centrist post-Iraq realists converge with the radicals of the left even as they converge with the radicals of the right. This is realism in the style not of Henry Kissinger but of Noam Chomsky. As in Chomsky, the aggression of America's adversaries is explained away as responses to American power. And as in Chomsky, the explanation often veers into apologies for monsters. Consider "Why the Ukraine Crisis is the West's Fault," an essay by Mearsheimer in *Foreign Affairs* in 2014. There he argues that the expansion of NATO and the European Union, along with American democracy-promotion, created the conditions for which the Kremlin correctly assessed that its strategic interests were threatened in Ukraine. And after street demonstrations in Kiev resulted in the flight of the Ukrainian president, Viktor Yanukovych, to Russia, Putin had little choice but to snatch Crimea from his neighbor. "For Putin," the realist writes, "the illegal overthrow of Ukraine's democratically elected and pro-Russian president — which he rightly labeled a 'coup' — was the final straw." Of course the heroic agitation of the Maidan was about as much of a coup as the Paris commune of 1871. But like Putin, Mearsheimer argues that this "coup" in Ukraine was supported by Washington. His evidence here is that the late Senator John McCain and former assistant secretary of state Victoria Nuland "participated in antigovernment demonstrations," and that an intercepted phone call broadcast by Russia's propaganda network RT found that Nuland supported Arseniy Yatsenyuk for prime minister and was positive about regime change. "No Russian leader would tolerate a military alliance that was Moscow's mortal enemy until recently moving into Ukraine," Mearsheimer writes. "Nor would any Russian leader stand idly by while the West helped install a government there that was determined to integrate Ukraine into the West."

What Mearsheimer leaves out of his essay is that Yanukovych campaigned for the presidency of Ukraine on a promise to integrate his country into the European Union, an entirely worthy goal. But he violated his pledge with no warning, and under Russian pressure; and his citizens became enraged. Nor does Mearsheimer tell his readers about the profound corruption discovered after Yanukovych fled. Ukrainians did not rise up because of the imperialist adventures of Victoria Nuland or the National Endowment for Democracy. They rose up because their elected president tried to bamboozle them by promising to join Europe only to join Russia. Mearsheimer also makes no mention of the Budapest memorandum of 1994, in which Russia, America, and the United Kingdom gave security assurances to Ukraine to protect its territorial integrity in exchange for relinquishing its Soviet-era nuclear weapons. The fact that Putin would so casually violate Russia's prior commitments should give fair-minded observers reason to fear what else he has planned. But Mearsheimer is not bothered by Putin's predations. Putin, Mearsheimer writes, knows that "trying to subdue Ukraine would be like swallowing a porcupine. His response to events there has been defensive, not offensive."

Mearsheimer's excuses for Putin and his failure to grasp the meaning of Ukraine's democratic uprising in 2014 illuminate a weakness in his broader theory of international relations. In Mearsheimer's telling, the only meaningful distinction between states is the amount of power they wield. States, he writes in his book *The Great Delusion*, "are like balls on a billiard table, though of varying size." He goes on to say that "realists maintain that international politics is a dangerous business and that states compete for power because the more power a state has, the more likely it is to survive. Sometimes that competition becomes so intense that war breaks out. The driving force behind this aggression is the structure of the international system, which gives states little choice but to pursue power at each other's expense." This is not a novel idea. Thucydides relates what the Athenians told the Melians: "the strong do what they can and the weak suffer what they must." For Mearsheimer, it does not matter that twenty years before its invasions of Crimea and Ukraine Russia had pledged to respect and protect Ukraine's territorial integrity. Russia was strong and Ukraine was weak. Russia's perception of the threat of an enlarged European Union mattered, whereas the democratic choice of Ukrainians did not. Realists are not moved by democratic aspirations, which are usually domestic annoyances to high strategy. Nor are they bothered by the amorality of their analysis of history.

As for American behavior around the world, the Thucydidean framework describes it, but — unlike Russian behavior — does not extenuate it. For the Quincy intellectuals, there is no significant difference between America and other empires. America is not exceptional. It is only a larger billiard ball. It stands, and has stood, for nothing more than its own interests. But this equivalence is nonsense. Important distinctions must be made. When France booted NATO's headquarters out of Paris in the middle of the Cold War, Lyndon Johnson did not order an army division to march on Paris. Trump's occasional outbursts aside, America does not ask countries that host military bases to pay tribute. After toppling Saddam Hussein, America did not seize Iraq's oil. Compare this to the Soviet Union's response to a dockworkers' strike in Poland, or for that matter to the Dutch East India Company. These realists do not acknowledge the value of preserving the system of alliances and world institutions that comprise the American-led world order, or the fact that they have often enriched and secured America's allies, and at times even its adversaries. In this respect they are not only anti-interventionist, they are also isolationists, in that they believe that the United States, like all other states, naturally and in its own best interest stands alone.

All of this is emphatically not to say that the American superpower has always acted with prudence, morality, and benevolence. There have been crimes, mistakes, and failures. There have also been national reckonings with those crimes, mistakes, and failures. No nation state has ever not abused its power. But behind these reckonings lies a larger historical question. Has America largely used its power for good? A great deal depends on the answer to that question. And the answers must be given not only by Americans but also by peoples around the world with whom we have (or have not) engaged. The valiant people on the streets of Tehran in 2009 who risked their lives to protest theocratic fascist rule shouted Obama's name — were they wrong? About Obama they were certainly wrong: while they were imploring him for help he was brooding about American guilt toward Mossadegh. But were they wrong about America? And the Ukrainians in the Maidan, and the Egyptians in Tahrir Square, and the Kurds, and the women of Afghanistan, and the masses in Hong Kong, and the Guaido movement in Venezuela, and the Uighurs in their lagers — why have they all sought American assistance and intervention? Perhaps it is because they know that the American republic was founded on a sincere belief that the freedom enjoyed by its citizens is owed to all men and women. Perhaps it is because they have heard that the United States created, and stood at the helm, of a world order that has brought prosperity to its allies and its rivals, and even sometimes came to the rescue of the oppressed and the helpless. The case can certainly be made that America in its interventions damaged the world — the anti-interventionists make it all the time — but the contrary case is the stronger one. And contrary to the anti-interventionists, there are many ways to use American power wisely and decisively: the choice is not between quietism and shock and awe. No, the people around the world who look to us are not deluded about our history. They are deluded only about our present.

American exceptionalism was not hubris. It was a statement of values and a willingness to take on historical responsibility. Nor was it in contradiction to our interests, though there have been circumstances when we acted out of moral considerations alone. It goes against the mood of the day to say so, but we must recover the grand tradition of our modern foreign policy. It is not remotely obsolete. Reflecting on the pandemic last spring, Ben Rhodes declared in *The Atlantic,* very much in the spirit of his boss, that the crisis created an opportunity to reorient America's grand strategy: "This is not simply a matter of winding down the remaining

273

9/11 wars — we need a transformation of what has been our whole way of looking at the world since 9/11." Rhodes said that he still wants America to remain a superpower. He proposed new national projects to fight right-wing nationalism, climate change, and future pandemics — all excellent objectives. He also questioned why America's military budget is several times larger than its budget for pandemic preparedness or international aid. But what if the world has not entirely changed, pandemic and all? What if the world that awaits us will be characterized by great power rivalry and persistent atrocities? What if corona does not retire Westphalia?

If you seek to know what the world would look like in the absence of American primacy, look at the world now. Hal Brands and Charles Edel make this point well in *The Lessons of Tragedy*: "It is alluring to think that progress can be self-sustaining, and that liberal principles can triumph even if liberal actors are no longer preeminent. To do so, however, is to fall prey to the same ahistorical mindset that so predictably precedes the fall." And so the first task of those seeking to counter American unexceptionalism is to resist the urge to believe that the past is entirely over, and to reject wholesale the old ends and the old means, and therefore to scale back America's commitments to allies and to decrease the military budget. Even when we are isolationist we are not isolated. There are threats and there are evils, and whatever should be done about them it cannot be that we should do little or nothing about them. We need to become strategically serious.

It was as recently as 2014 that Obama dismissed ISIS as a junior varsity team, and even he was forced to reconsider his narrative that the killing of Osama bin Laden was the epitaph for the 9/11 wars, when a more virulent strain of Islamic fascism emerged in the Levant. In the summer of 2014, he sent special operation forces back to Iraq and began the air power campaign against ISIS that continued through 2019. Would ISIS have come into being if America had kept a small force inside of Iraq after 2011 and continued to work quietly with Iraq's government to temper its sectarian instincts against the Sunni minority? It is impossible to know. What is known, though, is that in 2011 American officers and diplomats on the ground who had worked with Iraq's security forces warned that without some American presence in the country, there was a risk that the army would collapse; and it did. This same cautionary lesson also applies to Afghanistan. No serious person should trust the Taliban's promise that it will fight against al Qaeda if it were to take back power. And while it is true that the Afghan government is corrupt and often hapless, foreign policy consists in weighing bad and worse options. The worse option for Afghanistan is a withdrawal that leaves al Qaeda's longstanding ally a fighting chance to consolidate power and turn the country again into a safe haven of international terrorism and again oppress its people. This is not idle speculation.

The continuing battle against terrorism, which is a continuing threat, must not blind us, as it did George W. Bush, to the new era of great power rivalry. Americans must surrender the pleasant delusion that China and Russia will mature into responsible global stakeholders, or that outreach to Iran will temper its regional ambitions. In this respect Fukuyama was wrong and Huntington and Wieseltier were right. The pandemic has shown how China hollows out the institutions of the world order that so many had hoped would constrain and tame them. After prior pandemics, the United States invested more in its partnership with China and the World Health Organization, reasoning that as China industrialized it needed assistance to track new diseases before they were unleashed on the rest of the world. That system failed in late 2019 and 2020 not because China lacked the public health infrastructure to surveil the coronavirus. It failed because China is a corrupt authoritarian state that lied about the threat and punished the journalists, doctors, and nurses who tried to warn the world about it. This suppression of the truth cost the rest of the world precious time to prepare for what was coming. It turns out that states are not just billiard balls of varying sizes. If China were an open society, it would not have been able to conceal the early warnings. The nature of its regime is an important reason why covid19 was able to mutate into a global pandemic.

As former Soviet dissidents or Serbian student activists can attest, tyrannies appear invincible right up to the moment they topple. This does not mean that America should always use its power to speed this process along. Nor does this mean that America should lead more regime change wars like Iraq. The best outcome for countries such as Iran, China, and Russia is for its own citizens to reclaim their historical agency and take back their societies and their governments from their oppressors. But when moments arise that reveal fissures and weaknesses in the tyrant's regime, when there are indigenous democratic forces that are gaining ground, America must intensify and assist them. This is a matter of both strategy — the friendship of peoples is always better than the friendship of regimes — and morality. When opportunities for democratic change emerge in the world, the wiser strategy is to support the transition and not save the dictator. Again, this is not a license to invade countries or foment military coups. It is rather a recognition that any arrangements America makes with despots will at best be temporary. America's true friends are the states that share its values. But the triumph of the open society is not at all preordained. It requires historical action, a rejection of narcissistic passivity, in an enduring struggle. This historical action can take many forms, and it is not imperialism. It is the core of the republic's historical identity. It is responsible statecraft.

SALLY SATEL

Dark Genies, Dark Horizons: The Riddle of Addiction

In 2014, Anthony Bourdain's CNN show, *Parts Unknown*, travelled to Massachusetts. He visited his old haunts from 1972, when he had spent a high school summer working in a Provincetown restaurant, the now-shuttered Flagship on the tip of Cape Cod. "This is where I started washing dishes ...where I started having pretensions of culinary grandeur," Bourdain said in a wistful voiceover. For the swarthy, rail-thin dishwasher-turned-cook, Provincetown was a "wonderland" bursting with sexual freedom, drugs, music, and "a joy that only came from an absolute certainty that you were invincible." Forty years later, he was visiting the old Lobster Pot restaurant, cameras in tow, to share Portuguese kale soup with the man who still ran the place.

Bourdain enjoyed a lot of drugs in the summer of 1972. He had already acquired a "taste for chemicals," as he put it. The menu included marijuana, Quaaludes, cocaine, LSD, psilocybin mushrooms, Seconal, Tuinal, speed, and codeine. When he moved to the Lower East Side of New York to cook professionally in 1980, the young chef, then 24, bought his first bag of heroin on the corner of Bowery and Rivington. Seven years later he managed to quit the drug cold turkey, but he spent several more years chasing crack cocaine. "I should have died in my twenties," Bourdain told a journalist for *Biography*.

By the time of his visit to Provincetown in 2014, a wave of painkillers had already washed over parts of Massachusetts and a new tide of heroin was rolling in. Bourdain wanted to see it for himself and traveled northwest to Greenfield, a gutted mill town that was a hub of opioid addiction. In a barebones meeting room, he joined a weekly recovery support group. Everyone sat in a circle sharing war stories, and when Bourdain's turn came he searched for words to describe his attraction to heroin. "It's like something was missing in me," he said, "whether it was a self-image situation, whether it was a character flaw. There was some dark genie inside me that I very much hesitate to call a disease that led me to dope."

A dark genie: I liked the metaphor. I am a physician, yet I, too, am hesitant to call addiction a disease. While I am not the only skeptic in my field, I am certainly outnumbered by doctors, addiction professionals, treatment advocates, and researchers who do consider addiction a disease. Some go an extra step, calling addiction a *brain* disease. In my view, that is a step too far, confining addiction to the biological realm when we know how sprawling a phenomenon it truly is. I was reminded of the

Dark Genies, Dark Horizons: The Riddle of Addiction

shortcomings of medicalizing addiction soon after I arrived in Ironton, Ohio where, as the only psychiatrist in town, I was asked whether I thought addiction was "really a disease.

In September 2018, I set out for Rust Belt Appalachia from Washington, D.C., where I am a scholar at a think tank and was, at the time, a part-time psychiatrist at a local methadone clinic. My plan was to spend a year as a doctor-within-borders in Ironton, Ohio, a town of almost eleven thousand people in an area hit hard by the opioid crisis. Ironton sits at the southernmost tip of the state, where the Ohio River forks to create a tri-state hub that includes Ashland, Kentucky and Huntington, West Virginia. Huntington drew national attention in August 2016, when twenty-eight people overdosed on opioids within four hours, two of them fatally.

I landed in Ironton, the seat of Lawrence County, by luck. For some time I had hoped to work in a medically underserved area in Appalachia. Although I felt I had a grasp on urban opioid addiction from my many years of work in methadone clinics in Washington DC, I was less informed about the rural areas. So I asked a colleague with extensive Ohio connections to present my offer of clinical assistance to local leaders. The first taker was the director of the Ironton-Lawrence County Community Action Organization, or CAO, an agency whose roots extend to President Johnson's War on Poverty. The CAO operated several health clinics.

Ironton has a glorious past. Every grandparent in town remembers hearing first-person accounts of a period, stretching from before the Civil War to the early turn of the century, when Ironton was one of the nation's largest producers of pig iron. "For more than a century, the sun over Ironton warred for its place in the sky with ashy charcoal smoke," according to the *Ironton Tribune*. "In its heyday in the mid-nineteenth century there were forty-five [iron] furnaces belching out heat, filth, and prosperity for Lawrence County." After World War II, Ironton was a thriving producer of iron castings, molds used mainly by automakers. Other plants pumped out aluminum, chemicals, and fertilizer. The river front was a forest of smokestacks. High school graduates were assured good paying if labor-intensive jobs, and most mothers stayed home with the kids. The middle class was vibrant.

But then the economy began to realign. Two major Ironton employers, Allied Signal and Alpha Portland Cement, closed facilities in the late 1960s, beginning a wave of lay-offs and plant closings. The 1970s were a time of oil shocks emanating from turmoil in the Middle East. Inflation was high and Japanese and German car makers waged fierce competition with American manufacturers. As more Ironton companies downsized and then disappeared, the pool of living wage jobs contracted, and skilled workers moved out to seek work elsewhere. At the same time, the social fabric began to unravel. Domestic order broke down, welfare and disability rolls grew, substance use escalated. 281 Most high school kids with a shot at a future pursued it elsewhere, and the place was left with a population dominated by older folks and younger addicts.

Ironton continues to struggle. Drug use, now virtually normalized, is in its third, sometimes fourth, generation. Almost everyone is at least one degree of separation away from someone who has overdosed. Although precise rates of drug involvement are hard to come by, one quarter to one third is by far the most common answer I hear when I ask sources for their best estimate of people dealing with a "drug problem of any kind." Alluding to the paucity of hope and opportunity, one of my patients told me that "you have to eradicate the want — why people want to use — or you will always have drug problems."

When Pam Monceaux, an employment coordinator in town, asked me whether I thought addiction was "really a disease," she was thinking about her own daughter. Christal Monceaux grew up in New Orleans with her middle-class parents and a younger sister, and started using heroin and cocaine when she was nineteen. Pam blamed the boyfriend. "Brad sucked her in. Finally, she dumped him, went to rehab and did well, but a few months later took him back and the cycle began all over again." Eventually Christal's younger sister, who had moved to Nashville with her husband, persuaded her to leave New Orleans and join them. Pam, a serene woman who had over a decade's time to put her daughter's ordeal into perspective, said that relocating — or the "geographic cure," as it is sometimes called — worked for Christal. A new setting and new friends allowed her to relinquish drugs. She got married, had children, and lived in a $400,000 house. The happy ending was cut short by Christal's death at the age of forty-two of a heart attack. "If she could kick it for good when she was away from Brad and then when she moved to Nashville, how is that a disease?" Pam asked in her soft Louisiana drawl. "If I had breast cancer, I'd have it in New Orleans and in Nashville."

Unlike Christal, Ann Anderson's daughter had not left drugs behind for good. So, at age 66, Ann and her husband were raising their granddaughter, Jenna. Ann, who worked for my landlord, was bubbly, energetic, and, curiously, sounded as if she were raised in the deep South. The welcome basket she put together for me when I arrived, full of dish towels, potholders, and candies, foretold the generosity that she would show me all year. Ann makes it to every one of Jenna's basketball games. Jenna's mom lives in Missouri and has been on and off heroin for years. "I love my daughter, but every time she relapsed, she made a decision to do it," said Ann, matter-of-factly, but not without sympathy. "And each time she got clean she decided that too."

Another colleague, Lisa Wilhelm, formed her opinions about addiction based on her experience with patients. Lisa was a seen-it-all nurse with whom I had worked at the Family Medical Center located across highway 52 from the Country Hearth, a drug den that passed itself off as a motel. She did not ask for my opinion about addiction; she told me hers. "I think it is a choice. And I'll devote myself to anyone who made that choice and now wants to make better ones," Lisa said, "But it's not a disease, I don't think."

Then there was Sharon Daniels, the director of Head Start. Sharon managed programs for drug-using mothers of newborns and toddlers. "I see opportunities our women have to make a different choice," she said. She is not pushing a naive "just say no" agenda, nor is she looking for an excuse to purge addicted moms from the rolls. This trim grandmother with bright blue eyes and year-round Christmas lights in a corner of her office is wholly devoted to helping her clients and their babies. But she thinks that the term disease "ignores too much about the real world of addiction. If we call it a disease, then it takes away from their need to learn from it."

Before coming to Ironton, I had never been asked what I thought about addiction by the counselors at the methadone clinic at which I worked in Washington. I am not sure why. Perhaps abstractions are not relevant when you are busy helping patients make step-wise improvements. Maybe the staff already knew what I would say. On those rare occasions

Dark Genies, Dark Horizons: The Riddle of Addiction

when a student or a non-medical colleague asked me, generally *sotto voce,* if addiction were *really* a disease my response was this: "Well, what are my choices?" If the alternatives to the disease label were "criminal act," "sin," or "moral deprivation," then I had little choice but to say that addiction was a disease. So, if a crusty old sheriff looking to justify his punitive lock-'em-up ways asked me if addiction were a disease, I would say, "Why yes, sir, it is."

But Pam, Beckey, Lisa, and Sharon had no concealed motives. They were genuinely interested in the question of addiction. And they were fed up with the false choice routinely thrust upon them in state-sponsored addiction workshops and trainings: either endorse addicts as sick people in need of care or as bad actors deserving of punishment. With such ground rules, no one can have a good faith conversation about addiction. Between the poles of diseased and depraved is an expansive middle ground of experience and wisdom that can help explain why millions use opioids to excess and why their problem can be so difficult to treat. The opioid epidemic's dark gift may be that it compels us to become more perceptive about why there is an epidemic. The first step is understanding addiction.

Most people know addiction when they see it. Those in its grip pursue drugs despite the damage done to their wellbeing and often to the lives of others. Users claim, with all sincerity, that they are unable to stop. This is true enough. Yet these accounts tell us little about what drives addiction, about its animating causal core — and the answer to those questions has been contested for over a century. In the mid-1980s the Harvard psychologist Howard J. Shaffer proclaimed that the field of addiction has been in a century-long state of "conceptual chaos." And not much has changed. For behaviorists, addiction is a "disorder of choice" wherein users weigh benefits against risks and eventually quit when the ratio shifts toward the side of risk. For some philosophers, it is a "disorder of appetite." Psychologists of a certain theoretical stripe regard it as a "developmental" problem reflecting failures of maturity, including poor self-control, an inability to delay gratification, and an absence of a stable sense of self. Sociologists emphasize the influence of peers, the draw of marginal groups and identification with them, and responses to poverty or alienation. Psychotherapists stress the user's attempt at "self-medication" to allay the pain of traumatic memories, depression, rage, and so on. The American Society of Addiction Medicine calls addiction "a primary, chronic disease of brain reward, motivation, memory and related circuitry." For the formerly addicted neuroscientist Marc Lewis, author of *Memoirs of an Addicted Brain,* addiction is a "disorder of learning," a powerful habit governed by anticipation, focused attention, and behavior, "much like falling in love."

None of these explanations best captures addiction, but 285 together they enforce a very important truth. Addiction is powered by multiple intersecting causes — biological, psychological, social, and cultural. Depending upon the individual, the influence of one or more of these dimensions may be more or less potent. Why, then, look for a single cause for a complicated problem, or prefer one cause above all the others? At every one of those levels, we can find causal elements that contribute to excessive and repeated drug use, as well as to strategies that can help bring the behavior under control. Yet today the "brain disease" model is the dominant interpretation of addiction.

I happened to have been present at a key moment in the branding of addiction as a brain disease. The venue was the second annual "Constituent Conference" convened in the fall of 1995 by the National Institute on Drug Abuse, or NIDA, which is part of the National Institutes of Health. More than one hundred substance-abuse experts and federal grant recipients had gathered in Chantilly, Virginia for updates and discussions on drug research and treatment. A big item on the agenda set by the NIDA's director, Alan Leshner, was whether the assembled group thought the agency should declare drug addiction a disease of the brain. Most people in the room — all of whom, incidentally, relied heavily on NIDA-funding for their professional survival — said yes. Two years later Leshner officially introduced the concept in the journal: "That addiction is tied to changes in brain structure and function is what makes it, fundamentally, a brain disease."

Since then, NIDA's concept of addiction as a brain disease has penetrated the far reaches of the addiction universe. The model is a staple of medical school education and drug counselor training and even figures in the anti-drug lectures given to high-school students. Rehab patients learn that they have a chronic brain disease. Drug czars under Presidents Bill Clinton, George W. Bush, and Barack Obama have all endorsed the brain-disease framework at one time or another. From being featured in a major documentary on HBO, on talk shows and *Law and Order*, and on the covers of *Time* and *Newsweek*, the brain-disease model has become dogma — and like all articles of faith, it is typically believed without question.

Writing in the *New England Journal of Medicine* in 2016, a trio of NIH- and NIDA-funded scientists speculated that the "brain disease model continues to be questioned" because the science is still incomplete — or, as they put it, because "the aberrant, impulsive, and compulsive behaviors that are characteristic of addiction have not been clearly tied to neurobiology." Alas, no. Unclear linkages between actions and neurobiology have nothing to do with it. Tightening those linkages will certainly be welcome scientific progress — but it will not make addiction a brain disease. After all, if explaining how addiction operates at the level of neurons and brain circuits is enough to make addiction a brain disease, then it is arguably many other things, too: a personality disease, a motivational disease, a social disease, and so on. The brain is bathed in culture and circumstance. And so I ask again: why promote one level of analysis above all of the others?

Of course, those brain changes are real. How could they not be? Brain changes accompany any experience. The simple act of reading this sentence has already induced changes in your brain. Heroin, cocaine, alcohol, and other substances alter neural circuits, particularly those that mediate pleasure, motivation, memory, inhibition, and planning. But the crucial question regarding addiction is not whether brain changes take place. It is whether those brain changes obliterate the capacity to make decisions. The answer to that question is no. People who are addicted can respond to carrots and sticks, incentives and sanctions. They have the capacity to make different decisions when the stakes change. There is a great deal of evidence to substantiate faith in the agency of addicts. Acknowledging it is not tantamount to blaming the victim; it is, much more positively, a recognition of their potential.

The brain-disease model diverts attention from these

287

truths. It implies that neurobiology is necessarily the most important and useful level of analysis for understanding and treating addiction. Drugs "hijack" the reward system in the brain, and the patient is the hostage. According to the psychiatrist and neuroscientist Nora Volkow, who is currently the head of NIDA, "a person's brain is no longer able to produce something needed for our functioning and that healthy people take for granted, *free will.*" Addiction disrupts the function of the frontal cortex, which functions as "the brakes," she told a radio audience, so that "even if I choose to stop, I am not going to be able to." Volkow deploys Technicolor brain scans to bolster claims of hijacked and brakeless brains.

Rhetorically, the scans make her point. Scientifically, they do not. Instead they generate a sense of "neuro-realism" — a term coined by Eric Racine, a bioethicist at the Montreal Clinical Research Institute, to describe the powerful intuition that brain-based information is somehow more genuine or valid than is non-brain-based information. In truth, however, there are limits to what we can infer from scans. They do not allow us, for example, to distinguish irresistible impulses from those that were not resisted, at least not at this stage of the technology. Indeed, if neurobiology is so fateful, how does any addict ever quit? Is it helpful to tell a struggling person that she has no hope of putting on the brakes? It may indeed seem hopeless to the person caught in the vortex of use, but then our job as clinicians is to make quitting and sustained recovery seem both desirable and achievable to them.

We start doing this in small ways, by taking advantage of the fact that even the subjective experience of addiction is malleable. As Jon Elster points out in *Strong Feelings: Emotions, Addiction, and Human Behavior*, the craving for a drug can be triggered by the mere belief that it is available. An urge

becomes overpowering when a person believes it is irrepress-
ible. Accordingly, cognitive behavioral therapy is designed
precisely to help people understand how to manipulate their
environment and their beliefs to serve their interests. They
may learn to insulate themselves from people, places, and
circumstances associated with drug use; to identify emotional
states associated with longing for drugs and to divert attention
from the craving when it occurs. These are exercises in stabili-
zation. Sometimes they are fortified with anti-addiction
medications. Only when stabilized can patients embark on the
ambitious journey of rebuilding themselves, their relation-
ships, and their futures.

I have criticized the brain disease model in practically
every lecture I have given on this wrenching subject. I have
been relentless, I admit. I tell fellow addiction professionals
and trainees that medicalization encourages unwarranted
optimism regarding pharmaceutical cures and oversells the
need for professional help. I explain that we err in calling
addiction a "chronic" condition when it typically remits in
early adulthood. I emphasize to colleagues who spend their
professional lives working with lab rats and caged monkeys
that the brain-disease story gives short shrift to the reality
that substances serve a purpose in the lives of humans. And
I proselytize that the brain changes induced by alcohol and
drugs, no matter how meticulously scientists have mapped
their starry neurons and sweeping fibers, need not spell
destiny for the user.

Yet despite my strong aversion to characterizing addiction
as a problem caused primarily by brain dysfunction, I
genuinely appreciate the good ends that the proponents of
the brain model have sought to reach. They hoped that "brain
disease," with its intimation of medical gravitas and neurosci-

289

entific determinism, would defuse accusations of flawed character or weak will. By moving addiction into the medical realm, they can get it out of the punitive realm. And if addicts are understood to suffer from a brain disease, their plight will more likely garner government and public sympathy than if they were seen as people simply behaving badly. But would they? Research consistently shows that depictions of behavioral problems as biological, genetic, or "brain" problems actually elicit greater desire for social distance from afflicted individuals and stoke pessimism about the effectiveness of treatment among the public and addicted individuals themselves.

Evidence suggests that addicted individuals are less likely to recover if they believe that they suffer from a chronic disease, rather than from an unhealthy habit. More radically, there is a grounded argument to be made for feelings of shame, despite its bad reputation in therapeutic circles. "Shame is highly motivating," observes the philosopher Owen Flanagan, who once struggled mightily with alcohol and cocaine, "it expresses the verdict that one is living in a way that fails one's own survey as well as that of the community upon whose judgment self-respect is legitimately based." But under what conditions do feelings of shame end up prodding people into correcting their course, as opposed to making matters worse by fueling continued consumption to mute the pain of shameful feelings? The psychologists Colin Leach and Atilla Cidam uncovered a plausible answer. They conducted a massive review of studies on shame (not linked to addiction per se) and approaches to failure, and found that when people perceive that damage is manageable and even reversible shame can act as a spur to amend self-inflicted damage. They underscored what clinicians have long-known: only when patients are helped to feel competent — "self-efficacious" is the technical term — can they begin to create new worlds for themselves.

Thinking critically about the disease idea is important for conceptual clarity. But a clinician must be pragmatic, and if a patient wants to think of addiction as a disease I do not try to persuade them otherwise. Yet I do ask one thing of them: to be realistic about the *kind* of disease it is. Despite popular rhetoric, addiction is not a "disease like any other." It differs in at least two important ways. First, individuals suffering from addiction respond to foreseeable consequences while individuals with conventional diseases cannot. Second, this "disease" is driven by a powerful emotional logic.

In 1988, Michael Botticelli, who would go on to become President Obama's second drug czar over two decades later, was charged with drunk driving on the Massachusetts Turnpike. A judge gave him the choice of going to jail or participating in a treatment program. Botticelli made a decision: he went to a church basement for help, joined Alcoholics Anonymous, and quit drinking. Yet on CBS' *60 Minutes* he contradicted his own story when he drew an analogy between having cancer and being addicted. "We don't expect people with cancer to stop having cancer," he said. But the analogy is flawed. No amount of reward or punishment, technically called "contingency," can alter the course of cancer. Imagine threatening to impose a penalty on a brain cancer victim if her vision or speech continued to worsen, or to offer a million dollars if she could stay well. It would have no impact and it would be cruel. Or consider Alzheimer's, which is a true brain disease.

(True insofar as the pathology originates in derangements of brain structure and physiology.) If one held a gun to the head of a person addicted to alcohol and threatened to shoot her if she consumed another drink, or offered her a million dollars if she desisted, she could comply with this demand — and the odds are high that she would comply. In contrast, threatening to shoot an Alzheimer's victim if her memory further deteriorated (or promising a reward if it improved) would be pointless.

The classic example of the power of contingency is the experience of American soldiers in Vietnam. In the early 1970s, military physicians in Vietnam estimated that between 10 percent and 25 percent of enlisted Army men were addicted to the high-grade heroin and opium of Southeast Asia. Deaths from overdosing soared. Spurred by fears that newly discharged veterans would ignite an outbreak of heroin use in American cities, President Richard Nixon commanded the military to begin drug testing. In June 1971, the White House announced that no soldier would be allowed to board a plane home unless he passed a urine test. Those who failed could go to an Army-sponsored detoxification program before they were re-tested.

The plan worked. Most GIs stopped using narcotics as word of the new directive spread, and most of the minority who were initially prevented from going home produced clean samples when given a second chance. Only 12 percent of the soldiers who were dependent on opiate narcotics in Vietnam became re-addicted to heroin at some point in the three years after their return to the United States. Whereas heroin helped soldiers endure wartime's alternating bouts of boredom and terror, most were safe once they were stateside. At home, they had different obligations and available rewards, such as their families, jobs, friends, sports, and hobbies. Many GIs needed heroin to cool the hot anger they felt at being sent to fight for the losing side by commanders they did not respect. Once home, their rage subsided to some extent. Also, heroin use was no longer normalized as it was overseas. At home, heroin possession was a crime and the drug was harder and more dangerous to obtain. As civilian life took precedence, the allure of heroin faded.

We know the value of "contingencies." Hundreds of studies attest to the power of carrots and sticks in shaping the behavior of addicted individuals. Carl Hart, a neuroscientist at Columbia University, has shown that when people are given a good enough reason to refuse drugs, such as cash, they respond. He ran the following experiment: he recruited addicted individuals who had no particular interest in quitting, but who were willing to stay in a hospital research ward for two weeks for testing. Each day Hart offered them a sample dose of either crack cocaine or methamphetamine, depending upon the drug they use regularly. Later in the day, the subjects were given a choice between the same amount of drugs, a voucher for $5 of store merchandise, or $5 cash. They collected their reward upon discharge two weeks later. The majority of subjects choose the $5 voucher or cash when offered small doses of the drug, but they chose the drug when they were offered a higher dose. Then Hart increased the value of the reward to $20, and his subjects chose the money every time.

One of my patients, I will call her Samantha, had been using OxyContin since 2011 when she was working in the kitchen at Little Caesar's in downtown Ironton. The 20 mg pills belonged to her grandmother, whose breast cancer had spread to her spine. Samantha visited her grandma after work, watched TV

Dark Genies, Dark Horizons: The Riddle of Addiction

with her, and went through the mail. She would also remove three or four pills per day from the massive bottle kept by the fancy hospital bed that Samantha's brother moved into the living room. When Samantha's grandmother died in 2016, so did the pill supply. "I just couldn't bring myself to do heroin, and, anyway, I had no money for drugs," Samantha said.

When the pills were almost gone, Samantha drove to an old friend's house, hoping that the friend would give her a few Oxy's in exchange for walking Snappy, her arthritic chihuahua. "My friend wasn't home, but her creepy boyfriend Dave answered the door and told me he'd give me some Oxy's if I gave him a blow job." Samantha was feeling the warning signs of withdrawal — jitteriness, crampy stomach, sweaty underarms. Desperate to avoid full blown withdrawal, she gave a minute's thought to the proposition. "Then I felt revolted and I said no way and drove straight here because I knew I could start buprenorphine the same day," she said.

What of Samantha's "hijacked" brain? When she stood before Dave, her brain was on fire. Her neurons were screaming for oxycodone. Yet in the midst of this neurochemical storm, at peak obsession with drugs, Samantha's revulsion broke through, leading her to apply the "brakes" and come to our program. None of this means that giving up drugs is easy. But it does mean that an "addicted brain" is capable of making a decision to quit and of acting on it.

On Tuesday nights, I co-ran group therapy with a wise social worker named John Hurley. In one group session, spurred by a patient sharing that he decided to come to treatment after spending some time in jail, the patients went around the room reciting what brought them to the clinic. Without exception, they said that they felt pressured by forces inside or outside themselves.

"I couldn't stand myself."

"My wife was going to leave me."

"My kids were taken away."

"My boss is giving me one more chance."

"I can't bear to keep letting my kids down."

"I got Hep C."

"I didn't want to violate my probation."

Ultimatums of these kinds were often the best things to happen to our patients. For other addicts, the looming consequences proved so powerful that they were able to quit without any professional help at all.

The psychologist Gene Heyman at Boston College found that most people addicted to illegal drugs stopped using by about age thirty. John F. Kelly's team at Massachusetts General Hospital found that forty-six percent of people grappling with drugs and alcohol had resolved their drug problems on their own. Carlos Blanco and his colleagues at Columbia University used a major national database to examine trends in prescription drug problems. Almost all individuals who abused or were addicted to prescription opioids also, at some point in their lives, had a mental disorder, an alcohol or drug problem, or both. Yet roughly half of them were in remission five years later. Given low rates of drug treatment, it is safe to say that the majority of remissions took place without professional help.

These findings may seem surprising to, of all people, medical professionals. Yet it is well-known to medical sociologists that physicians tend to succumb to the "clinicians' illusion," a habit of generalizing from the sickest subset of patients to the overall population of people with a diagnosable condition. This caveat applies across the medical spectrum. Not all people with diabetes, for example, have brittle blood sugars — but they will represent a disproportionate share of

295

the endocrinologist's case load. A clinician might wrongly, if rationally, assume that most addicts behave like the recalcitrant ones who keep stumbling through the emergency room doors. Most do not. Granted, not everyone can stop an addiction on their own, but the very fact it can be done underscores the reality of improvement powered by will alone: a pathway to recovery rarely available to those with conventional illness.

The second major difference between addiction and garden-variety disease is that addiction is driven by powerful feelings. Ask an alcoholic why she drinks or an addict why he uses drugs and you might hear about the pacifying effect of whisky and heroin on daunting hardship, unremitting self-persecution, yawning emptiness, or harrowing memories. Ask a patient with Parkinson's disease, a classic brain disease, why he developed the neurological disorder and you will get a blank stare. Parkinson's is a condition that strikes, unbidden, at the central nervous system; the patient does not consciously collude in bringing it about. Excessive use of a drug, by contrast, serves some kind of need, an inner pain to be soothed, a rage to be suppressed. It is a response to some sort of suffering.

Memoirs offer portals into the drama of addiction. One of my favorites is *Straight Life,* by the master alto saxophonist Art Pepper. Self-taught on the instrument by the age of thirteen, Pepper endured a childhood of psychological brutality at the hands of a sadistic alcoholic father, an icicle of a grandmother, and an alcoholic mother who was fourteen years old when he was born and who did not hide her numerous attempts to abort him. "To no avail," he writes. "I was born. She lost."

What preoccupied him as a child was "wanting to be loved and trying to figure out why other people were loved and I wasn't." Pepper's self-loathing bubbled like acid in his veins. "I'd talk to myself and say how rotten I was," he wrote. "Why do people hate you? Why are you alone?" At 23, after years of alcohol and pot, he sniffed his first line of heroin through a rolled up dollar-bill and the dark genie dissolved. He saw himself in the mirror. "I looked like an angel," he marveled. "It was like looking into a whole universe of joy and happiness and contentment."

From that moment on, Pepper said, he would "trade misery for total happiness... I would be a junkie...I will die a junkie." Indeed, he became a "lifelong dope addict of truly Satanic fuck-it-all grandeur," in the words of his passionate admirer, the critic and scholar Terry Castle. He was in and out of prison for possession charges. Pepper lived without heroin for a number of years after attending Synanon, a drug-rehabilitation center in California, from 1969 to 1972 and was treated with methadone for a period in the mid-1970s. Eventually, though, he returned to drugs, mainly consuming massive amphetamine, and died from a stroke in 1982. He was 56.

Addicts can appear to have everything: a good education, job prospects, people who love them, a nice home. They can be people who "are believed to have known no poverty except that of their own life-force," to borrow the words of Joan Didion, and yet suffer greatly. The malaise is internal. Or they can be in dire circumstances, immiserated by their lives, moving through a dense miasma. "There was nothing for me here," said one patient whose child was killed in a car accident, whose husband cheated on her, and who was trapped in her job as a maid in a rundown motel with an abusive boss. OxyContin made her "not care." She reminded me of Lou Reed's song "Heroin":

Dark Genies, Dark Horizons: The Riddle of Addiction

Wow, that heroin is in my blood
And the blood is in my head
Yeah, thank God that I'm good as dead
Oooh, thank your God that I'm not aware
And thank God that I just don't care

Pharmacologists have long classified opioid drugs as euphoriants, inducers of pleasure, described often as a feeling of a melting maternal embrace, but they could just as easily be called obliviants. According to the late Harvard psychiatrist Norman Zinberg, oblivion seekers yearned "to escape from lives that seem unbearable and hopeless." Thomas De Quincey, in *Confessions of an English Opium Eater*, which appeared in 1821, praised opium for keeping him "aloof from the uproar of life." Many centuries before him Homer had likely referred to it in the *Odyssey* when he wrote that "no one who drank it deeply...could let a tear roll down his cheeks that day, not even if his mother should die, his father die, not even if right before his eyes some enemy brought down a brother or darling son with a sharp bronze blade," When the Hollywood screen-writer Jerry Stahl surveyed his life in 1995 in his memoir *Permanent Midnight*, he concluded that "everything, bad or good, boils back to the decade on the needle, and the years before that imbibing everything from cocaine to Romilar, pot to percs, LSD to liquid meth and a pharmacy in between: a lifetime spent altering the single niggling fact that to be alive means being conscious." Drugs helped him to attain "the soothing hiss of oblivion."

According to ancient myth, Morpheus, the god of dreams, slept in a cave strewn with poppy seeds. Through the cave flowed the river Lethe, known as the river of forgetfulness, also called the river of oblivion. The dead imbibed those waters to forget their mortal days. Unencumbered by memory, they floated free from the aching sadness and discomforts of life. The mythological dead share a kinship with opioid addicts, oblivion-seekers, and all their reality-manipulating cousins. The difference, mercifully, is that actual people can "un-drink" the numbing waters. *Aletheia*, truth, is a negation of *lethe*, the Greek word for forgetting. Recovery from addiction is a kind of unforgetting, an attempt to live in greater awareness and purpose, a disavowal of oblivion.

Addiction is a cruel paradox. What starts out making life more tolerable can eventually make it ruinous. "A man may take to drink because he feels himself a failure," said Orwell, "but then fail all the more completely because he drinks." The balm is a poison. Drugs that ease the pain also end up prolonging it, bringing new excruciations — guilt and grief over damage to one's self, one's family, one's future — and thus fresh reason to continue. The cycle of use keeps turning. Ambivalence is thus a hallmark of late-stage addiction. The philosopher Harry Frankfurt speaks of the "unwilling addict" who finds himself "hating" his addiction and "struggling desperately...against its thrust." This desperate struggle is what Samuel Taylor Coleridge, himself an opium addict, called "a species of madness" in which the user is torn between his current, anguished self who seeks instant solace and a future self who longs for emancipation from drugs. This explains why the odds of treatment drop out are high — over half after six months, on average. The syringe of Damocles, as Jerry Stahl described the vulnerability to relapse, dangles always above their heads. Many do not even take advantage of treatment when it is offered, reluctant to give up their short-term salvation. They fear facing life "unmedicated" or cannot seem to find a reason for doing so. My friend Zach Rhoads, now a teacher in Burlington, Vermont, used heroin for five years beginning in his early twenties and struggled fiercely to quit. "I had to convince myself that such effort was worth the trouble," he said.

Thomas De Quincey consumed prodigious amounts of opium dissolved in alcohol and pronounced the drug a "panacea for all human woes." For Anthony Bourdain, heroin and cocaine were panaceas, defenses against the dark genie that eventually rose up and strangled him to death in 2018. But not all addicts have a dark genie lurking inside them. Some seek a panacea for problems that crush them from the outside, tribulations of financial woes and family strain, crises of faith and purpose. In the modern opioid ordeal, these are Americans "dying of a broken heart," in Bill Clinton's fine words. "They're the people that were raised to believe the American Dream would be theirs if they worked hard and their children will have a chance to do better — and their dreams were dashed disproportionally to the population as the whole." He was gesturing toward whites between the ages of 45 and 54 who lack college degrees — a cohort whose life-expectancy at birth had been falling since 1999. They succumbed to "deaths of despair," a term coined by the economists Anne Case and Angus Deaton in 2015, brought on by suicide, alcoholism (specifically, liver disease), and drug overdoses. Overdoses account for the lion's share. The white working class has been undermined by falling wages and the loss of good jobs which have "devastated the white working class," the economists write, and "weakened the basic institutions of working-class life, including marriage, churchgoing, and community."

Looking far into the future, what so many of these low income, under-educated whites see are dark horizons. When communal conditions are dire and drugs are easy to get, epidemics can blossom. I call this dark horizon addiction. Just as dark genie addiction is a symptom of an embattled soul, dark horizon addiction reflects communities or other concentrations of people whose prospects are dim and whose members feel doomed. In Ironton, clouds started to gather on the horizon in the late 1960s. Cracks appeared in the town's economic foundation, setting off its slow but steady collapse.

Epidemics of dark horizon addiction have appeared under all earthly skies at one time or another. The London gin "craze" of the first half of the eighteenth century, for example, was linked to poverty, social unrest, and over-crowding. According to the historian Jessica Warner, the average adult in 1700 drank slightly more than a third of a gallon of cheap spirits over the course of a year; by 1729 it was slightly more than 1.3 gallons per capita, and hit 2.2 gallons in 1743. A century later, consumption had declined, yet gin was still "a great vice in England," according to Charles Dickens. "Until you improve the homes of the poor, or persuade a half-famished wretch not to seek relief in the temporary oblivion of his own misery," he wrote in the 1830s, "gin-shops will increase in number and splendor."

During and after the American Civil War, thousands of men needed morphine and opium to bear the agony of physical wounds. In his *Medical Essays*, the physician Oliver Wendell Holmes, Sr., a harsh critic of medication, excepted opium as the one medicine "which the Creator himself seems to prescribe." The applications of opium extended to medicating grief. "Anguished and hopeless wives and mothers, made so by the slaughter of those who were dearest to them, have found, many of them, temporary relief from their sufferings in opium," Horace B. Day, an opium addict himself, recorded in *The Opium Habit* in 1868. In the South, the spiritual dislocation was especially profound, no doubt explaining, to a significant degree, why whites in the postbellum South had higher rates of opiate addiction than did those in the North — and also, notably, one reason why southern blacks had a lower rate of opiate addiction, according to the historian David T. Courtwright. "Confederate defeat was for most of them an occasion of rejoicing rather than profound depression."

A similar dynamic was seen when Russia's long-standing problem with vodka exploded during the political instability and economic uncertainty of the post-Communist era. The majority of men drank up to five bottles a week in the early 1990s. Back home, heroin was a symptom of ghetto life for millions of impoverished and hopeless Hispanics and blacks in the 1960s and 70s, followed by crack among blacks in the mid-80s. The rapid decline of manufacturing jobs for inner city men, writes the historian David Farber in his recent book *Crack*, "helps explain the large market of poor people, disproportionately African Americans, who would find crack a balm for their troubled, insecure, and often desperate lives."

Children raised by dark horizon parents often bear a double burden. Not only do they suffer from growing up with defeated people in defeated places where opportunities are stunted and boredom is crushing. Often they are casualties of their parents' and their grandparents' addictions. One of my patients, Jennifer, described herself as a "third generation junky." Patches of acne clung to her cheeks, making her look younger than thirty. Her maternal grandmother managed well enough with an ornery husband who drank too much on weekends until he lost his job at a local casting plant in the 1970s and became a full-fledged alcoholic, bitter, aimless, and abusive to his wife. The grandmother worked cleaning motel rooms and began staying out late, using pills and weed. Jennifer's mother, Ann, was the youngest in a household that had devolved into havoc.

When Ann was sixteen, Jennifer was born. Not one reliable adult was around. "No one really cared if I went to school," Jennifer recalls. No one urged her to succeed or expressed confidence in her. "I learned that when something bothered you, you got high." Her mother, Ann, was aloof, Jennifer said, except for the stretch they were both in jail at the same time: she was 19, her mother was 42. "My mother was assigned to be the chaperone for my group of inmates," Jennifer recalled. "She did my laundry and saved me extra food in jail. It was the only time she acted like a mom towards me." Children raised in such homes are greatly disadvantaged. The absence of a steady protector in their lives often derails their developing capacity for tolerating frustration and disappointment, controlling impulses, and delaying gratification. They have difficulty trusting others, forming rewarding connections with others and they often see themselves as damaged and worthless. When adults around them do not want to work regularly, children cannot imbibe the habits of routine, reliability, and dependability. At worst, the cycle repeats itself, inflicting wounds across generations and communities as their collective disenchantment with the future mounts. Sociologists call this "downward social drift."

The germ theory of addiction: that is my term for one of the popular if misbegotten narratives of how the opioid crisis started. It holds that the epidemic has been driven almost entirely by supply — a surfeit not of bacteria or viruses, but of pills. "Ask your doctor how prescription pills can lead to heroin abuse," blared massive billboards from the Partnership for a Drug-Free New Jersey that I saw a few years ago. Around that time, senators proposed a bill that would have limited physician prescribing. "Opioid addiction and abuse is commonly happening to those being treated for acute pain, such as a broken bone or wisdom tooth extraction," is how they justified the legislation.

Not so. The majority of prescription pill casualties were never patients in pain who had been prescribed medication by their physicians. Instead, they were mostly individuals who were already involved with drugs or alcohol. Yes, some actual patients did develop pill problems, but generally they had a history of drug or alcohol abuse or were suffering from concurrent psychiatric problems or emotional distress. It is also true, of course, that drug marketers were too aggressive at times and that too many physicians overprescribed, sometimes out of inexperience, other times out of convenience, and in some cases out of greed.

As extra pills began accumulating in rivulets, merging with pills obtained from pharmacy robberies, doctor shopping, and prescription forgeries, a river of analgesia ran through various communities. But even with an ample supply, you cannot "catch" addiction. There must be demand — not for addiction, per se, but for its vehicle. My year in Ironton showed me that the deep story of drug epidemics goes well beyond public health and medicine. Those disciplines, while essential to management, will not help us to understand why particular people and places succumb. It is the life stories of individuals and, in the case of epidemics, the life story of places, that reveal the origins. Addiction is a variety of human experience, and it must be studied with all the many methods and approaches with we which we study human experience.

Dark genies can be exorcised and dark horizons can be brightened. It is arduous work, but unless we recognize all the reasons for its difficulty, unless we reckon with the ambiguity and the elusiveness and the multiplicity of addiction's causes, unless we come to understand why addicts go to such lengths to continue maiming themselves with drugs — compelled by dark genies, dark horizons, or both — their odds of lasting recovery are slim, as are the odds of preventing and reversing drug crises. The complexity of addiction is nothing other than the complexity of life.

MOSHE HALBERTAL

A Democratic Jewish State, How and Why

The question of whether Israel can be a democratic Jewish state, a liberal Jewish state, is the most important question with which the country must wrestle, and it can have no answer until we arrive at an understanding of what a Jewish state is. A great deal of pessimism is in the air. Many people attach to the adjective "Jewish" ultra-nationalistic and theocratic meanings, and then make the argument that a Jewish democratic state is a contradiction in terms, an impossibility. On the left and on the right, among the elites and the masses, people are giving up on the idea that both elements, the particular and the universal, may co-exist equally and prominently in the identity of the state. This way of thinking is partly responsible for the recent convulsions in Israeli politics, for the zealotry and the despair that run through it. Yet it is an erroneous and unfruitful way of thinking. It rigs the outcome of this life-and-death discussion with a tendentious and dogmatic conception of Judaism and Jewishness.

There is another way, a better way, to arrive at an answer to this urgent and wrenching question. Let us begin by asking a different one, a hypothetical one. Let us imagine the problem in a place that is not Israel or Palestine. Could a Catalan state, if it were to secede from Spain, be a democratic Catalan state, a liberal Catalan state? Catalan nationalism is a powerful force, and many Catalans wish to establish an independent state of their own with Barcelona as its capital, based on their claim that they constitute a distinct ethnocultural group that deserves the right to self-determination. Though recent developments in Spain have shown that the establishment of an independent Catalan state is far from becoming a reality in the near future, let us nonetheless consider what it might look like. In this future state — as in other European nation-states, such as Denmark, Finland, Norway, Germany, the Czech Republic, and others that have a language and state symbols that express an affinity to the dominant national culture — the Catalan language would be the official language, the state symbols would be linked to the Catalan majority, the official calendar would be shaped in relation to Christianity and to events in Catalan history, and the public education of Catalans would insure the vitality and the continuity of Catalan culture, transmitting it to the next generation. Revenues from taxation would be distributed solely among Catalan citizens and not across Spain, and the foreign policy of the Catalan state would reflect the interests of the ethnocultural majority

A Democratic Jewish State, How and Why

of the state. It is very probable that Catalunya's immigration policy, like that of all contemporary European and Scandinavian states, would attempt to safeguard the Catalan majority in its sovereign territory.

It is important to note that these aspects of a Catalan state would not reflect anything unusual in the modern political history of the West. The Norwegians, for example, demanded all these characteristics of statehood in 1907, when they seceded from Sweden (under threat of war) since they saw themselves as a separate national group. In the matter of identity, Catalunya, like Norway, would not be a neutral state in any meaningful fashion, and there is no reason that it should be a neutral state. Members of the Catalan group deserve a right to self-determination, which includes a sovereign territory inhabited by a Catalan majority in which a Catalan cultural public space is created and the culture of the majority is expressed.

But this is not all we would need to know about a Catalan nation-state that purports to be a democracy. The test of the question of whether Catalunya, or any other state, is democratic is not dependent upon whether it is neutral with respect to identity. Its moral and political quality, its decency, its liberalness, will be judged instead by two other criteria. The first is whether its character as a nation-state results in discriminatory policies towards the political, economic, and cultural rights of the non-Catalan minorities that reside within it. The second is whether Catalunya would support granting the same right of self-determination to other national communities, such as the Basques. Adhering to these two principles is what distinguishes democratic nation-states from fascist ones.

Ultra-nationalist states are sovereign entities in which the national character serves as a justification for depriving minorities of political, economic and cultural rights. In the shift to ultra-nationalism that we are witnessing around the world today, such states also attack and undermine the institutions that aim at protecting minorities — the independent judiciary, the free press, and NGO's dedicated to human and minority rights. In addition, ultra-nationalists states do not support granting rights of self-determination to nations that reside within them or next to them. They generally claim that no such nations exist, or that the ethnic groups that call themselves a nation do not deserve the right to self-determination.

The legitimacy of Israel as a nation-state should be judged just as we would judge any other nation-state, according to these two principles. If, in the name of the Jewish character of the state, the Arab minority in Israel is deprived of its rights, the very legitimacy of the State of Israel as a Jewish nation-state will be damaged. Discrimination in the distribution of state resources in infrastructure, education, and land, and the refusal to recognize new Arab cities and villages in the State of Israel, threatens to transform it from a democratic nation-state into an ultra-nationalist state. Such a threat to the democratic character of the state is posed also by recent legislative attempts (which fortunately have failed) to demand a loyalty oath solely from Israel's Arab citizens. The threat is heightened by a political plan put forth by elements of the Israeli radical right, which, in a future agreement with the Palestinians, would deny Israeli citizenship to Israeli Arabs, by virtue of a territorial exchange that would include their villages in the territory of a future Palestinian state. This is to act as if the Israeli citizenship of the Arabs of Israel is not a basic right, but a conditional gift granted

A Democratic Jewish State, How and Why

to them by the Jewish nation-state — a gift that can be rescinded to suit the interests of Jewish nationalism. The Nation-State law that was passed by the Israeli parliament in 2018, which formulates the national identity of the country in exclusively Jewish terms, is an occasion for profound alarm, in particular in its glaring omission of an explicit commitment to the equality of all Israeli citizens, Jews and Arabs alike. Such a commitment to the equality of all citizens was enshrined in Israel's Declaration of Independence, the founding document that to this day contains the noblest expression of the vision of Israel as Jewish and democratic. The commitment to the equality of all citizens might be legally and judicially ensured in relation to other basic laws in Israel's legal system, yet its striking absence from this latest official articulation of the character of the state is yet another marker of the drift to ultra-nationalism.

The structural discrimination manifested in these examples constitutes an unjustified bias against the Arab citizens of Israel. It also serves to undermine the very legitimacy of the Jewish state. A Jewish nation-state can and must grant full equality to its Arab citizens in all the realms in which it has failed to do so until now. It must recognize them as a national cultural minority, with Arabic as a second official language of the state and the Islamic calendar as an officially recognized calendar. The public educational system must be devoted, among other goals, to the continuity of the Arab cultural traditions of Israel's citizens.

In the recent elections held in Israel, three within a single year, the participation of the Arab citizens of Israel in the vote increased by 50%, reaching very close to the percentage of the vote among Jewish citizens. This is a wonderful and encouraging sign of the greater integration of the Arab population in larger Israeli politics. As a result the Joint List, the Israeli

Arab party, which encompasses different ideological and political streams in the Arab community of Israel, increased its seats in Israel's Knesset from ten to fifteen — an extraordinary achievement. But its positive impact was undone by the disgraceful failure of the left and center to form a government with the Joint List on the grounds that a government that rests on the Arab vote is unacceptable. Thus was lost an historic opportunity to integrate the Arab minority as an equal partner in sharing governmental power.

As is true of all other legitimate democratic nation-states, the second condition that Israel must maintain is the recognition of the right of the Palestinian nation to self-determination in Gaza and the West Bank — the same right that Jews have rightly demanded for themselves. The denial of such a right, and the settlement policy that aims at creating conditions in which the realization of such a right becomes impossible, similarly damage the legitimacy of Israel as a Jewish nation-state. The Trump plan for peace includes, among its other problematic aspects, the annexation of the Jordan Valley to the state of Israel, which would constitute yet another significant impediment to the possibility of a two-state solution. If any Israeli government includes such an annexation in its plans, it will also create *de facto* conditions that will undermine the possibility of a Jewish democratic state in the future.

It is important to stress that the fulfillment of the first condition — equal rights to minorities — is completely within Israel's power. Discrimination against citizens of your own country is always a self-inflicted wound. The second condition, by contrast, the recognition of the Palestinian right to self-determination, is not exclusively in the hands of Israel. The conditions of its realization are much more complicated. It depends to a significant degree upon Palestinians' willingness to live side by side with the State of Israel in peace and security. The situation with regard to the possibility of such co-existence is difficult and murky and discouraging on the Palestinian side — and yet Israel must nevertheless make clear its recognition of the Palestinian right to self-determination, not least for the simple reason that achieving it will lend legitimacy to Israel's own claim to the same right.

If democracy and decency do not require cultural neutrality from a nation-state, then how should the identity of the majority be recognized in such a state without vitiating its liberal principles? There are four ways, I believe, that the Jewish nature of the State of Israel should be expressed. The first is to recognize the State of Israel as the realization of the Jewish national right to self-determination. In this era, when the meaning of Zionism is mangled and distorted in so many quarters, it is important to recognize what Zionism incontrovertibly is: a national liberation movement aimed at extracting a people from the historic humiliation of dependence on others in defining their fate. That remains its central meaning. Zionism gave one of the world's oldest peoples, the Jewish people, the political, military, and economic ability to define themselves and defend themselves.

The most fundamental feature of Israel as a Jewish state resides, therefore, in its responsibility for the fate of the Jewish people as a whole. If the responsibility of the State of Israel were confined only to its citizens, it would have been only an Israeli state. In light of this responsibility to a people, it has the right and the duty to use the state's powers to defend Jews who are victimized because they are Jews.

The second feature that defines Israel as a Jewish state is the Law of Return. This law, which was established in 1950, and is intimately connected to the first feature of national self-determination, proclaims that all Jews, wherever they are, have a right to citizenship in the State of Israel, and can make the State of Israel their home if they so desire. The State of Israel was created to prevent situations — plentiful in Jewish history — in which Jews seeking refuge knock on the doors of countries that have no interest in receiving them. For the same reason, Palestinian refugees in the Arab states ought to have immediate access to citizenship in the state of Palestine when it is established.

Yet the justification of the Law of Return does not rest exclusively on conditions of duress. If national groups have a right to self-determination — the right to establish a sovereign realm where they constitute the majority of the population, and where their culture develops and thrives — it would be odd not to allow Jews or Palestinians a right of citizenship in their national territory. It is also important to emphasize that the Law of Return is legitimate only if accompanied by other tracks of naturalization. If the Law of Return were the only way of acquiring Israeli citizenship, its exclusively national character would harm the rights of minorities and immigrants who are not members of the ethnic majority. Safeguarding the ethnocultural majority in any state is always severely constrained by the rights of minorities. Thus the transfer of populations, or the stripping of citizenship by the transfer of territory to another state, are illegitimate means of preserving a majority. It is crucial, therefore, that other forms of naturalization exist as a matter of state policy, including granting citizenship to foreign workers whose children were born and grew up in Israel, and to men and women who married Israeli citizens.

A Democratic Jewish State, How and Why

The third expression of the Jewishness of the State of Israel relates to various aspects of its public sphere, such as its state symbols, its official language, and its calendar. These symbolic institutions are derived from Jewish cultural and historical symbols, including the menorah and the Star of David; Hebrew is the official language; Israel's public calendar is shaped according to the Jewish calendar; and the Sabbath and Jewish holidays are official days of rest. Yet a democratic state demands more. The public expression of the majority culture must go along with granting official status to the minority cultures of the state, including Arabic as the second official language of the state of Israel, and recognizing the Islamic calendar in relation to the Arab minority. Again, official symbols and practices that have an affinity to the majority culture exist in many Western states: in Sweden, Finland, Norway, Britain, Switzerland and Greece, the cross is displayed on the national flag. In all those cases, the presence of state symbols that are connected to the religion and culture of the majority does not undermine the state's democratic and liberal nature. In many of those states, however, there are powerful political forces that wish to limit democracy to the dominant ethnicity. The historical challenge in these multiethnic and volatile societies — and Israel also faces this challenge — is to prevent the self-expression of the majority from constraining or destroying the self-expression of the minority.

The fourth essential feature of a democratic nation-state, and the most important one, relates to public education. In the State of Israel, as a Jewish state, the public system of education is committed to the continuity and reproduction of Jewish cultures. I emphasize Jewish cultures in the plural, since Jews embrace very different conceptions of the nature of Jewish life and the meaning of Jewish education. In its commitment to Jewish cultures, the State of Israel is not different from many modern states whose public education transmits a unique cultural identity. In France, Descartes, Voltaire, and Rousseau are taught, and in Germany they teach Goethe, Schiller, and Heine. The history, the literature, the language, and sometimes the religion of different communities are preserved and reproduced by the system of public education, which includes students of many ethnic origins. Jews who happen to be German, American, or French citizens and wish to transmit their tradition to their children must resort to private means to provide them with a Jewish education. In Israel, as in other modern states (though not in the United States), such an education should be supported by state funds. This commitment does not contradict — rather, it requires — public funding for education that, alongside the public education system, insures the continuity of the other traditions represented in the population of the state, the Islamic and Christian cultures of the Arab minority in Israel. The culture of a minority has as much right to recognition by the state as the culture of the majority.

There are voices that maintain that the only way to secure Israel's democratic nature is to eliminate its Jewish national character and turn it into a state of all its citizens, or a bi-national state. This sounds perfectly democratic, but it would defeat one of the central purposes of both national communities. In this territory there are two groups that possess a strong national consciousness — Jews and Palestinians; and there is no reason not to grant each of them the right of self-determination that they deserve. Moreover, a state of all its citizens in the area between the Jordan River and the Mediterranean Sea would, in fact, be an Arab nation-state with a large Jewish minority. It would become a place of exile

A Democratic Jewish State, How and Why

for the Jewish minority. Historical experience in this region, where national rights and civil liberties are regularly trampled, suggests that Greater Palestine would be one of the harshest of all Jewish exiles.

Honoring the status of the Arab citizens of Israel and espousing the establishment of a Palestinian state ought not to focus on — and does not require — the impossible and unjust annulment of the Jewish character of the State of Israel. It should focus instead on the effort to create full and rich equality for the Arab minority in Israel, and on the possibility of establishing a Palestinian nation-state alongside the state of Israel.

In a Jewish state, the adjective "Jewish" carries within it another crucial challenge to liberal democracy, which is not tied to its national content but to its religious implications. This Jewish character, or the religious meaning of the adjective "Jewish," might harm the freedom of religion in the state. Indeed, some currents in Israeli Judaism — and some religiously inspired ideological and political trends in the Jewish population of Israel — constitute a powerful and complex challenge to Israeli liberalism. Some voices assert that the Jewish identity of the state justifies granting the weight of civil law to Jewish law, and the use of the coercive machinery of the state for the religious purposes of the dominant community.

But a Jewish state conceived in this way could not be democratic in any recognizable manner, for two reasons: it would harm both the religious freedom of its citizens and the religious pluralism of the communities that constitute it. The attempt to "Judaize" the state through religious legislation, above and beyond the four features mentioned above, would undermine Israel's commitment to liberalism and destroy some of its most fundamental founding principles. It would take back the pluralism that was explicitly and stirringly guaranteed in Israel's Declaration of Independence.

Since the nineteenth century, Jews have been deeply divided about the meaning of Jewish identity and their loyalty to Jewish law. Jews celebrate the Sabbath in a variety of ways. They disagree ferociously about basic religious questions, including the nature of marriage and divorce. Any attempt to use the power of the state to adjudicate these deep divisions would do inestimable damage to freedom of religion and freedom from religion. In this case it would be the freedoms of Jews that would be violated.

The role of the state is not to compel a person to keep the Sabbath or to compel her to desecrate it. The state must, instead, guarantee that every person has the right to behave on the Sabbath as she sees fit, as long as she grants the same right to individuals and communities who live alongside her. All attempts at Judaizing the state through religious legislation — such as the law prohibiting the selling of bread in public during Passover, or the law prohibiting the raising of pigs — are deeply in error, since it is the obligation of a liberal democratic state to allow its citizens to decide these matters autonomously, as they see fit.

The Sabbath, like other Jewish holidays, ought to be part of the official calendar of Israel as a Jewish state. A shared calendar, with Islamic and Christian holidays on it too, is an essential feature of the life of a state, and it enables a kind of division of cultural and spiritual labor, a pluralist form of cooperation among its citizens. If state institutions do not function during the Sabbath, it is not only because we would like religious citizens to be able to take equal part in the running of those

317

institutions, but also because Israel ought to respect the Jewish calendar. The same applies as well to factories and businesses that must be shuttered during days of rest.

Such a policy, moreover, should be supported not for religious reasons, but owing to secular concerns about fairness. First, it allows equal opportunity to workers and owners who wish to observe the Sabbath. Historically, in the various Jewish exiles, the observance of the Sabbath sometimes caused Jews a great deal of economic hardship owing to the advantage that it conferred upon competitors who did not observe the same day of rest. In a Jewish state, Jews who observe the Sabbath ought to be free from such an economic sacrifice. The second reason for closing businesses and factories on the Sabbath concerns the rights of workers. The institution of the Sabbath is more widespread than most Jews know, and it is consistent with universal ethical considerations. Constraining the tyranny of the market over individual and family life by guaranteeing a weekly day of rest for workers and owners is common in European states which, in accordance with the Christian calendar, enforce the closing of businesses on Sunday. In a similar spirit, factories, malls, stores, and businesses ought to be closed during the Sabbath in a Jewish state — but art centers, theaters, museums, and restaurants should continue to function, so that Israeli Jews may choose their own way of enjoying the day of lovely respite.

The abolition of the coercive power of the state in matters of religion should be applied as well to the primary domain of religious legislation in Israel: divorce and marriage. The monopoly granted to rabbinical courts in issues of divorce and marriage must finally be terminated. It is an outrageous violation of the democratic and liberal ethos of the state. Alongside religious marriage, Israel must recognize civil marriage. Such a reform would allow a couple that cannot marry according to Jewish law to exercise their basic right to form a family. It would also recognize the legitimate beliefs of many men and women who do not wish to submit to the rabbinical court, which is often patriarchal in its rulings and financially discriminates against women in divorce agreements.

The claim of some religious representatives that establishing civil marriage would cause a rift among Jews, since members of the Orthodox Jewish community would not be able to marry Jews who did not divorce according to rabbinical procedure, is not persuasive. Many Jews all over the world marry and divorce outside the Orthodox community, and this is *de facto* the case in Israel as well, since many Israelis obtain civil marriages outside Israel, or live together without marrying under the jurisdiction of the rabbinate. The establishment of two tracks of marriage and divorce, religious and secular-civil, would not create division, which already exists in any case, but it would remove the legal wrong caused to Israelis who cannot practice their right to marry within Jewish law, and it would liberate those who aspire to gender equality from the grip of the rabbinical courts.

I should confess that my analysis of the place of religion in Israel does not rest exclusively upon my liberal commitments. It is grounded also in my concern for the quality of Jewish life in Israel. Religious legislation has had a devastating impact on Jewish culture and creativity in Israel. The great temptation to settle the debate over modern Jewish identity through the coercive mechanism of the state justifiably alienates major segments of the Israeli public from Jewish tradition, which comes to be perceived by many Israelis as threatening their way of life. The deepening of alienation from the tradition, and its slow transformation into hostility, suggests that the more Jewish the laws of Israel become, the less Jewish the citizens of Israel become.

The Israeli parliament is not the place to decide the nature of the Sabbath, or which Jewish denomination is the authentic representation of Judaism, or who is a legitimate rabbi. Such controversies have corrupted the legislature, creating cynical political calculations in which religious matters have served as political payoffs to maintain government coalitions. The unavoidable debate on Jewish culture and religion must move from parliament to civil society. The nature of Jewish life in Israel must be determined by individuals and communities who will themselves decide how to lead their lives without interference from the state. For instance, there is no law in Israel prohibiting private transportation during the sacred day of Yom Kippur, yet the sanctity of the day is generally observed without any coercion. Wresting Judaism from the control of the politicians will unleash creative forces for Jewish renewal and allow for new ways of refreshing the tradition and extending its appeal.

Among the precious and time-honored institutions of Judaism which have been corrupted by the state is the rabbinate. The methods used for nominating and choosing the chief rabbis, and the rabbis of cities and neighborhoods, demonstrates that the rabbinate has turned into a vulgar patronage system, used by politicians to distribute jobs to their supporters. In many places, there is no affinity between the state-appointed rabbis and their residents. It is urgently in the interest of both Judaism and Israel that the state rabbinate be abolished.

I do not support the total separation of religion and state as practiced in the United States. It seems to me that the model of some European countries is better suited to Israel. The establishment of synagogues and the nomination of rabbis ought to be at least partially supported by public funds, in the same way that museums, community centers, and other cultural activities are supported by the state. But this funding should be distributed in accordance with the communities' needs and preferences, without allowing for a monopoly of any particular religious denomination over budgets and positions. Each community should choose its own rabbi according to its own religious orientation, as was the practice of Jewish communities for generations. And these same protections of freedom of religion must be granted to Muslim and Christian communities of Israel.

Israel can and should be defined as a Jewish state, where the Jewish people exercises its incontrovertible right to self-determination; where every Jew, wherever he or she lives, has a homeland; where the public space, the language, and the calendar have a Jewish character; and where public education allows for the continuity and flourishing of Jewish cultures. These features do not at all undermine the democratic nature of the state, so long as Israel's cultural and religious minorities are also granted equal and official recognition and protection, including state funding of Muslim and Christian public education systems, and the recognition of Arabic as a second official language of the state and the Muslim and Christian calendar as state calendars. In this sense, there is nothing contradictory or paradoxical about the idea of a Jewish democratic state.

The pessimism is premature. These essential principles can be reconciled and realized. Yet there are significant limits in such an experiment that must be vigilantly respected. Any attempt to "Judaize" the state of Israel beyond those limits would transform it into an undemocratic nation-state, and compromise its liberal nature, and undo its founders' magnificent vision, and damage the creative Jewish renewal that may emerge from the great debate about modern Jewish identity. The tough question is not whether a Jewish state can be both democratic and liberal, but rather what kind of Jewish state do we wish to have.

JOSHUA BENNETT

Owed To The Tardigrade

*Some of these microscopic invertebrates shrug off temperatures
of minus 272 Celsius, one degree warmer than absolute zero.
Other species can endure powerful radiation and the
vacuum of space.*
*In 2007, the European Space Agency sent 3,000 animals
into low Earth orbit, where the tardigrades survived
for 12 days on the outside of the capsule.*

THE WASHINGTON POST,
"THESE ANIMALS CAN SURVIVE UNTIL THE END
OF THE EARTH, ASTROPHYSICISTS SAY"

O, littlest un-killable one. Expert
death-delayer, master abstracter

of imperceptible flesh. We praise
your commitment to breath.

Your well-known penchant
for flexing on microbiologists,

confounding those who seek
to test your limits using ever more

abominable methods: ejection
into the vacuum of space, casting

your smooth, half-millimeter frame
into an active volcano, desiccation

on a Sunday afternoon, when the game
is on, & so many of us are likewise made

sluggish in our gait, bound to the couch
by simpler joys. *Slow-stepper,* you were

called, by men who caught first
glimpse of your eight paws walking

through baubles of rain. *Water bear.*
Moss piglet. All more or less worthy

mantles, but I watch you slink
through the boundless clarity

of a single droplet & think
your mettle ineffable, cannot

shake my adoration
for the way you hold fast

324

to that which is so swiftly
torn from all else living,

what you abide in order
to stay here among the flailing

& misery-stricken, the glimpse
you grant into limitless

persistence, tenacity
under unthinkable odds,

endlessness enfleshed
& given indissoluble form.

Owed To The Tardigrade

JOSHUA BENNETT

Reparation

How are you feeling is always your opening question
& you know me. I always take it the wrong way
when you say it like that.

I hear you asking for damage reports, the autobiography
of this pile of brown rubble bumbling on

about his father's beauty, this chasm splitting
the voice in his unkempt head & the one
which enters the realm of the living.

You are good to me, & this kindness, I think, is not reducible
to our plainly economic relation, the yellow carbon
receipt at the end of each session a reminder
that we aren't just girls
in the park catching up, estimating the cost
of our high school errors.

I never call you my *analyst*, because
that makes me sound like a body
of work, some extended meditation
approaching theory, if only asymptotically.

Anyways. I'm alright today. I remembered
to eat breakfast, & went for a run uptown.
I gave myself credit for trying to change.

Something in me awakened, today,
ready for liftoff. It sang.

Trash

General consensus in our home
was candy or soda would kill us,

or else rot our constitutions in some
larger, metaphysical sense. *Body & soul,*

to cite the old wisdom. In protest,
my big sister & I would sneak the stuff

through customs whenever we could:
Swedish Fish & ginger beer, Kit-Kats,

Mary Janes & Malta lining the sides
of each pocket like the contraband

spoils they were, smallest joys,
our solitary arms

in this war against the invisible
wall our parents built to bar

the world of dreams. Now that
we are older, the mystery is all

but gone. We were poor. Teeth
cost. In the end, it was the same
as any worthwhile piece
of ancient lore: love obscured

by law, our clumsy hands
demanding heaven, forgetting

the bounty in our bellies, the miracles
our mother made from Jiffy mix

& cans of salmon, all the pain
we never knew we never knew

held there, against our will,
in the citadel of her care.

DAVID THOMSON

The Wonder of Terrence Malick

The best American film of 2019, *A Hidden Life*, was little seen, and nominated for nothing. Why be surprised? Or assume that our pictures deserve awards any more than the clouds and the trees? Try to understand how movies may aspire to a culture that regards Oscars, eager audiences, and fame as relics of our childhood. The ponderous gravity of *The Irishman* and its reiterated gangster fantasy, the smug evasiveness of *Once Upon a Time … in Hollywood*, were signs that old movie habits were defunct. *Parasite* was no better or worse than cute opportunism. It was a wow without an echo. Whereas *A Hidden Life* was like a desert, known about in theory but ignored or avoided.

I use that term advisedly, for Malick is a student who knows deserts are not dull or empty. They are places that can grow the tree of life as well as any forest. Simply in asking, what is hidden here?, Terrence Malick was leading us to ponder, *What should a movie be?*

He had never volunteered for conventional schemes of ranking. His creative personality can seem masked or obscure, but his reticence is portentous too, and it belongs to no one else. Had he really taught philosophy at M.I.T. while doing a draft for *Dirty Harry*? Please say yes: we so want our auteurs to be outlaws. His self-effacement, his famous "elusiveness," was often seen as genius. Yet some early admirers felt he had "gone away" in the twenty-first century, or migrated beyond common reach. People regarded his private and idiosyncratic work as egotism, no matter how beautiful it might be. Some were disinclined even to try *A Hidden Life* after the inert monuments that had preceded it. But it was — I say it again — the best American film of 2019, a masterpiece, and it invited us to try and place Malick, and to ponder if our "map" was part of the problem. To put it mildly, *A Hidden Life* does not seem American (or even Austrian, where it was set and filmed). It is occurring in cultural memory as a sign of what we might have been.

There was never a pressing reason to make up our minds about Malick. He was casual, yet lofty; he might be an artist instead of a regular American moviemaker in an age when it was reckoned that tough pros (like Hawks and Hitchcock) made the best pictures. Thus he began with two unwaveringly idiosyncratic films — *Badlands* in 1973 and *Days of Heaven* in 1978. He took in

The Wonder of Terrence Malick

their awed reception and then stopped dead for twenty years, and let his reputation become an enigma. Did he really prefer not to appear with his movies, or give helpful interviews, so that he could be free to pursue ornithology and insect life? Was he unpersuaded by careerist plans, or cleaning up in the manner of Spielberg or Lucas? In never winning an Oscar, he has made that statuette seem a stooge.

It has always been hard to work out his intentions. Going on the titles, *Badlands* could be a perilous vacation, while *Days of Heaven* might promise transcendence. In the first, across the empty spaces of the Dakotas and Montana, Kit Carruthers found his daft halcyon moment of aimlessness while being taken for James Dean, while in the latter, in its gathering of rueful magic hours, we encountered a broken family where a guy was shot dead, his girl was thinking of being a hooker to survive, and the kid sister was left alone with her mannered poetry (like Emily Dickinson voiced by Bonnie Parker). In its locusts and fire, and a screwdriver thrust in the farmer's fragile chest, *Days of Heaven* spoke to the ordeal of frontier people in 1916 going mad, skimming stones at entropy, or posing for the pictures in *Wisconsin Death Trip* (published by Michael Lesy in the year *Badlands* opened). The two films together said that America was an inadvertently gorgeous place full of terrors.

Those early films were filled with love and zest for drab characters buried in the hinterland yet nursing some elemental wonder. But decades later, in 2012, *To the Wonder* felt like a crushing title for a film that had lost touch with ordinary poetry. Its women were models fleeing from *Vogue*. Whereas Sissy Spacek as Holly in *Badlands* (twenty-four yet doing fourteen without strain or condescension) was somehow routine as well as brilliant. Her unwitting insights hovered at the brink of pretension, but any doubt we had was lost in captivation for this orphan who packed vivid party dresses for her violent spree into emptiness. This was after Kit had shot her father dead, not just because dad didn't approve of a garbage collector outlaw going with his Holly, but because he hadn't the patience to listen to the rambling solo that was so folksy and menacing — "Oh, I've got some things to say," Kit promised. "Guess I'm lucky that way."

And Holly did feel wonder for this vagrant actor. It was there in the flat adoration that Spacek offered him. She slapped his face for killing Dad, but then went along with him, too matter of fact to pause over spelling out love, but utterly transported by this signal for young getaway. *Badlands* was akin to *Bonnie and Clyde*, but you felt that Kit and Holly were in a marriage they did not know how to express. And they were sustained by Malick's amused affection. He was close to patronizing his couple, maybe, making them babes in the woods in a surreal frame, but he felt their romance as much as he was moved by sunsets and the childish tree houses that they built. They were savage yet humdrum, and Kit's killings were as arbitrary or impulsive as his funny chat. Yes, he was psychotic and headed for the electric chair, but the sweet interior desolation of their America understood them and treated them kindly. When Kit was captured at last, the horde of cops, sheriffs, and soldiers recognized that he was a cockeyed hero, the escapee they had dreamed of.

One can love *Bonnie and Clyde*, but that love story is self-conscious about its lust for fame; it really was the heartfelt cry of Beatty and Dunaway and a generation yearning to be known. *Badlands,* by contrast, is so casual or inconsequential, and so appreciative of a wider span of history, the one we call oblivion. It has a notion that vagrancy and lyricism were responses to the heart of it all, the vast stretch of land where

The Wonder of Terrence Malick

badness is as implicit as beauty. Bonnie and Clyde do not notice where they are, but Kit and Holly are specks in an emptiness as infinite as breathing. It's only now, in retrospect, that the film seems so intoxicated with talk and its futile liberty, when Malick was headed towards a sadder future in which his stunned characters said less and less, and sometimes became so reduced to half-stifled sighs you wished they'd shut up. That early Malick loved loose talk. Compared with the directors of the early 1970s he was like a muttering Bartleby alone in a crew of insistent press-agented Ahabs.

This leaves you wondering how few authentic outsiders American film has permitted.

Malick was thirty-five when *Days of Heaven* opened, the son of a geologist, born in a small town in Illinois, of Assyrian and Lebanese descent. He graduated from Harvard, and then went on to Oxford as a Rhodes scholar, without getting any degree there. The general estimate is that he was brilliant, as witness his published translation of Heidegger's *The Essence of Reasons*. But who has read that book, or is in a position to judge the translation? So it's part of the uncertain myth that includes our wondering over whether Malick has had private money. Or some lack of ordinary need for it. How has he seemed so unprofessional?

He is credited with the script for *Pocket Money* (1972), a Stuart Rosenberg film with Paul Newman and Lee Marvin that is more odd than striking. But it led to *Badlands,* for which he had some money from the young producer Edward Pressman, from the computer pioneer Max Palevsky, and from a few people he knew. All of which meant it wasn't a regular production like other films of 1973 — *The Exorcist, Mean Streets, The Sting, American Graffiti, The Way We Were.* Caught between two parts of *The Godfather*, it didn't seem to hear them or know them. *Badlands* may have cost $300,000. Warner Brothers bought the picture and released it: it closed the New York Film Festival in 1973, and if it perplexed audiences, there was a sense that something rare and insolent had passed by. *Badlands* didn't care what we felt: suspense and attention were mere horizons in its desert, not luxury hotels. It was an American product, but it had a more hushed European ambition. You could label it a Western if you were ready to agree that Hollywood, born and sited in the West, never knew or cared where it was.

Some tried to see *Badlands* as a slice of picaresque life. We knew it was derived from a real case, a minor outrage on the remote prairie. In 1957-1958, in Nebraska mostly, the nineteen-year-old Charles Starkweather had killed ten people with fourteen-year-old Caril Ann Fugate as his companion. Fugate actually served seventeen years in prison, no matter that in the movie she says she married her lawyer. (That was a prettification or a kind of irony.) And there was more real grounding in the steady assertion that Martin Sheen's Kit was a lookalike for James Dean and therefore rooted in popular culture. Kit and Holly dance to Mickey and Sylvia singing "Love is Strange," from 1956.

Strange was only half of it. In 1973, the feeling that sex was at hand on the screen was still pressing. As Kit took off with Holly, it was natural to think they would soon be fucking. Malick allowed an offhand obligation to that craze — $300,000 carried some box office responsibility — but he was too unimpressed or philosophical to get excited about it. Married three times by now, he doesn't do much sex on screen. "Did it go the way it's supposed to?" Holly asks Kit about their unseen

335

coupling. "Is that all there is to it? Well, I'm glad it's over." All said without prejudice to their affinity or their being together.

The absent-minded talk meant more than the way Sissy Spacek secured the top button on her dress "afterwards." After all, her character was fifteen and he was twenty-four. Yet they were both children in Malick's art. And then, like kids, they lost interest in their adventure, even in sex, the sacrament in so many pictures of the 1970s. The novelty of *Badlands* was its instinct that life was boring or insignificant. And that was asserted amid a culture where movies had to be exciting, urgent, and "important."

Malick knew that "importance" was bogus. Or he had his eye on a different order of significance. And other truths and differences were inescapable in his film: that no runaway kids had the temerity or the rhythm for talking the way these two did; that stranger than "Love is Strange" was the way Carl Orff and Erik Satie played in their summer as warnings against "realism." The people in the film were not just movie characters, they were shapes in a mythology.

A similar thing happened in *Days of Heaven* with its triangle of attractions, where Richard Gere, Brooke Adams, and Sam Shepard seemed unduly pretty for the Texas Panhandle. Malick had narrative problems on that picture which he solved or settled by summoning the voice of Linda Manz's kid sister — a laconic, unsentimental, yet dreamy observer of all the melodrama. (The voice was sister to Holly, too.) She was part of the family, but her voiceover let us feel the narrative was already buried in the past, and nothing to fret over. Life itself was being placed as an old movie.

Days of Heaven was extreme in its visualization: it included a plague of locusts, which was an epic of cinematography and weird special effects, involving showers of peanut shells and characters walking backwards. But the quandary of the Brooke Adams character, in love with two men, both unlikely in the long term, was the closest Malick had come to novelistic drama. I still feel for Shepard's farmer, a rich man at a loss with feelings, though Malick had the sense to save the reticent Shepard from "acting." Instead he was simply photographed, as gaunt and theoretical as his great house planted on the endless prairie. Just as he was shy of sex, so Malick the director was hesitant over what the world called story.

No great American director has carried himself with such indifference as to whether he was being seen, let alone understood. To see Malick's work has always been a way of recognizing that the obvious means of doing cinema — appealing stories with likeable actors that move us and make money — was not settled in his mind. I think that is one reason why he stopped for twenty years — just to remain his own man, and not to yield to the habit of eccentric beauty in case it became studied, precious, or crushingly important.

Thus, in 1998, *The Thin Red Line* seemed to believe in a new kind of authenticity and directness. Wasn't it "a war movie"? Didn't it make more money than Malick has ever known? Wasn't it about killing the enemy, that blessed certainty that films provide for fearful guys? It offered Guadalcanal in 1942, and it came from a James Jones novel, the writer of *From Here to Eternity*, which for someone of Malick's age really was the Pacific War, despite being short on combat and going no farther west than Hawaii. *The Thin Red Line* is the infantry, landing on an island, and reckoning to take its peaks and destroy the enemy. It is a man's world that male audiences might relax with. There are only fragmentary glimpses of women left at home — a rapturous shot of an occupied dress on a summer swing, something that would become an emblem of happiness in Malick's work.

But nothing competes with the ferocity of Colonel Tall, played by Nick Nolte in the most intense performance in a Malick picture, as a commander whose orders were abandoned and denied. That is not how war films are supposed to work: no one ever challenged John Wayne at Iwo Jima or Lee Marvin in *The Big Red One*. But Malick's thin red line is less conventional or reliable. It finds its example in the wistful instinct to desert on the part of a common soldier, Private Witt (Jim Caviezel). For Jones, Witt was an extension of the brave victim Prewitt whom Montgomery Clift played in *From Here to Eternity*, but for Malick the lonely private is another version of Bartleby, who gives himself up finally not just in heroism but in almost yielding to hesitation.

Maybe this was once a regular combat picture, to be set beside the work of Sam Fuller or Anthony Mann. But not for long: inscape pushes battle aside for a contemplation of tropical grasses tossing in the wind, insect life, parrots and snakes, intruded on for a moment by war but not really altered by it. Malick has an Emersonian gift for regarding human affairs from the standpoint of nature. It is in the perpetuity of nature that Malick perceives the strangeness, and the humbling, in Earth's helpless duration. This war prepares us for the bizarre little dinosaurs in *The Tree of Life,* and the unnerving perspective in which we observe or suffer the earnestness of Sean Penn in that film.

That touches on a fascinating atmosphere attached to Malick and his blithe treatment of stars. In his long absence from the screen, the glowing characters in those first two films seemed to attract actors, as if to say it might be them,

338

too. He seemed as desirable for them as Woody Allen — and sometimes with a similar diminution of felt human reality. He must have been flattered that so many stars wanted to work for him; he may have forgotten how far he had excelled with newcomers or unknowns. Still, I found it disconcerting when John Travolta or George Clooney suddenly turned up in spiffy, tailored glory in *The Thin Red Line*, and one had the feeling with *The Tree of Life* that Sean Penn was vexed, as if to say, "Doesn't Terry know I'm Sean Penn, so that I deserve motivation, pay-off, and some scenes, instead of just wandering around?" Led to believe he was central to *The Thin Red Line*, Adrien Brody was dismayed to find he had only a few minutes in the finished film.

Was this just an experimenter discovering that his film could remain in eternal post-production? Or was it also a creeping indifference to ordinary human story? Was it an approach that really required novices or new faces? How could big American entertainments function in this way? How was Malick able to command other people's money on projects that sometimes seemed accidental or random, on productions that had several different cuts and running times? He seemed increasingly indecisive and fond of that uncertainty, as if it were a proof of integrity. Was he making particular films, or had the process of filming and its inquiry become his preoccupation? How improvisational a moviemaker is he? And what were we to make of its end products — or was "the end" a sentimental destination mocked by the unshakable calm of duration? How could anyone get away with *The Thin Red Line* costing $90 million and earning back only a touch more? I could make a case for *The Thin Red Line* as Malick's best film and the most intellectually probing of them all. But "best" misses so many points. To shoot it, Malick had gone to the jungles

The Wonder of Terrence Malick

of northern Queensland and even the Solomon Islands. The weapons and the uniforms seemed correct, but the hallowed genre of war movie was perched on the lip of aestheticism and absurdity and surrealism.

As a world traveler and a naturalist — his nature films are certainly among his most marvelous achievements — Malick was especially sensitive to terrain. For *The New World,* in 2005, he went to the real sites, the swampy locations, of early settlement in Virginia. He researched or concocted a language such as the natives might have spoken. His tale of John Smith, Pocohontas, and John Rolfe has many enthusiasts for its attempt to recreate a time so new then and so ancient now. This was also a historical prelude to the wildernesses in *Badlands* and *Days of Heaven.* It might even begin to amount to a history of America.

I had worries about the film, and I have never lost them. Its Pocohontas was exquisite and iconic, even if the picture tried to revive her Powhartan language. But the actress, Q'orianka Kilcher, was also part German, part Peruvian, raised in Hawaii, a singer, a dancer, a stunt performer, a princess of modernity, with evident benefit of cosmetics and a gymnasium. Whereas Sissy Spacek in *Badlands* had a dusty, closed face credible for the look of a kid from Fort Dupree in South Dakota in the 1950s, uneducated, indefatigably unradiant, born bored, more ready for junk food than primetime fiction. That background was what made Holly so absorbing, and it was Kilcher's emphatic beauty that shifted *The New World* away from urgency or naturalism. It was as if Angelina Jolie or Joan Crawford were pretending to be the Indian maiden.

In a way, Pocohontas was the first adult female in Malick's work, but was that a warning sign that maybe he didn't fathom grown up women once they had got past the wry baby talk that makes the first two films so endearing? *The New World* did not really have much caring for Native Americans, for women, or for the challenge of Europeans determined to take charge of any viable Virginia. It was a film that opted for the picturesque over history, whereas *Badlands* and *Days of Heaven* lived on a wish to inhabit and understand America in the unruly first half of the twentieth century as a wilderness succumbing to sentimentality. But the picturesque has always been a drug in cinema, and it had been lurking there in the magic hours in *Days of Heaven*.

There was a gap of six years before the pivotal *The Tree of Life,* perhaps Malick's most controversial film. Here was a genuinely astonishing picture, ambitious enough to range from intimacy to infinity. In so many ways, it was an eclipsing of most current ideas of what a movie might be. At one level, it was entirely mundane, the portrait of two parents and their three sons in a small town in Texas in the 1950s. For Brad Pitt (a co-producer on the project), the father was a landmark role in which he allowed his iconic status to open up as a blunt, stubborn, unenlightened man of the 50s. Jessica Chastain was the mother, and she was placid but eternal — she was doing her pale-faced best, but surely her part deserved more substance to match not just Pitt but the wondrous vitality of the boys (Hunter McCracken, Finnegan Williams, Michael Koeth, and Tye Sheridan).

All his working life, Malick has excelled with the topic of children at play, and as emerging forces who jostle family order. Don't forget how in his first two pictures adult actors were asked to play child-like characters. The family scenes in *The Tree of Life* are captivating and affirming with a power that is all the more remarkable because the subject of the film is the family's grief at the death of one of these children. *The Tree of Life* insists that the death of a child is a cosmic event. Not long after the young man's death is announced, and before the story of the family is told in flashback, there is an unforgettable yet pretentious passage shot with almost terrifying vividness from nature — the bottom of the sea, the fires of a volcano, the reaches of space — accompanied by religious music. With an epigraph from Job, the real subject may be sublimity itself.

No one had ever seen a film quite like it. Reactions were very mixed. The picture won the Palme d'Or at Cannes; it had many rave reviews; it did reasonable business. There were those who felt its perilous edging into pretension and a sweeping universality in which the movie vitality of the family succumbed to the melancholy of grazing dinosaurs who had never been moviegoers. But there were more viewers who recognized an exciting challenge to their assumptions. *The Tree of Life* prompted a lot of people in the arts and letters to revise their ideas about what a movie might be. Pass over its narrative situation, this was a film to be measured with Mahler's ruminations on the universe or with the transcendent effects of a room full of Rothkos.

And then Malick seemed to get lost again. He veered away from the moving austerity of *Days of Heaven* to a toniness more suited to fashion magazines. There was widespread disquiet about his direction, owing to the modish affectation in *To the Wonder* (2012), *Knight of Cups* (2015) and *Song to Song* (2017). From a great director, these seemed confoundingly hollow films that almost left one nostalgic for the time when Malick worked less.

Ironically, *To the Wonder* is the one film for which he has owned up to an autobiographical impulse. It grew out of hesitation over his third and fourth wives, presented in the

342

movie as Olga Kurylenko and Rachel McAdams, two unques-
tioned beauties. McAdams delivers as good a performance as
Brooke Adams in *Days of Heaven*, but there are moments where
her character's frustrations could be interpreted as the actress'
distress over poorly written material. Malick was now running
scared of his ear for artful, quirky talk. But the women in *To
the Wonder* are betrayed by the worst example of Malick's
uninterested stars. Ben Affleck is the guy here, allegedly an
"environmental inspector." That gestural job allows some
moody depictions of wasteland and some enervated ecstasy
over the tides around Mont-Saint-Michel in France. Yet the
situation feels the more posed and hollow because of Affleck's
urge to do as little as possible. His hero is without emotional
energy; he deserves his two women as little as male models
earn their expensive threads in fashion spreads. The film's
clothes are credited to the excellent Jacqueline West, but they
adorn a fatuous adoration of affluence.

West was part of Malick's modern team: the film's
producer was Sarah Green; the engraved photography was by
the extraordinary Emmanuel Lubezki; the production design
was from Jack Fisk still, who had held that role since *Badlands,*
where he met and then married Sissy Spacek; the aching music
was by Hanan Townshend in a glib pastiche of symphonic
movie music — it was so much less playful or spirited than the
score for *Badlands*. The only notable crew absentee was Billy
Weber, who has been the editor on many Malick pictures. *To
the Wonder* is said to have earned $2.8 million at the box
office, and it's hard to believe it cost less than $20 million. If
that sounds like a misbegotten venture, wait till you struggle
through it and then wonder what let Malick make another
film in the same clouded spirit, *Knight of Cups*. And then
another: *Song to Song*, the ultimate gallery of beautiful stars,

343

supposedly about the music world of Austin, which came off semi-abstract no matter that Malick had lived there for years.

Any sense of experience and vitality seemed to be ebbing away. Was he experimenting, or improvising, or what? The several loyalists involved, as well as those players who were filmed but then abandoned, might say it was a privilege to be associated with Terry. I long to hear some deflating rejoinders to that from Kit Carruthers. There was a wit once in Malick that had now gone missing. I say this because a great director deserves to be tested by his own standards, which in Malick's case are uncommonly high. Even with the more adventurous Christian Bale as its forlorn male lead — a jaded movie screen-writer — *Knight of Cups* is yet more stultifyingly beautiful and Tarot-esque, with a placid harem of women (from Cate Blanchett to Isabel Lucas, from Imogen Poots to Natalie Portman), all so immediately desirable that they do not bother to be awake. Richard Brody said it was "an instant classic," which only showed how far "instant" and "classic" had become invalid concepts. The film earned a touch over $1 million, and it had disdain for any audience. It was a monument to a preposterous cinephilia and to a talent that seemed in danger of losing itself.

Those are harsh words, but I choose them carefully, after repeated viewings, and in the confidence that *Badlands, Days of Heaven* and *The Thin Red Line* are true wonders. The Terrence Malick of early 2019, passing seventy-five, was not a sure thing. And then he retired all doubt about his direction and released his fourth great film; and surely four is enough for any pantheon.

Malick had been contemplating *A Hidden Life* and the historical incident upon which it is based for a few years. In 1943, Franz Jagerstatter was executed in Berlin for refusing to take an oath of loyalty to Adolf Hitler. He was a humble farmer high in the mountains of northern Austria, where he lived with his wife, his three daughters, his sister-in-law, and his mother. They were valued members of a small community and worked endlessly hard to sustain their meager living. They were devout Catholics, and Franz had done his military service without thinking too much about it. His farm and his village are surrounded by breathtaking natural beauty, and Malick lingers long over the fields and the peaks and the clouds in a way that teaches us that even Nazism is ephemeral.

The film has few long speeches in which Jagerstatter spells out his reluctance to honor the Nazi code. He is more instinctive than articulate. He knows the fate he is tempting; he understands the burden that will put upon his wife and children; he appreciates that he could take the oath quietly and then do non-combatant service. It is not that he understands the war fully or the extent of Nazi crimes. He is not a deliberate or reasoned objector. But just as he feels the practical truths in his steep fields and in the lives of his animals, and just as he is utterly loyal to his wife, so he believes that the oath of allegiance will go against his grain. He does not show a moral philosophy so much as a moral sense. He cannot make the compromise with an evasive form of words.

There is no heavy hint in *A Hidden Life* of addressing how Americans in our era might withhold their own allegiance to a leader. But the film rests on a feeling that such cues are not needed for an alert audience living in the large world. We are living in a time that will have its own Jagerstatters. That is part of the narrative confidence that has not existed in Malick since

The Wonder of Terrence Malick

Days of Heaven. It amounts to an unsettling detachment: he shares the righteousness of Jagerstatter, but he does not make a fuss about his heroism. In the long term of those steep Alps and their infinite grasslands, how much does it matter? Do the cattle on the farm know less, or are they as close to natural destiny as the farmer's children?

That may sound heretical for so high-minded a picture. And there is no escaping — the final passages are shattering — how Jagerstatter is brutalized and then hung by the Nazi torturers and executioners. The Catholic church would make a saint of him one day, and Malick has taken three hours to tell what happened, but the film has no inkling of saintliness or a cause that could protect it. The farmer's wife, rendered by Valerie Pachner as sharp and uningratiating, does not need to agree with her man, or even to understand him. People are alike but not the same, even under intense pressure. No one could doubt Malick's respect for Jagerstatter, and August Diehl is Teutonically tall, blond, and good-looking in the part. But he is not especially thoughtful; his doubts over the oath are more like a limp than a self-consciously upright attitude. Certainly the old Hollywood scheme of a right thing waiting and needing to be done leaves Malick unmoved; he would prefer to be a patient onlooker, a diligent chronicler, attentive and touched, but more rapt than ardent, and still consumed by wonder.

Malick has admitted how often he had got into the habit of working without a script (or a pressing situation), so that he often filmed whatever came into his head. But he seems to have learned how far that liberty had led him astray. So *A Hidden Life* has as cogent a situation as those in *Badlands* and *Days of Heaven*. That does not mean those three films are tidy or complacent about their pieces clicking together. They are all as open to spontaneity and chance as *The Thin Red Line*. But

346

just as it is trite and misleading to say that *The Thin Red Line* was a film about war, so *A Hidden Life* feels what its title claims: the existence of an inwardness that need not be vulgarized by captions or "big scenes." The film concludes with the famous last paragraph of *Middlemarch*, about the profound significance of "hidden lives" and "unvisited tombs." Yes, this is what a movie, a heartbreaking work, might be for today. As for its relative neglect, just recall the wistful look on the dinosaur faces in *The Tree of Life*.

We can do our best, we can make beauty and find wisdom, without any prospect of being saved from oblivion.

JULIUS MARGOLIN

The Doctrine of Hate

Julius Margolin was born in 1900 in Pinsk. After studying philosophy in Germany in the 1920s he moved to Poland with his family, where he became active in Revisionist Zionism and published a Yiddish book on poetry. From there he and his family moved to Palestine. For economic reasons, Margolin returned to Poland in 1936, where he was trapped by the Nazi invasion, and was eventually imprisoned in Soviet labor camps. In July, 1945 he was released and made his way back to Tel Aviv, where he wrote a pioneering memoir of the Gulag and died in 1971. The full text of Journey into the Land of the Zeks and Back *was not published in his lifetime.*

After my release from Maxik's hospital, having had an opportunity to rest, and armed with certification as an invalid, I returned to the camp regime. In Kruglitsa, a certified invalid with a higher education has a wealth of possibilities. You can choose: assist the work supervisor in compiling the lists of personnel in the brigades; work in the Cultural-Educational Sector (KVCh); or be an orderly in the barrack. Until a prisoner is taken off the official work register, he will not be sent to such unproductive work. The place for a healthy, able person is in the forest or field, where hands and shoulders are needed. The work boss will not allow an able-bodied worker to have an office or service job. An invalid is another matter. Whatever he is able and willing to do without being obliged to do so is a pure gain for the state.

At first, I was amused at the accessibility of work from which I had been barred as a third-category worker. When they found out that Margolin had been deactivated, people immediately invited me to work in various places, and I succumbed to temptation. An invalid is allotted the first level food ration and 400 grams of bread. By working, I received the second level and 500 grams.

For an entire month, I tried various places. After a ten-week stay in the hospital, it was pleasant to be occupied and to be listed in a job. After a month, however, I came to feel that I had been deactivated for a reason. I lacked strength. The job with the work supervisor dragged on until late at night. Work at the KVCh entailed being in motion all day, making the rounds of the barracks, rising before reveille. As a worker in the Cultural-Educational Sector, I had to get up an hour before everyone else: by the time the brigades went out to work, I had to list on the huge board at the gate the percentage of the norm that each brigade had fulfilled the previous day.

The Doctrine of Hate

A worker calculated these norms in the headquarters at night and, before going to sleep, he left the list for me in a desk drawer in the office. The camp was still sleeping, the dawn reddened behind the barracks, and the guards were dozing on the corner watchtowers, when I would climb with difficulty onto a stool that I had placed in front of the giant chart and begin writing in chalk on the blackened board the figures for the twenty brigades.

This work bored me. The thought that as an invalid I was not obliged to endure this misery gave me no rest. I had been an invalid for an entire month and had not yet utilized the blessed right to do nothing; I had not taken advantage of my marvelous, unbelievable freedom. In the middle of the summer in 1943, I declared a grand vacation. At the same time, it represented a great fast: 400 grams of bread and a watery soup. It was June. Blue and yellow flowers bloomed in the flowerbeds in front of the headquarters; under the windows of the infirmary, the medical workers had planted potatoes and tobacco. In the morning, the patients crawled out to the sun and lay on the grass in their underwear or sunned themselves in the area around the barracks. When I went by, barefoot, in my mousy gray jacket without a belt, fastened by one wooden button near the collar, they shouted to me: "Margolin, you're still alive? We thought you were gone already!"

Without stopping, I went on to the farthest corner of the camp territory. I had a blanket, a little pencil, and paper. There was lots of paper: in the past month, I had hoarded a respectable amount. I even had a little bottle of ink from my work in the KVCh. I would take a rest from people, the camp, work, and eternal fear. I lay on my back, watching the clouds float above Kruglitsa. A year earlier, I had worked in the bathhouse and ran into the forest for raspberries. Amazingly, then I was able to carry three hundred buckets of water a day. That year depleted me. Now there were no raspberries, but neither did I have to drag water buckets. I was satisfied; it was a profound rest.

In the summer of 1943, a storm raged over Kursk, and Soviet communiqués spoke of gigantic battles, as if all the blood receded from this great country and flowed to the single effort in that one spot. One hardly saw healthy males in Kruglitsa. Women guarded the prisoners and conducted the brigades to work. Gavrilyuk, who the past summer had been a Stakhanovite wagoner, now, like me, had been retired from work, and women prisoners worked as wagon drivers in camp. Women, like reservists, went to the first line of work. We knew from the newspapers that, throughout the country, women were working as tractor drivers, in factories, and in the fields. The free men held the battle front while the male prisoners in the camp melted like snow in the spring sun and descended under the ground. I knew that in another year I would be weaker than I was at present. If the war dragged on, I would die and not even know how it ends. Out of pure curiosity, I wanted to make it to the end of the war.

That summer, my first grand interlude as an invalid, I wrote "The Doctrine of Hate." That summer I was preoccupied with thoughts about hate. Lying in the grass behind the last infirmary, I returned to the topic from day to day and turned out chapter after chapter. I experienced a profound and pure enjoyment from the very process of thought and from the awareness that this thinking was outside-the-camp, normal, free thought, despite my current conditions and despite the barbed wire fence and guards. This was "pure art." There was no one to whom I could show it or who could read what I was writing, and I felt pleasure from the very activity of formulating my thoughts, and as the work advanced I also felt

The Doctrine of Hate

proud that to a certain degree I was prevailing over hatred, was able to grasp it, and to subject it to the court of Reason.

This subject was dictated by my life. What I had endured and seen around me was a true revelation of hate. In my previous life, I only heard or read about it, but I never encountered it personally. Neither racial nor party hatred had crossed the threshold of my peaceful home. In camp, for the first time, I heard the word "kike" directed at me, felt that someone wanted me to perish, saw victims of hate around me, and witnessed its organized apparatus. In camp, I, too, for the first time learned to hate.

Now it was time for me to elaborate all this material theoretically. How simple it would be to go away from the haters to that bright kingdom of warmth and humanity in which I, unawares, lived before the Holocaust. It is natural for a person to live among those who love and are loved by him, not among enemies and haters. But this was not my fate. Nor was I able to resist hatred actively. The only thing that remained free in me was thought; only by thought could I respond. There was nothing else I could do but try to understand the force that wanted to destroy me.

I was less interested in the psychology of individual hatred than in its social function, its spiritual and historical meaning. I saw hatred as a weapon or as a fact of contemporary culture.

The most important thing, with which I began, was the dialectic of hate. Hatred is what unites people while dividing them. The link via hate is one of the strongest in history. Souls come together in hate like the bodies of wrestlers — they seek each other like wrestlers in a fight. You cannot understand hate as pure negation, because if we merely do not love or do not want something, we simply walk away from it and try to eliminate the unnecessary and unpleasant from our life. There was something in my hatred of the camp system that forced me to think about it, and I knew that my hatred would not let me forget it even when I got out of here. Hate arises in conditions when we cannot escape. Hate is a matter of proximity. Personal, class, or national hatred — it is always between cohabitants, between neighbors, between Montague and Capulet, over borderline and frontier.

The paradox of hate is that it leaves us in spiritual proximity to that which we hate until, ultimately, there arises rapprochement and similarity. Sometimes, the hate itself turns out to be merely a concealed fear of what attracts us, as in Catullus' poem *Odi et amo*, as in Hamsun's "duel of the sexes," as in a lackey's hatred for the lord, and finally, in antisemitism of the maniacal type, when people cannot do without the Jews. Here is an acute example. Adolf Nowaczyński, a talented Polish writer, was a malicious hater of everything Jewish. When he approached old age, he took off for Palestine to see things with his own eyes, and it turned out that he felt quite good in Tel Aviv. This man's life would have been empty without Jews. If they had not existed, he would have had to invent them, and ultimately that is what he did all his life. There is hatred toward fascism and even hatred of communism that derives from a certain moral closeness and, in any case, leads toward it over time. We cannot hate what is absolutely incomprehensible and alien. The incomprehensible arouses fear. Hatred, however, needs an intimate knowledge and multiplies it, and it endlessly forces us to take an interest in what we detest.

This was the paradox of hatred that I examined from all sides while lying in the sun in the corner of the camp yard. Hatred was not only before me — it was also inside me. In

The Doctrine of Hate

me, however, it was different from the hatred against which my entire being rebelled. It thus was necessary to differentiate the various forms of hatred, in order to distinguish between the hatred that was inside me and what to me was an odious and evil hatred.

I began by identifying some bogus and altered forms, the pseudo-hatred that only obscures the essence of the matter. I saw that an inapt item or something with an external resemblance paraded under the label of hatred. Away with counterfeits!

First: juvenile hatred, *odium infantile*. Children are capable of the most fierce, frantic hatred, but that is only "ersatz," not serious. Juvenile hatred is a momentary reaction, an acting out. It boils up in an instant and passes without leaving a trace; it rises and bursts like a soap bubble. In essence, it is an outburst, a fit of emotional distress. This is precisely the reason why, in its mass manifestation, by virtue of its qualities of easy arousal, easy manageability, and evanescence, it is particularly suitable for the purposes of cold-blooded producers of this hatred and inciters, who always mobilize it in the masses when it is necessary to stimulate them to an extraordinary effort, to struggle in the name of changing goals. Hatred goes to the masses, flows along the channels of calculated propaganda, but it is all on the surface; it has neither depth nor stability. Left to itself, it dies out or unexpectedly changes direction, as in 1917, when the masses, filled by Tsarist governments with pogromist and front-line hatred, turned against the government itself. The savage hatred of the incited mass, like fuel in a car, turns the wheels of the military machine, but the ones at the steering wheel are calm and cool.

Ripe, mature hatred does not have the nature of a momentary reaction; it is a person's automatic, internally determined and stable position. It does not exhaust itself in one ferocious outburst but gnaws at a person's entire life and lurks behind all his manifestations and deeds. Psychologically it is manifested in a thousand ways. From open hostility to blind nonrecognition, all shades of dislike, malice, vengefulness, cunning and envy, mockery, lies, and slander form the vestments of hatred, but it is not linked exclusively with any one of them. There is no specific feeling of hatred; in its extreme form, it ceases to need any kind of "expression."

A child's hatred is expressed in screaming, foot stamping, and biting. The hatred of a savage, which is the same as a child's hatred, elementary, bestial fury, is expressed in a pogrom, in broken skulls and bloodletting. There is, however, mature hatred that is expressed only in a polite smile and courteous bow. Perfect hatred is Ribbentrop in Moscow, kissing the hands of commissars' wives, or Molotov, smiling at the press conference. We adults have learned to suppress and regulate manifestations of our hatred like a radio receiver, turning it off and on like a light switch. Our hatred is a potential force; therefore, it can be polite and calm, without external manifestations, but woe to the one who shakes an enemy's extended hand and walks along with him.

The second form of pseudo-hatred is *odium intellectuale*: the hatred of scientists, philosophers, and humanists — it is the hatred of those incapable of hating, the academic hatred of intellectuals, which was introduced as an antidote and placed as a lightning rod against barbarism. This vegetarian, liter-

The Doctrine of Hate

ary hatred would have us hate abstract concepts — not an evil person but the evil in man, not the sinner, but sin. This hatred unceasingly exposes vices and fallacies, mistakes and deviations against which we are ordered to fight. This theoretical hatred completely fences itself off from the practical. Unfortunately, the street does not understand these fine distinctions: mass hatred recognizes only that enemy whose head one can break.

Humanism in its essence cannot oppose hatred. We know of two attempts in the history of culture to eliminate hatred from human relations: "nonresistance to evil" and the view that the end does not justify immoral means. Passive resistance to evil, however, invariably switches to active resistance against the bearers of evil, and the question of "ends and means," with its artificial division of the indivisible, remains intractable so long as we do not know what specific means are being used for precisely what goals. Historically, butchers and murderers invariably used abstract, theoretical hatred for their own purposes, expertly contriving to turn every intellectual product into a weapon of mass murder and unlimited slaughter.

Christ drove the money lenders out of the Temple. His successors excommunicated the heretics from the church and lit the bonfires of the Inquisition, up to Torquemada and that papal legate who, upon suppressing the Albigensian heresy, said, "Kill all of them; God will recognize his own." The Encyclopédistes and Rousseau hated vice and believed in the triumph of virtue. The French Revolution introduced the guillotine. Marx started with the liquidation of classes and of exploitation in human relations. His followers turned Marxism into a formula of mass terror, when a "class" is destroyed not as an economic category but as millions of living, innocent people. "Kill them all; history itself will revive what it needs." The process contains a tragically inevitable progression, and, unavoidably, the warrior-humanist becomes a captive of an alien element, as in the case of Maxim Gorky in the role of a Kremlin dignitary. The teachers either capitulate in the face of the conclusions that the pupils derive from their lessons or perish in prison or on the scaffold.

Odium intellectuale, the theoretical hatred of scholars, thus either fails to achieve its goal or leads to results that are diametrically opposite to the original intention. Luther throws an inkpot at the devil. The devil turns the philosopher's ink into blood and a sea of tears.

The third form of hate that I isolated in my analysis is *odium nationale*, the well-meaning hatred of those who take up arms in order to halt the force of evil. Evidently, there was never a dark force that did not try to pass itself off as just and worthy. Evidently, we have no other means of distinguishing between good and evil than by Reason and Experience, which teach us to recognize the essence of phenomena from their manifestations and consequences. There is, thus, a hatred that is rational and transparent in all its manifestations. It is clear to us why and when it arises. Its logical basis is at the same time the reason for its conditional nature, as it disappears along with the causes that evoked it. This hatred is so secondary and reactive that we can easily designate it as counter-hatred. We do not need it intrinsically, but when an enemy imposes it upon us, we do not fear to take up the challenge, and we know that there are things in the world that are worth fighting against — the passion and force of survival which do not yield to the enemy's force and passion but have nothing in common with them in their inner essence.

Having thus carefully differentiated the historically present forms of pseudo-hatred — mass-juvenile and intellectual-abstract, and the rational counter-hatred of the warrior — I approached the eyeless monster that at the time of my imprisonment had spread over all of Europe.

Unlike the superficially emotional, infantile hatred of the crowd, the theorizing hatred of the intellectual, and the sober, clear conviction of the defenders of humankind, there is a force of primal and pure hatred, active despite its blindness, and blind despite its initiative, and the more active the less causally provoked. It fears only the light of day. Reason is its natural enemy.

Haters of the world are united in their negation of freedom of the intellect. The mark of Cain by which one can recognize genuine hate is scorn of free thought, rejection of the intellect. For Hitlerism, free thought is "a Jewish invention"; for the Inquisition, it is a mortal sin; for the ideologues of communism, it is counterrevolution and bourgeois prejudice. Every basis for such hate is imaginary and pseudo-rational. It is therefore natural that the people who established forced-labor camps in Russia simultaneously eradicated freedom of discussion and the right of independent investigation there.

In a pure, undiluted form, hatred is self-affirmation via another's suffering. People become haters not because their surrounding reality forces them to that. There is no sufficient basis for hatred in the external world. There is nothing in the world that could justify the annihilation of flourishing life and proud freedom undertaken by Hitler, the fires of the Inquisition, or the prisons and pogroms and the camp hell of the Gestapo and the NKVD.

There is a pyramid of hate, higher than the Palace [of the Soviets] that is being constructed in Moscow at the cost of hundreds of millions while people are dying of starvation in the camps. At the base of this pyramid are people similar to children, wild savages, like the one who hit me with a board on the road to Onufrievka, or the SS man who shot my elderly mother on the day the Pinsk ghetto was liquidated. These people rape, destroy, and murder, but tomorrow they themselves will be the most mild and obedient and will serve the new masters and believe the opposite of what they believed yesterday, and others — just like them — will come to their homes to murder and rape. Above these people stand others who teach them and entrust them to do what they do. Above them are still others, who engage in ideology and theoretical generalizations, and those embellishers, who service the hatred, deck it out, put it to music, and dress it in beautiful words.

Ultimately, however, at the very top of the pyramid stands a person who needs all this: the incarnation of hatred. This is the organizer, the mastermind, the engineer and the chief mechanic. He has assembled all the threads in his hands, all the subterranean streams and scattered drops of hatred; he gave it direction, a historic impetus and scope. At his signal, armies cross borders, party congresses adopt resolutions, entire peoples are exterminated, and thousands of camps are erected. And he may be kind and sweet: he may have six children as Goebbels did or a "golden heart" like Dzerzhinsky's, an artistic nature like Nero's or Hitler's, and the Gorkys and Barbusses will not stop slobbering over him. He, however, decreed that somewhere people must suffer. He executed them in his mind when no one yet knew about his existence. Even then he needed this.

This brings up a central question in the doctrine of hate: What is the makeup of a person, a society, an epoch if naked hatred has become such a necessity for them, if the senseless torment- ing of their victims becomes a necessary condition of their own existence? It is not at all easy to answer this question if one does not adduce the familiar so-called arguments that the German people "were defending themselves against the Jews," that the Inquisition was "saving souls," or that Stalin is re-edu- cating and reforming "backward and criminal elements" with the help of the camps. This is obvious nonsense. Of course, I in no way harmed the Germans or needed a Stalinist re-education, but even if that had been the case, it would not justify the gas chambers or turning millions of people into slaves. Germany did not need the gas chambers; the Russian people did not need the camps. But they are truly necessary for the big and little Hitlers and Himmlers, Lenins and Stalins, of the world. What, indeed, is going on?

One must clearly recognize that the people holding the keys of power are fully aware of and admire the extent of the avalanche of human and inhuman suffering that seems like an elemental misfortune to us little people. Those people are responsible for its existence every minute and second. They have started it and control it, and it exists not because of their ignorance or impotence but precisely because they know well what they are doing, and they are doing precisely what meets their needs. Only a dull, wooden German lacking imagina- tion, such as Himmler, needed to visit Auschwitz in person in order to look through a little window of the gas chamber to see how hundreds of young Jewish girls choked to death, girls who had been specially dispatched to execution that day for that purpose. People of the Kremlin do not need to observe personally; they have statistics about the camp death toll.

There is no answer to why this is necessary other than to analyze the known pathological peculiarities of human nature. There is no rational, "economic," or other explanation of hatred. The logic of hatred is the logic of madness.

That man [Stalin] hates: He cannot do without this attitude to people; without it, he suffocates. Hate is the oxygen that he breathes. Taking hatred away from him would leave him destitute.

That man hates, which means that some kind of inner weakness develops into hate, the result of some organic problem. Some kind of lack, defect, or unhappiness may remain within the bounds of his sense of self, but it may also spread to his social milieu and be transmitted to other people. There are wounded people, vulnerable classes, ready to turn into breeding grounds of collective hate. There are situations when people, groups, or societies are unable or unwilling to look truth in the face.

In Vienna, young Hitler discovered that the Jews are responsible for depriving him and the German people of their deserved place in the sun. This is preposterous but, indisputably, this man started with some feeling of pain; he was deeply hurt. Had he wanted the truth, he would have found a real cause, but the truth was too much for him to bear. He therefore began to search for external guilty parties. Here the mechanism of hate begins to operate. The real pain turns into an imagined insult. An enemy and offender must be found.

The need for an enemy is radically different from the need for a struggle that is characteristic of every strong person. Strong people seek an arena, an outlet for strength. The hater seeks offenders to accuse. On the one hand, the need for a struggle engenders courage and initiative. On the other, the need to deal with a cunning enemy engenders aggressiveness and malice. The offender is always nearby. If he is not visible, that means he is in disguise and must be unmasked.

All haters are great unmaskers. Instead of a mask, however, they tear off live skin, the true nature, and they replace reality with a creation of their inflamed fantasy. Hatred starts with an imaginary unmasking and ends with real flaying, not in theory but in practice.

The analysis of our epoch given by Marx and developed by Lenin crossed all bounds of a reasonable interpretation of reality. Pseudo-rational theory turned into a Procrustean bed that did not accommodate real life. It is sufficient to compare the tirades of *Mein Kampf* with Lenin's passionate polemics and his thunderous charges against capitalism to sense their psychological affinity. It is the language of hate, not of objective research. We can learn as much about reality from Marxist-Leninist scholastics as we can from the *Protocols of the Elders of Zion*.

Every hatred that reworks pain into insult carries out "transference," in the language of modern psychoanalysis. The source of the pain is internal but we transfer it to the outside. Others are to blame when things go wrong for us, when our plans do not succeed and our hopes are crushed. We thus find an outlet, a relief, but only an illusory one. Hate acquires an address — a false one. Revenge, dictated by hate, misses the mark, like a letter sent to an incorrect address. Hatred engenders a constantly hungry vengefulness.

An imagined or real hatred becomes a pretext for hateful acts if a person has a need and desire to hate. Sooner or later, this need will be expressed in aggression. Even if there is a real cause at the basis of the hatred, it is always incommensurable with the repression; and vengeance born of hate far exceeds what is acceptable to reason and normal human psychology. Genuine revenge, as we know from history, entails the search for, and the attainment of, expiation. The act of revenge is a final one, closing the account. Blood is washed away by blood, and the insult is compensated by insult. The need for another's suffering, which forms the essence of hate, derives from the illusion that, in this way, one's suffering will be suppressed and mental equilibrium will be restored.

But because the connection between one's own misfortune and another's guilt is imaginary, no acts that derive from hatred stifle it, and it turns into abiding, eternal mental anguish. There no longer are Jews in German and Polish cities, but things did not become easier because of this. Millions of people have been destroyed in Soviet camps, and the world gradually realizes that hatred of capitalism does not derive from its criminality because the crimes of communism are just as great. There is neither benefit nor satisfaction from the crimes that are carried out, nor is there a way out as long as hatred spins in a vicious circle.

The people who wrecked my life and turned me into a slave in the summer of 1940 did not know me, and I did not know them. But hatred formed between us. It was not their personal hatred but the collective creation of the epoch, a Leninist-Stalinist concoction, an abstract poison that penetrated the flesh and blood of the generation. Indifferently, calmly, and with bureaucratic dispassion, they carried out their deeds. The same people would have been capable of torturing me. Indifference to human life and dignity, as if it were a matter of an animal at a slaughter house, is the highest measure of concentrated hate. It is a violent, monstrous but completely

363

objective murderous force, which derives from a hopeless attempt to build one's own cursed existence on the misfortune and death of those around.

In order to find support in the external world, this deadly force needs to falsify it. The world is not suitable as is. It is literally true that Streicher and Goebbels could not hate Jews because they did not know them at all. If they had known this people with true, live knowledge, this hatred could not have developed. Their hatred related to that distorted, deformed notion of the Jewish people that they themselves had created and that was dictated by their need to hate. In the institutions of the National Socialist Party, in the Erfurt Institute, there were enormous piles of material about the Jewish people, but the thousands of pieces served them only to create a monstrous mosaic of slander.

In the same way, the people who sent me to this camp did not know me. Their hatred consisted precisely of their not wanting to know me and not having hesitated to turn my life and face into a screen onto which to project an NKVD film: "A threat to society, a lawbreaker. Henceforth this person will be not what he thought he was but what we want him to be and what we shall make of him." In order to erase my existence as they did, one had to harbor a great, formidable hatred of humanity.

Until we uproot this hatred, it will not stop slandering people and their real impulses, will not cease circling around us, seeking out our every weakness, mistake, and sin, which are numerous, not in order to understand us and to help us but in order to blame us for its own thirst for cruelty and blood.

Pathological hate reflects the primal instinct of the rapacious beast who knows that he can appease his agonizing hunger by the warm blood of another. Millennia of cultural development infinitely distanced and complicated this instinct by pseudo-rational sophistry and self-deception. Human rapaciousness exceeded that of the beasts, differing from it in that it manifested itself under senseless pretexts in the name of imaginary goals. The struggle against hatred is thus not limited by humankind's biological nature but encompasses all the specifically inhuman, the perversions, and the lies that comprise the anomaly of highly developed culture and cannot be destroyed until its existence becomes common knowledge.

Free and perspicacious people someday will destroy hatred and create a world where no one will need to hate or oppose hatred. The human striving for freedom is incompatible with hate. Without going into complex definitions of freedom, one can agree that as it develops, freedom will steadfastly expel lies and hatred not only from the human heart but also from human relationships and the social order. Opposition to lies and hatred is thus already the first manifestation of human freedom.

Having finished my investigation of hatred with this proud phrase, I turned over onto my back and looked around: I was lying in a meadow, on green grass at the end of the camp. The forbidden zone started five steps away and a tall palisade with barbed wire spread around. Several prisoners swarmed in the forbidden zone; they were cutting the grass and digging up earth. Under the windows of the hospital kitchen formed a line of medics with buckets for soup and kasha.

In the most minuscule hand, I erased all dangerous hints. I read it with the eyes of the security operative: it was an "antifascist" document written by a stranger, but it was not blatantly counterrevolutionary. Understandably, there was not a word about Soviet reality in this manuscript. I had to keep in mind that it could be taken away at any moment in a search.

But I had pity on my manuscript. There was no chance of hiding a work of that size for a long time in the camp. Suddenly, I had a fantastic idea. I got up and went to the KVCh, where two girls were sitting at two tables.

"What do you want?"

"This is what I want," I said slowly. "I have a manuscript of about a hundred pages. ... I am an academic and wrote something in my specialty. In the barrack, you know, it's dangerous. They'll tear it up to use for rolling cigarettes. I want to give it to the KVCh for safekeeping. When I leave here, you'll return it to me."

The girl was taken aback. She and her friend looked at me in dull astonishment, suspiciously, as at someone abnormal. In the end, she went to the phone and asked the guardhouse to connect her to the security supervisor.

"Comrade supervisor, someone came here, brought a manuscript, and asks that we take it for safekeeping. He says that he is a scientific worker."

She repeated this several times over the telephone, then she turned to me:

"Your name?"

I gave it.

The girl conveyed my name, listened to the answer, and hung up the receiver. "The supervisor said," she turned to me, hardly keeping back laughter, "'let him throw his manuscript into the outhouse'."

CLARA COLLIER

Plagues

Consider the plague. I mean the actual, literal, bubonic plague, the disease caused by the bacterium *Yersinia pestis*. In this pestilential season the subject has been impossible to avoid, because so many people are calling coronavirus "plague" — even though, as pandemics go, they have almost nothing in common. Plague has an astonishingly high fatality rate — between 50% and 80% of its victims die — but is rarely transmitted directly from person to person, traveling instead through the bites of infected fleas. Covid19, by contrast, is much more contagious but significantly less fatal. And there are other distinctions. While the plague comes with painful, swollen tumors, running sores, and putrid secretions, coronavirus leaves no visible marks on the body. Most victims will survive it. Some might never even know they had it.

There has also been plenty of talk about Ebola and AIDS and influenza and what all of them have to tell us about the present crisis. (I have no intention of interpreting the present crisis). But plague has retained a special hold on the imagination. To Thomas Dekker, the Elizabethan hack pamphleteer, it was simply "the sicknesse," a disease with "a Preheminence above all others...none being able to match it for Violence, Strength, Incertainty, Suttlety, Catching, Universality, and Desolation." The Black Death is still the most deadly pandemic in recorded history. At its height, between 1348 and 1351, the disease may have killed half the population of Eurasia. It has only two close rivals for sheer morbidity: the Spanish influenza of 1918-1919 and the smallpox pandemic brought to the Americas by Europeans after 1492. Both events caused untold human suffering, but neither left behind the same long history of written records. That was because the plague kept coming back. Its periodic recurrences swept through Europe with devastating regularity until the 1770s, and continued to ravage the Ottoman Empire into the 1850s. For almost five centuries, it was not unusual for cities to lose a quarter of their population in a year.

So when Asiatic cholera spread to Europe in the 1830s, a century after the last plague outbreak, it was swiftly termed "the new plague." Newspapers from 1918 proclaimed that influenza was "just like a plague of olden times." Yellow Fever was called "the American plague" when it struck Philadelphia in 1793, and early coverage of AIDS in the 1980s demonized its victims by calling it "the gay plague." Like coronavirus, none of these diseases are particularly similar to bubonic plague.

They have different symptoms, causes, biological agents, and epidemiologies. What they share is a particular social profile: all are epidemic diseases of unusual suddenness and severity. They take populations by surprise. Cholera was the most feared disease of the nineteenth century, not the more deadly and more familiar tuberculosis. Endemic childhood illnesses killed more people than the plague before the invention of vaccination, but they did not inspire nearly the same terror. Fear of plague is not just about death or pain: more fundamentally, it is the fear of not knowing what comes next.

Unsurprisingly, plague literature is currently having a moment. Publishers have announced a flood of upcoming books about the coronavirus experience. Recent months-have seen rising sales of everything from Boccaccio's *Decameron* to Dean Koontz's *The Eyes of Darkness* (a novel about a fictional bioweapon called the Wuhan-400 virus). Camus' *The Plague* is a best-seller in Italy and Korea; Penguin is currently issuing a reprint. For a couple of days in March, Defoe's *A Journal of the Plague Year* was actually sold out on Amazon.

Defoe might not be the best-selling plague author of the moment (though it's close), but he has almost certainly been the most reviewed. After all, the *Journal* is the original plague novel, and arguably the only genuine historical narrative of the lot. By reading Defoe, we can tell ourselves a story about what really happened in 1665, when the Great Plague swept through London — and by extension, what has really happened to us now. In just a few days I read that it "speaks clearly to our time," offers "some useful perspective on our current crisis," and gives an "eerie play-by-play" of recent events. And at times, reading the *Journal* really did give me an uncomfortable sense of familiarity. Vague rumors of the plague reach London. The threat is discussed, then dismissed. The government

369

waffles. Deaths start to mount through the winter of 1664 and the spring of 1665. By the time quarantines are established, schools closed, and public events banned, it's too late to prevent the worst. There is flight, uncertainty, panic, and lots of hoarding. Grocery shopping is perilous — careful vendors make sure never to touch their customers and keep jars of vinegar on hand to sanitize coins. Quack doctors peddle toxic "cures" and citizens obsess over mortality statistics. Everyone is constantly terrified and also somehow really bored.

And then there is the famous ending:

A dreadful plague in London was
In the year sixty-five,
Which swept an hundred thousand souls
Away; yet I alive!

I suspect that this is the true appeal of plague literature: the narrator always survives to tell the story. The glimpses of the present that we find in Defoe or Camus or Manzoni have a kind of talismanic effect, somewhere between a mirror and a security blanket. The more similarities we find — and judging by the current spate of writing about plague literature, there are always a great deal of "striking parallels" — the easier it is to tell ourselves that things will play out the same way. This, too, shall pass. My copy of the *Journal* is only 192 pages long and at the end of it the outbreak is over.

There is nothing wrong with seeking this kind of comfort, but it does make me wonder: what is hiding behind the reassuring promise of human universals? If you read a lot of plague novels, you will notice that they tend to hit similar beats. The threat is dismissed, things get worse, quarantines are imposed, city-dwellers flee, the rule of law breaks down, we learn a very valuable lesson about man's inhumanity to man and emerge on the other side not unscathed but wiser. Another advantage of fiction over reality is that everything occurs for a reason. Epidemics create a natural backdrop for extreme heroism or extreme selfishness. The disease itself, an inhuman killer that turns fellow-survivors into existential threats, naturally lends itself to allegorical interpretation. Plague is a divine punishment (Defoe) or a parable for totalitarianism (Camus). If we expand the genre a little, it is the inevitability of mortality (Edgar Allen Poe), a device to pare civilization down to stark moral binaries (Stephen King), or whatever it is Thomas Mann is doing in *The Magic Mountain* — it is anything at all, that is, except a real disease. By treating fiction as a window into the past, we substitute a particular author's attempt to make meaning out of meaninglessness for the full, complicated, messy range of responses which every outbreak has inspired.

A Journal of the Plague Year is a particularly strong object lesson in the creative and purposeful appropriation of history. Defoe was five years old in 1665, too young to remember the epidemic in much detail. He wrote the book almost sixty years later, in response to an outbreak of the plague in Marseilles. Then as now, it was a good time for plague writing: 50,000 of the city's 90,000 inhabitants had perished, and fears were high that the disease would cross the channel. Parliament issued new quarantine laws. Public fasts were proclaimed. The book was an instant success. Defoe paints a truly apocalyptic picture of London in the grip of the worst outbreak in its history: mass hysteria, corpses rotting in the streets, infants smuggled out of infected houses by desperate parents, the agonized screams of the dying in an unnaturally quiet city. Above it all, there is the omnipresent fear that an incidental touch or stray breath from a seemingly healthy person could spread the contagion.

Critics have spent the better part of the past three hundred years debating just how accurate this portrait really is. Defoe liked to mix fact and fiction. Just four years earlier, he had published *Robinson Crusoe* as an authentic travelogue (it sold thousands of copies). The *Journal* also purports to be a factual account, "written by a Citizen who Continued All the While in London." When the book was published in 1722, the great plague was still within living memory, and Defoe's account rang true enough that his contemporaries largely accepted it as fact. His pseudonymous narrator, H.F., freely cites real mortality statistics, veiled or overt references to historical figures, and anecdotes found in genuine accounts of the plague year. Few scholars would go as far as his most peevish defender, Watson Nicholson, who asserted in 1919 that "there is not one single statement in the Journal, pertinent to the history of the Great Plague in London, that has not been verified" — but there is no denying that Defoe did his research.

At the same time, Defoe's concerns in the novel have at least as much to do with the present as the past. In the first place, horror sells. Defoe, who ghost-wrote the memoirs of a notorious thief to sell at his execution, was well aware of the commercial value of ghoulishness. He also had definite opinions about public health legislation. Defoe was a vocal advocate of the government's new and highly unpopular maritime quarantine laws, which included an embargo on trade with plague-stricken countries. In the *Journal*, he portrays the similar restrictions put in place in 1665 as necessary life-saving measures. True, he acknowledges, they are costly and inconvenient — but that hardly seems relevant in the face of his catastrophic account of the alternative.

While in favor of maritime quarantine, Defoe was one of a growing number of critics in the seventeenth and early eighteenth centuries who opposed the practice of imprisoning whole families in their homes at the first sign of infection. Some of the book's most bone-chilling anecdotes are devoted to this "cruel and Unchristian" practice, which increased death tolls, he argued, by shutting up the healthy with the sick, and was in any case ineffective, since the plague was most contagious before its symptoms were evident. (Notably, household quarantine was not one of the provisions adopted in the controversial Quarantine Act of 1721. Here, too, H.F.'s recommendations for containing the disease support the tottering Whig government.)

Defoe's account of London in 1665 reflects the particular political conditions of London in 1722, but it also draws on a much older tradition of English Protestant plague writing.

By 1665, plague was a very familiar occurrence. "It was a Received Notion amongst the Common People that the Plague visited England once in Twenty Years, as if after a certain Interval, by some inevitable Necessity it must return again," wrote Nathaniel Hodges, one of the few physicians to remain in London during the Great Plague. In fact, its recurrences were even more frequent: an elderly Londoner in 1665 would have witnessed seven plague outbreaks in his or her lifetime, and only one interval of more than two decades without a visitation.

The plague inspired unequaled terror, accompanied by intense religious fervor. Since it was universally accepted that the disease was a manifestation of divine vengeance, plagues made for powerful rhetorical tools in sectarian disputes. Under Queen Mary, plague was the consequence of Protestantism; when Queen Elizabeth restored the Anglican church, it was blamed on Catholics. Nonconformists were especially well-placed to take advantage of the revivals which nearly always accompanied outbreaks. Thomas Vincent, a Puritan minister who continued to preach in London through the worst months of 1665, noted that his sermons had never been so well-attended: "If you ever saw a drowning man catch at a rope, you may guess how eagerly many people did catch at the Word, when they were ready to be overwhelmed." It didn't hurt that Puritanism stressed emotional piety with an emphasis on sin, punishment, and predestination — all popular themes during outbreaks of a horrific disease that seemed to strike at the virtuous and the wicked indiscriminately.

For Anglican and Nonconformist ministers alike, the plague was an opportunity to frighten a very receptive audience back into God's good graces. Their grotesque eyewitness accounts and graphic descriptions of the suffering of plague victims warned readers of the consequences if they failed to repent. Defoe was raised a Calvinist and once intended to pursue a career as a minister. His stock of metaphors, anecdotes, and moral tales recalls the preachers and pamphleteers of earlier outbreaks. Like them, the *Journal* features lengthy excurses on the plight of the poor, the corruption and hypocrisy of the court, the benefits of piety and charity, and the grisly details of what a bubo really looks like up close. Defoe waxes especially poetic on the stench they emit while being lanced.

The authors of these materials were quite willing to exaggerate certain details in the interest of leading their readers to religion. In reality, the Great Plague subsided gradually, with deaths returning to pre-plague levels by February 1666. Defoe, in one of his few outright falsehoods, has the plague end abruptly: "In the middle of their distress, when the condition of the city of London was so truly calamitous, just then it pleased God ... to disarm this enemy." This sudden reprieve cannot be attributed to medicine, public health, or anything but "the secret invisible hand of Him that had at first sent this disease as a judgement upon us." This is where Defoe drops the pretense that he is writing a history book. His words are a warning to the reader: beware. Quarantine laws are all to the good, but if you do not repent, nothing on earth can save you.

The Great Plague provoked just as much apocalyptic preaching as any other outbreak, but intense religiosity was not the only or even the dominant response. Indeed, the biggest difference between Defoe's *Journal* and the diaries of actual plague survivors is how much less the plague features in them. When we consider the scope of the disaster — 100,000 dead, large-scale quarantines, the total cessation of public life — it is hard to imagine how anyone who lived through it could think about anything else. Remarkably, they could and they did. "It is true we have gone through great melancholy because of the great plague" wrote Samuel Pepys, the least inhibited diarist in seventeenth-century England, but "I have never lived so merrily (besides that I never got so much) as I have done this plague time."

The *Journal* picks up in September 1664, with the first rumors of an attack of the plague in Holland. Pepys doesn't mention the plague at all until the end of April 1665, and then drops the subject entirely for another month. By summer, the traditional peak of the plague season, the epidemic had grown impossible to ignore. John Evelyn, another diarist, first brings up the plague in his entry for July 16: "There died of the plague in London this week 1,100; and in the week following, above 2,000. Two houses were shut up in our parish." Both men shared Defoe's interest in mortality statistics. The numbers punctuate Evelyn's diary for the next few months: "Died this week in London, 4,000." "There perished this week 5,000." "Came home, there perishing near 10,000 poor creatures weekly." But between them, life goes on. Evelyn goes about his business as a commissioner for the care of sick and wounded sailors and prisoners of war. (Unsurprisingly, he is very busy.) He pays social calls. His wife gives birth to a daughter. The plague clearly weighed on his mind, but Evelyn treats it matter-of-factly. The disease is frightening, inconvenient, and a nuisance at work, but it is not the end of the world.

Throughout the months of August and September, Pepys manages to fit a regular diet of plague-related anxiety in and around more important topics such as food, sex, and earning large quantities of money. He worked as a naval administrator, and the Anglo-Dutch war provided good opportunities for business. In his diary, Pepys is equally assiduous in recording plague mortality, monetary gains, and the "very many fine journys, entertainments and great company" which he consistently manages to provide for himself. The frequent, intense, and jarring juxtaposition of life and death makes for a bizarre reading experience. In a typical entry, Pepys enjoys a venison pasty with some business associates, complains of a mild cold, spends a pleasant evening with his family, and remarks that fatalities have jumped by almost 2,000, bringing this week's total to 6,000 — though the true number is probably higher.

It's not that Pepys is insensitive to the suffering around him — in fact, he seems keenly aware of it. He records his grief at the deaths of friends and servants, his own fears, the dismal mood in the city. At the same time, he seems to possess a preternatural ability to experience everything fully, from existential dread to a particularly good breakfast. For him, the greatest disaster in living memory is just another part of life. In his entry for September 3, which I can't help but quote at length, Pepys describes his morning toilette: "Up; and put on my coloured silk suit very fine, and my new periwigg, bought a good while since, but durst not wear, because the plague was in Westminster when I bought it; and it is a wonder what will be the fashion after the plague is done, as to periwiggs, for nobody will dare to buy any haire, for fear of the infection, that it had been cut off of the heads of people dead of the plague." What indeed will the plague do to periwiggs? The question is so delightfully specific. Nobody but a fashion-conscious seventeenth-century Londoner could possibly think to ask it. In its concreteness it sticks in my mind more than any given passage in Defoe, or any observation about the universal effects of epidemics. Here the disease is human-scale, an event in a particular place and a particular time, a cause of small vanities as well as mass tragedies.

The specific has more sticking power than the general — which is another reason we look to Defoe. The Great Plague of London seems so familiar to modern readers not because there is some fundamental human response to outbreaks of infectious diseases, but because the reactions it inspired were so different from the medieval outbreaks that came before it. Everything from enforced isolation to widespread fear of infection and attempts to understand the plague's progress were relatively new developments. The practice of quarantine emerged in northern Italian city states in the aftermath of the Black Death, along with systematic methods of state surveillance, recorded death tallies, and dedicated plague hospitals. This apparatus of plague regulation diffused gradually throughout Europe. By the turn of the seventeenth century, England had official mortality statistics and punitive sanctions to enforce home quarantine.

The outbreak of 1665 marked another transition. Rather than an unpredictable act of providence, the plague became a predictable act of providence: while still a manifestation of divine punishment, it was carried out through natural means and could be discussed in detached and objective terms. (This development also began in Italy, but there is no great English-language novel of the plague in sixteenth-century Milan.) The Great Plague was the first outbreak in which the discourse of naturalism prevailed, and medical treatises on plague outnumbered religious ones. This medical literature included recipe books of cures and prophylactics, lengthy volumes on the nature of the disease, and theoretical debates carried out in pamphlets and broadsides. While medical writers all acknowledged God as the "first cause" of the epidemic, they established a clear separation between religious and naturalistic inquiry.

It is tempting for the modern reader, looking back on the past with the benefit of hindsight and germ theory, to treat religious etiologies of plague as a response to a lack of available medical explanations. In fact, early modern Londoners had no shortage of naturalistic causes to choose from. A list by Gideon Harvey, a Dutch-born and Cambridge-educated member of the Royal College of Physicians, includes "great Inundations, Stinks of Rivers, unburied Carcases, Mortality of Cattel, Withering of Trees, Extinction of Plants, an extraordinary multiplication of Froggs, Toads, Mice, Flies, or other Insects and Reptils, a moist and moderate Winter, a warm and moist Spring and Summer, fiery Meteors, as falling Stars, Comets, fiery Pillars, Lightnings, &c. A ready putrefaction of Meats, speedy Moulding of Bread, briefness of the Small Pox and Measles, &c." Other proposed sources of the plague included rotten mutton, imported carpets, and a particular dog in Amsterdam.

William Boghurst, an apothecary who remained in London during the plague, took a cynical view of these lengthy traditional lists: "because they would bee sure to hitt the nayle, they have named all the likely occasions they could think of." Noticing that most of the commonly listed causes related to dirt or rot, he traced the origin of the plague to corrupt particles lurking in the earth. Like many others, his theory combined the two dominant explanatory frameworks for disease in Early Modern Europe. The classical explanation, derived from the Greek physician Galen, connected plagues and other infectious diseases to miasma, or poisonous effusions from rotting organic matter. The more modern contagionist view held that the plague could be transferred invisibly from person to person. Boghurst believed that outbreaks began when miasmas rose from disturbed earth, and quickly spread through contagion. In a similar vein, Harvey wrote that "the Plague is a most Malignant and Contagious Feaver, caused through Pestilential Miasms."

The fear of contagion drove Londoners to measures that even Boghurst considered excessive. He complained of the extreme lengths to which his patients would go to avoid even incidental contact: "for example, what care was taken about letters. Some would sift them in a sieve, some wash them first in water and then dry them at the fire, some air them at the

379

top of a house, or an hedge, or pole, two or three days before they opened them ... some would not receive them but on a long pole." He was right — though he had no way of knowing it — that the plague bacterium does not live for very long on paper. But frightened citizens were eager to implement the mass of medical knowledge suddenly made available to them.

As we have seen, this enthusiasm for information had a statistical bent. The city of London started to publish weekly bills of mortality during the outbreak of 1592. During times of plague, Londoners enthusiastically read, reprinted, and circulated the bills, which they used to track the progress of the disease from parish to parish. In 1662, John Graunt published the first statistical analysis of the data in his *Natural and Political Observations Made upon the Bills of Mortality*. Graunt argued that the number of deaths which the bills attributed to the plague during past outbreaks was inaccurate, and speculated that reporting was less than reliable. When the plague struck again in 1665, many Londoners adopted a similarly critical attitude to the reported death rates, suggesting that some groups (Quakers, the poor) might be undercounted, or that fatalities from other diseases were being reported as plague deaths.

The weekly bills gave rise to one of the weirder genres of English plague publishing: the "Lord Have Mercy" broadside, named for the title which nearly all of them shared. These documents, which were reprinted almost identically in each outbreak, usually included a prayer, a woodcut, some remedies, maybe a poem, and mortality statistics from six or seven previous visitations. Examples from 1665 typically featured data from 1592, 1603, 1625, 1630, 1636, 1637, and the current week. They also included pre-printed headings for the next few weeks or months for the reader to fill in as the epidemic wore on.

For anyone who has checked the numbers, again, just to see if they have changed, it is not hard to imagine what people got out of this practice. But the historical data is harder to interpret. Knowing how many people died in 1636 is not particularly useful in 1665. Why did Londoners want this? And why did they want it again and again in exactly the same form? Of course, this is the central question of plague literature in general. When historians discuss it, they tend to use phrases like "conventional and derivative" or "a vast and repetitive outpouring." It is, famously, boring.

In outbreak after outbreak, plague tracts featured the same assortment of prayers, cures, and exhortations to repent. They also shared the same stories. Some served as cautionary tales: a wealthy man refuses to assist a plague victim and immediately falls ill. Another is struck down after boasting about his own safety. Premature interment is a common theme. One of Defoe's anecdotes concerns a drunk piper who passes out in the streets and is loaded onto a dead-cart, only to wake up just as he is about to be buried. In another variant of the story, he is tossed into a plague pit and terrifies the sexton the next morning by calling out from the grave. In yet another, he is thrown out of a tavern for fear that his dead-sleep will be mistaken for actual death and the whole establishment will be declared infected.

The same tale appears in the memoirs of Sir John Rareseby, a bona fide survivor of the plague of 1665, who certainly believed it to be both true and current. "It was usual for People to drop down in the Streets as they went about their Business," he reports, and it may well have been — but the tale of the drunk piper also appears in plague tracts from 1636 and 1603. Repeated over decades or even centuries, these stories imposed a kind of narrative order on outbreaks. The residents

381

of an infected city knew what to expect when the plague came. They were so familiar with the cultural scripts that they began to see them everywhere.

The extent to which first-person plague narratives draw on earlier accounts makes it difficult to tease out the subjective experience of individual survivors. "To a degree, interpretations and responses to plague were copied and taught, not reinvented and coined afresh whenever plague occurred," the historian Paul Slack has observed. When Samuel Pepys and John Evelyn talk about grass growing in the streets of London in 1665, they are quoting Paul the Deacon a thousand years earlier (whether they know it or not), and nearly everybody is citing Thucydides nearly all of the time. His account of the plague in Athens in 430 B.C. is the source of innumerable plague tropes, from the image of bodies lying unburied in the streets to the moral lesson that the disease brings about the collapse of social order. As with Sir John Raresby, there is no reason to believe that later chroniclers used these commonplaces intentionally to mislead. Expectations have a powerful ability to shape perception. Through them, the disease is tamed, familiarized, and given meaning.

We are among the first human beings for whom the experience of a disease outbreak so severe and wide-ranging is outside of living memory. Our generation has inherited no familiar stock of coronavirus parables; no script that tells us exactly why we are suffering; no sheets of mortality statistics with an empty space left over for next time. Our fascination with plague literature is a sign that some things never change: this desire to tell and retell stories puts us in the company of every other set of survivors in recorded history. The instinct to impart structure and purpose to a fundamentally purposeless crisis might be the only truly universal response to life in a pandemic. That we should feel it so strongly is all the more remarkable in a society as blissfully and unprecedentedly pandemic-free as the developed world was at the beginning of the twenty-first century. But no more: now we have narrative resources of our own, stories of contagion and endurance and recovery, to bequeath to the vulnerable who come after us. When faced with the unimaginable, we did what we have always done: look back.

SHAWN McCREESH

The Hatboro Blues

To the memory of friends

The first thing I remember thinking about what we now call "the opioid crisis" is that it was making everything really boring. It was 2010, I was in eleventh grade and at a house party about which I had been excited all week. I had with me a wingman in the form of my buddy Curt, and a fresh pack of smokes, and — please don't think less of me — 750 milliliters of Absolut blueberry vodka. In short, all that was needed for a good night.

And yet the party was a bust. It seemed that every third kid was "dipped out," as we called those in drug-induced comas, lit cigarettes still dangling from their lips. Even the terrible rap music wasn't enough to wake them. Nobody was fighting, nobody was fornicating, nobody was doing much of anything. There was nothing about this sorry shindig that set it apart from many others just like it which were still to come, but it sticks in my mind now for a melancholy reason: It was the point at which I realized that something was very wrong.

What follows is not some hardcore *Requiem for a Dream* kind of yarn. Different movies apply. My high school experience was plenty *Dazed and Confused,* but with shades of *Trainspotting* and maybe a flash of *Drugstore Cowboy.* It was like *The Breakfast Club,* if Claire had carried Percocet in her purse and the dope in Bender's locker had been white, not green. This is a story about how a kid who enters high school as a Led Zeppelin-loving pothead can leave four years later with a needle sticking out of his arm. (Or not leave at all). It is a tale of a town and a generation held hostage by Purdue pharma — the story of every place on the edge of a big East Coast city flushed with cheap heroin and prescription pills in the mid-to-late aughts. Maybe you already know how it goes.

Fifteen miles north of Philadelphia's City Hall sits Hatboro. It is a majority-white town with an average per capita income of $35,000 per year. A set of train tracks dissecting the town can shoot you into the city in a few minutes and for a couple of bucks. My elementary school, Crooked Billet, was named after a Revolutionary-era battle that took place on its grounds on May 1, 1778. Every year on that day kids don tricorn hats and sing songs about America. The town is part of a larger school district encompassing a neighboring township called Horsham, which gets much wealthier as it creeps closer to Philadelphia's Main

Line. In high school, some kids lived in McMansions and drove new cars, others took the bus. The public schools were good.

I was raised, along with a younger brother and sister, by a single mom who worked as a hairdresser and a waitress. I spent every other weekend with my father, who lived in the next town over and founded a tree and landscaping company and later worked in real estate. We qualified for the free lunch program at school, and some years were tougher than others, but we were not poor and always had everything we needed. One week every summer was spent on vacation in Wildwood, New Jersey. I began my career as a busboy in an Italian restaurant when I was fourteen and kept the job all through high school. Later I became the first person in my family to go to college.

It started off as your regular suburban experience, innocent enough. I smoked my first cigarette on the same day as my first toke of pot, in the last week of eighth grade. The cigarette was a Marlboro Red, provided by a friend's older sister whom everyone thought was hot. (Regrettably, I smoke them to this day). Weekends were spent with my three best friends, guzzling Canadian whisky lifted ever-so-gently from a parent's liquor cabinet and chain-smoking in various parking lots. We were long-haired little gremlins who liked to venture into the city for Warped Tour, Ozzfest, and Marilyn Manson. We loved Cypress Hill and named my friend's $45 bong "King Zulu." We hated the rich fucks (that was our term of art for them) who wouldn't shut up about tie-dying their shirts for the next Dave Matthews concert.

Sandwiched between a scrap-metal yard and the Revolutionary-era battleground turned elementary school were the aforementioned train tracks and a pathetic patch of mud and trees we called "the woods." It was to us what the country club was to that other Pennsylvanian, John O'Hara: a place to get soused and settle scores. A few yards down the tracks lived a homeless Vietnam veteran whom we'd christened "the Bum." He would walk with us to a local bar to buy forty-ounce bottles of beer — usually Olde English or Steel Reserve — in exchange for a couple of bucks. (Bars in Pennsylvania sell beer-to-go, and many of them still allow you to smoke inside.) My best friend at the time was legendary for being able to down an entire forty in under sixty seconds. We played a clever game called "Edward Fortyhands," in homage to the Tim Burton movie, in which a forty-ounce bottle would be duct-taped to each hand and use of both your mitts would not be regained until the bottles were emptied. A guy named James at the local Hess gas station would sell us cigarettes underage and one woman who operated the McDonald's drive-thru traded Newports for dollar-menu items. The world was our malt liquor-soaked oyster.

Another hangout was a place we called "Chronic Bay." (We were heavily into Dr. Dre's "The Chronic" back then.) It was a pond-sized storm drainage ditch located behind a sewage processing plant and an abandoned Sam's Club that was shielded from view by a tree line. It smelled, literally, like shit, but it was the perfect place to smoke weed and drink fortys undetected. Our soundtrack at the time included lots of Sublime, Biggie Smalls, and some tragically awful emo albums. Most of my friends were skaters who loved to watch "Baker 3" on repeat. Those were the carefree days when everything felt like a party, the days before pregnancies and overdoses. Nobody was dying, or making their mom sad, or falling asleep behind the wheel, or stealing from their grandparents, or going to jail.

People used to talk a lot about pot as a "gateway drug," but I think about what came next in terms of floodgate drugs: the floodgates of an over-prescribed society opened, and suddenly drugs were everywhere. Some people would learn where or how to draw the line, but others could not see it; and crossing it became a death sentence. After booze and weed we all started to play around with prescription pills in a way that was always getting ratcheted up. It started light, with Klonopin ("K-pins"), and then Xanax.

The first time I took Xanax was in a McDonald's parking lot. I took both of the two milligram "bars" my friend Sam plopped in my hand, felt pretty damn loose, and then my memory disappeared.

Most of my friends liked to eat pills, some more than others. In the first month of eleventh grade, in 2009, a black comedy called *Jennifer's Body* starring a salacious Megan Fox as a demonic succubus, came out in theaters. A friend named Becky piled us into her Honda Accord for a trip to the movies. Most kids sneak candy or soda into the movie theater. Our clandestine appetites were different. We popped Klonopin and smuggled into the theater a backpack stocked with "Four Loko," the fruity malt liquor concoction that contained so much caffeine that its manufacturer was later forced by the FDA to tweak its recipe, because people were dropping dead after drinking it. Why would anyone pay money to see a movie in this state? Most of us were passed out before the credits rolled. But that's just how we rolled. Everything seemed like an occasion to get "fucked up," even standardized testing. Before the PSATS, Sam ate so many Xanax "bars" that halfway through the test he dropped his sharpened number 2 pencil and told the proctor that if she didn't let him out of the classroom he was going to vomit all over her. (She let him out.)

Sharon was a year older than me and lived in the neighborhood. The year her mother was sent to jail, Sharon's house became our free-for-all party pad and experimentation fort. Sharon's scratchy baritone made for the perfect imitation mom-voice, so she could supply an alibi to any anxious parent inquiring about their child's whereabouts. It always worked, including on my own mother. One night at Sharon's we couldn't get our paws on any preferred substances, and so Collin, our friend with the stickiest fingers, had a brainstorm: He would go to the home of a girl he was seeing and raid her parent's medicine cabinet. After he came back with a bottle of what we thought was pharmaceutical-grade sleeping medication, we decided to divvy up the bottle, pop all the pills at once, wash them down with fortys, and have a contest to see who could stay awake the longest. Fingers were crossed that we would be rewarded with hallucinations. But things went awry and it was only later, after consulting our handy-dandy Pillfinder ("Worried about some capsules found in your teenager's room? Not sure about those leftover pills still in the bathroom cabinet? There's a good chance that our Pill Identification Wizard (Pill Finder) can help you match the imprint, size, shape, or color and lead you to the detailed description in our drug database") that we realized the Seroquel we had ingested was not knock-off Ambien but an antipsychotic medication used to treat schizophrenia. Oh well.

Meanwhile, all the regular stuff associated with teenage development continued apace. I had some bad haircuts, kept decent grades, and rarely missed a day of work at the restaurant. (There was that one time, when Collin, Sam, and I each ate an eighth of magic mushrooms at midnight, went out to play in a state-of-emergency blizzard, and I missed a brunch shift the next morning. Otherwise I was a model employee and my bosses loved me.) I was the same bookish kid I had always been, devouring every *Harry Potter* and *Lord of the Rings* book in the library. I shared a room with my little brother. I hung a *Pulp Fiction* poster on my wall and bought CDs at the mall. I lost my virginity. I got my permit and then my license. My father bought me a 1999 Nissan Maxima with 190,000 miles on it for $2,000 and taught me how to drive a stick shift.

Wheels meant freedom and access — to fine things, like trips to the shore, but to trouble, too. Now that our group was mobile, all my friends suddenly became two-bit drug dealers. Usually they had only an ounce or less of pot to peddle, but sometimes more. I held a pound of weed for the first time when a friend asked me to drive to nearby Norristown to pick it up and stash it in the trunk of my car. (Incentive: "I'll fill your gas tank and smoke you up on the way.") Most days after school my Maxima was transformed into a roving dispensary of marijuana and other delights. One night I decided to vacuum the thing and install some new air fresheners. Miraculously, the next day the school announced a surprise search of the grounds by the police and their drug-sniffing dogs. Midway through science class a principal knocked on the door and beckoned for me. The whole classroom shifted to watch as I traipsed out, fate unknown. We walked down the hall in silence and approached the exit to the parking lot, where a sortie of my buddies — who didn't know I had just wiped "the whip," as we called the car — had congregated with looks of abject terror on their faces to watch the pooches encircle my lemony-scented ride. Even though it had been cleaned, the dogs couldn't help but stop on their adventure through the school's parking lot. You can imagine the dismay of the principal and the officers upon finding nothing harder than a

390

pack of cigarettes and some "Rohto Arctic" eye drops inside. As I say, a miracle.

One friend, high on something or other, crashed his car through a storefront on the town's Main Street. Later, after a new facade was constructed, we joked that he had merely given the place a free facelift. (No one was seriously injured.) Another time I was cruising around with my friend Ethan when a drug dealer named Pete got in touch. For reasons that now seem inexplicable, we thought Pete was cool and that his imprimatur meant something. At the time he was dating Diana, a beautiful brunette and a real Calamity Jane who had flitted in and out of our crew since the early days of eighth-grade summer, when she would never turn up any place without a Gatorade bottle full of vodka and a pack of Newport 100s. So when she dialed me up to say that Pete had an $800 bag of cocaine from which a modest profit could be made, and did I want to move it for him, I had to take a minute to think about it. Ethan and I both looked at each other and blithely shrugged, but my gut told me it was maybe a bad idea to become a coke dealer. Besides, I had a job already, a real one. I said I was honored but politely declined and hung up the phone.

Then Ethan's cell started to ring — it was Diana. He said yes, dropped out of school the next week, and started selling the pile of white powder, gram by gram. This posed two problems for the rest of us: We liked coke and we had no self-control. By the time the weekend rolled around, half the bag had disappeared up our little noses. Even worse, Ethan's mother found the rest under his bed, freaked out and flushed it. We dodged Pete for as long as possible, and then he turned up on Ethan's front lawn with a couple goons and baseball bats. Poor Ethan's parents were left with no choice but to call the cops. Pete eventually backed off, but Ethan's credit around town was pretty low afterward and there were more than a few parties to which we couldn't bring him.

Drugs beget drugs and things begin to blur. The halcyon days of fat blunts and warm beer in the woods were firmly in the rearview. Movie shorthand again: if the ninth and tenth grades were *Fast Times at Ridgemont High*, junior and senior year were more like *Valley of the Dolls*, all the Spicolis turned to fiendish Neely O'Hara's. And it was not just my raggedy clique that was gobbling pills like Pac Man. The vicissitudes of the Lacrosse team and the Richie Rich kids from up the way seemed to mirror our own. Next came Percocet, an opiate, and therefore in the same drug family as heroin. "Perc 10s" and blueish "Perc 30s" could be crushed up and snorted. Luckily for me, I disliked the way Percocet made me feel. I didn't enjoy the stomach pains, the itches, the bouts of narcolepsy — or the feeling that I was an actual drug user as opposed to a dumb kid having fun.

When you are a teenager, it is of course easy to make bad choices, because you feel invincible. Maybe the worst decision one could make in pilltown was to try OxyContin. You can have fun, as we all did, with Klonopin, coke, Xanax, Percocet, Ecstasy, and tabs of acid, but there is usually no coming back from OxyContin. A seventeen-year-old doesn't stand a chance. Adults who are prescribed it for legitimate reasons barely stand a chance. Oxycontin's not a drug that one can "dabble" in. It is synthetic heroin in pill form manufactured by a gigantic pharmaceutical corporation, and in Hatboro it wasn't hard to find 40 milligram doses of it — "OC 40s" for short, or the double dosage "OC 80s." Ingested orally, Oxycontin is meant to mete out pain relief over a number of hours, but the "extended release" could be circumvented for an instantaneous high by crushing and then snorting the pills.

In 2010, when I was in eleventh grade, Purdue Pharma tweaked its production so that the pills could no longer be crushed. It was like trying to plug a sinkhole with a wine cork. (Studies would later argue that this tweak only pushed people more quickly to heroin.) By then we all knew someone who was a full blown "jawn head," as we called those addicted to OC's. Maybe it was the kid next to you in homeroom who stopped showing up to school. Maybe it was a friend from the grade above. Maybe it was an older sibling. There was a stupid rap song called "OxyCotton" extolling the joys of OC's and it became a kind of unofficial anthem of my high school, Hatboro-Horsham High School, now nicknamed "Heroin High." The song was a menacing joint by an otherwise obscure rapper named Lil Wyte. One verse, rapped by Lord Infamous, went like this:

Scarecrow, scarecrow what's that you're popping
A powerful pill they call Oxycontin
But it's so tiny and it catch you dragging
Haven't you heard big things come in small packages
I prefer the oranges with the black OC
Take two and you cannot move up out your seat
Some people melt 'em down in a needle and shoot 'em up
But I pop 'em with Seroquel like glue, I am stuck

This was hardly just a street drug, though. With so many people's parents being over-prescribed opiates, nabbing pills out of a medicine cabinet became my generation's version of raiding the liquor cabinet. In this way one of my earliest friends, Danny, got hooked. He lived two streets over and was in the grade above me. We'd known each other since we were in diapers. "In the beginning it was fun, there's no two ways about it," he now recalls. "If it wasn't fun, we wouldn't have done it. I don't know if that was the only way we knew how to have fun or if we just took it to another level. Kids in different parts of the country will drink and party and take it to a certain level and there's nothing else readily available so it fizzles out. Around here, it's like you partied and then you met older kids and the older kids were doing this, and then, somehow — peer pressure, wanting to fit in and be cool — you somehow got into that." The way he said it, "somehow" was another word for inevitably.

I never touched the stuff, not because I was smarter than anyone else, I was just more of a wimp. I was already trepidatious owing to some unpleasant experiences with Percocet, and OxyContin seemed genuinely frightening. By now the kind of havoc that the drug could unleash was everywhere apparent, and snuffing the fun out of house parties was just the start. An older brother type with whom I had worked at the restaurant since the day I was hired was no longer funny, smart, or cool: He was a confirmed and abject jawn head, a zombie. It was heartbreaking to watch someone's personality dim and die before he was even old enough to vote. You had to look out for your own, and my best buddies and I made a pact that, no matter how far we pushed our partying, we would stay away from OC's. Still, everything was being warped around us. Even our mood music morphed from metal, grunge, and 90's hip hop into the real hood stuff coming out of North Philly at the time, mix tapes about "trapping" and being "on the block" and pushing drugs 365 24/7 rain or shine. I hate to sound like Tipper Gore, but I believe that the music, if it did not directly influence us, at least reflected the spiraling and trashy subculture of an ostensibly nice town littered with drug baggies.

Hatboro is just across the city line and a thirty-minute drive from the open air drug markets of North Philly, known as "the badlands." That is where all the heroin comes from once it is pulled from the docks and flooded through the streets. OxyContin is expensive, but a $10 "stamp bag" of heroin does the trick just as well. And so before long, in a kind of irreversible entailment, all the jawn heads devolved into dope heads, actual heroin addicts. Ground zero for dope was — and still is — an intersection called "K & A," where Kensington and Allegheny Avenues meet in the Kensington neighborhood. The streets that spiderweb out from that junction are an addict's bazaar, a warren of narrow blocks in which dealers sit on porches shouting out their merchandise to passersby. You don't even have to know someone to collect. When cops roll down the block, the dealers simply retreat back inside. This is the hellish district in which suburban mothers go looking for their heroin-addicted children, bringing them peanut butter and jelly sandwiches or a new coat if they can't coax them to come home. Half the kids on those streets are from towns just like mine.

I started hanging out in the city more when Becky — she who had driven us to the movies to see *Jennifer's Body* — began dating Matt. He was a year older, out of school, and living in a one-bedroom apartment on Rising Sun Avenue, about a fifteen-minute drive from the open air drug markets. Now drugs were more attainable than ever. A new cast of shady characters floated into our orbit and the old ones just got shadier. One night at Matt's I pawned some of the Xbox 360 games I had received for Christmas to purchase a bag of ecstasy pills that turned out to be cut with methamphetamines. The

395

red pills emblazoned with stars and the green ones imprinted with palm trees kept me, Sam, and Collin up all night — Sam vomited every hour on the hour and we pondered bringing him to the emergency room — and sent us into horrible withdrawal the next morning. It was the worst I had ever felt in all my short life. The kid who sold us the dirty E-pills, also named Matt, had his newborn baby with him that night. I can still remember Matt fishing for a Newport in his pocket while handing me his baby and saying "Here, you look like you're good with kids." That Matt is dead now. When I bumped into the baby's mother at a bar last year, we didn't even bother mentioning that fact. It was the order of things. The other Matt became an addict and a father and then, last I heard, got clean. Becky has two rugrats herself and just sent out wedding invitations.

Until then, the city had always loomed large in our suburban imaginations as the place where we would spend the best nights of our lives. We used to head into the city to see our favorite bands at the Electric Factory or the Theater of the Living Arts on South Street. It was where the best cheesesteaks were, and the Italian market, and the Flyers and Melrose Diner. It was the home of magic. But then going to "the city" meant dipping into a dangerous neighborhood for drugs — a different kind of home for a different kind of magic. We were slowly being blasted. It was on another night at Matt's when my own sense of invincibility was finally shattered. After polishing off a bottle of vodka we took a drive to K & A for some more provisions. I parked the car while Matt walked up the block. He came back empty handed, but with two cops in tow. They pulled up next to my Maxima, yanked us out, slapped handcuffs on our wrists, and searched my car. There was nothing to find, but one cop grabbed my red Verizon enV3 flip phone, turned to me and asked, "Who am I calling, Mom or Dad?" I thought for a second and then gulped, "Dad."

The cop left a voicemail on my father's phone, gripped me up and spat, "Now go back to the suburbs and stick to smoking your fucking grass, white boy." When I got home, my father was nothing but rage. He yelled so loud I can still remember the foundations of the house shaking. I try to imagine what the voicemail said: "Hey, we've got your loser son down here trying to buy narcotics in a neighborhood where people are shot in broad daylight. Where did you think he was, the mall?" When I reflect on that episode now, what is most shocking to me is the blatant and incontrovertible white privilege. Here we were, teenagers drinking and driving and looking for drugs, a menace to ourselves and to anyone who might encounter us, and my interaction with the police amounted not to a rap sheet or a bullet but parental concern and an actual slap on the wrist.

For me, the alarm had sounded. What on earth was I doing in North Philly or with people like Matt? I really harbored no desire to destroy myself. I really was hungry for life. Despair was never my affliction, so why was I acting as if it was? And so I stopped going to the city and cut out everything except pot and booze — a renunciation which, given the habits of most of my friends, was practically monastic. The fact that I had been scared straightish did not mean that anyone else was. The opposite was the case. Things were getting worse. Rehab stints to the local clinic, court mandated or otherwise, became a rite of passage for hard partiers. This meant that Suboxone, a drug just as powerful as heroin that is used to wean one off it, entered an already bleak picture. One day after school I watched as Ethan and Curt split one tiny Suboxone pill, letting it overpower them to the point that they could barely walk or keep from vomiting. Hard drugs were no longer the realm of upperclassmen, either. When Curt's parents went out of town, we threw a party at his place and were deeply unsettled to discover a fifteen-year-old freshman girl snorting lines of heroin in the upstairs bathroom. We were the moralists! It was an odd sensation for us to be clutching our pearls at the ripe old age of eighteen, but that episode shocked even us.

My story is coming to its end. In the years after I graduated, the bill for a class of kids hooked on heroin came due. One of the first people with whom we ever smoked weed in eighth grade overdosed and died. So did the kid who used to sell it to us. Two of the most beloved girls in town, lifelong friends who grew up on the same block as each other, both overdosed and died. Danny overdosed a number of times, he was even found turning purple on the floor of a Rite Aid bathroom once, and against all odds he is now sober. (To this day his mother carries two forms of Narcan in her purse because you never know.) Diana, who was dating the drug dealer Pete, descended further into addiction, stole from friends, and fell off the map altogether. One day last year I received a frantic Facebook message from her mother, who was reaching out to Diana's old school friends for any clues as to her whereabouts. She finally turned up a few months ago newly sober, and posted a long status on Facebook about how, at her lowest, she had picked up a meth addiction, weighed less than ninety pounds, and was hearing voices. Her ex-boyfriend Pete lost his little brother to dope. The list of the lost goes on. And not only of the young. Some of the parents were just addicted as their children. My mom's ex-boyfriend, who was like a stepfather to me during the years when I was in middle school, became an addict and is now dead. The man she dated when I was in eleventh grade ended up addicted to opiates. As for any judgment about the quality of anyone's parenting: I have come to believe that no level of awareness about the danger could have prevented it. You can keep a close eye on your child, but when drugs are ubiquitous, when they are a central feature of social life, when the surrounding culture confers prestige upon them, the best you can do is cross your fingers and pray.

A whole vocabulary has sprung up to convey the shared experience of addiction, a vernacular of the carnage. When I go home and visit with old friends, there is always a grim roll call conducted over beers. "When was the last time anyone heard from her?" "Oh, I heard she's still really bad." There is a lot of sorrowful shaking of heads. Another one I've heard often and with nonchalance: "So, guess who's a dopehead nowadays?" Social media has become a surreal forum for this conversation, too. Facebook newsfeeds are so peppered with remembrances and R.I.P posts that you might not even pause while scrolling past one. Many of them include poorly cropped angel wings or some variant of "Heaven just gained another angel," a phrase so anodyne and overused I consider it Hatboro's version of a Hallmark card. These were the clichés of social destruction. In the years since I graduated, heroin has been largely edged out by fentanyl, a synthetic opioid that is much easier to overdose on than your garden-variety dope. Meth, which was never around in my picaresque youth, has found a big market in the suburbs, too.

The crisis is in your face everywhere you go. It is the driver next to you at a stoplight falling asleep at the wheel. It is the dopehead in line in front of you at the 7-Eleven or the grieving mother of one of your school chums standing behind you.

The Hatboro Blues

Who should we turn to? God, perhaps; but look at His record. The government, perhaps; but look at its record.

To confront the addiction of the despairing produces its own variety of despair. Along with some of my closest friends from back then, I marvel that we made it out when so many of our comrades did not. Melancholy permeates my town. And it is never really over. One of those friends recently became a cause for concern among our circle after he was fired for dipping out at work, just the way we did at house parties in eleventh grade. He is not returning anyone's calls, and word is that he has stopped paying some of his debts. It beggars belief: opiates *now*, after everything we remember? But we are too sober to delude ourselves about what is possible in our town, and in other towns. We have seen this movie before.

LEON WIESELTIER

Steadying

For some time now it has felt like history is itself the pandemic. In our country and elsewhere, it has been in overdrive, teeming with evils, flush with collapses, abounding in fear and rage, a wounding contest between the sense of an ending and the sense of a beginning, between inertia and momentum, with all the terribilities of ages of transition. What is going has not yet gone and what is coming has not yet come. We have become connoisseurs of convulsion. At sea is our new sea.

For better and for worse, axioms and assumptions are dying everywhere around us. Such vertiginous hours always come with both clarities and confusions — there is no promise of illumination. The guidance we need in our circumstances will not be provided by the circumstances themselves: they are too many and too contradictory and too volatile; passion increasingly unconstrained and power increasingly unconstrained. As the sense of injustice grows, injustice seems to keep pace with it. There is a piercing sensation of flux, of uncontrollable effects and unmanageable consequences. The masks on our faces are emblems of an entire era of vulnerability. The most important thing, therefore, is that we keep our heads. A disequilibrium of history demands an equilibrium of mind. Steadiness in the midst of turbulence is not complicity with the existing order. "History marches more quickly than the healing of our wounds," wrote Vladimir Jankelevitch; and it is precisely in such binges of history that we must teach ourselves to sort through the true and the false, the good and the bad, the continuities and the discontinuities, the right statues and the wrong statues, the humane and the utopian.

Everything will be different: this is a ubiquitous sentiment. In all our upheavals — social and epidemiological — so much seems to be wrong and so much seems to be slipping away that one may be forgiven for enjoying a fantasy of total change. All these horrors, all these outrages, all these marches, and the world stays the same? So the first thing that needs to be said in the effort to keep our heads is that everything never changes. More, the idea that everything will change usually plays into the hands of those who want nothing to change. The cycle of revolution and reaction has never been the most effective engine of progress. Nothing suits the interests of the old regime like utopianism. The thirst for change will not be slaked by the cheap whiskey of apocalyptic thinking. The only certain outcome of the apocalyptic temper is catharsis, and one way of describing the decline of our politics in recent decades is that it has increasingly become a politics of catharsis, in which crisis is met mainly by emotion. (Populism is just mass emotionalism, and the emotions are often ugly ones.) Apocalypse is not an analysis, it is the death of analysis. It sets the stage only for salvation, but salvation must never become a political goal. This is especially true in a democratic society, where the only saviors are, alas, ourselves.

Thus it is that the struggle against injustice imposes upon us a paradoxical psychology: it demands both impatience and patience. Impatience about injustice, patience about justice. This is hard to do. It looks too much like, and in many cases it may well be, complacence. It is certainly difficult to preach incrementalism to the injured. So why not be impatient about justice, too? There are historical and practical reasons why not. History is stained by tales of instantaneous justice, by the consequences of the rush to perfection, by the victims of the victims. The ethical calculus of means and ends is never teleologically suspended, if just causes are to remain just. Nor is it a quantitative calculus: when I first studied the modern history of the Jews I drew a variety of conclusions from the Dreyfus affair, and one of them, which was an important moment in my moral education, was that Zola and his comrades appropriately threw an entire country into crisis for the sake of *one man*. Similarly, due process is not a legal formality, a procedural exercise that slows the way to a satisfying climax; it is the very honor of a liberal society.

More concretely, the establishment of justice involves not only revisions in opinions but also revisions in institutions. A dreary point! But anyone who denies the institutional dimension, in all its exasperating machinery, is not serious about the change. Paroxysms, unlike laws, vanish. This was the year in which the campaign for racial justice found support in virtually all the sectors of American society, with the exception of the White House — an unprecedented national epiphany that cannot be dismissed as "performative," because culture matters; but the road from protest to policy is long and winding. It is not a betrayal of the ideal of social justice to tread carefully and tenaciously, with a mastery of the scruples and the methods that would make a reform defensible and durable. Tenacity is what patience looks like in the middle of a struggle.

I will give an example of the complicated nature of the mentality of change. One of the consequences of recent social movements in America — #MeToo (which came also to my door, with its lesson and its excess) and Black Lives Matter — has been to reveal how poorly we understand each other. Or more precisely, they have exposed the extent to which the failure to understand others may be owed to the failure to understand oneself — the limitations of one's own standpoint, the comfortable assumption that one appears to others as one wishes to appear to them, or to oneself. This is nonsense, though sometimes you learn so the hard way. There are limits to our epistemological jurisdiction. The failure to observe these limits is solipsism, and we all begin as solipsists, awaiting correction by social experience.

Our epistemological jurisdiction stops at the encounter with another person. She is another epistemological kingdom, not more perfect but certainly different, with something important to add, and a perceptual contribution to make. I may like to think that I am what I present myself to be, but I am also what she sees me to be, because she sees me as I cannot, or will not, see myself. I am never in control of my self-representation and never complete in my self-awareness. We always show more of ourselves than we think we do, which is why we may learn from the responses of others. We spill beyond our intentions and our conceits, and what we gain from this overflow is criticism.

But criticism, too, must be assessed critically — there is no exemption. The enlightenment that one acquires from the judgments of others is owed only to their accuracy. It is certainly not warranted by the belief that a person's identity or socio-economic position or experience of hardship confers an absolute authority, a special relationship to truth, a vatic privilege. What a simple world it would be if pain were a sufficient guarantee of credibility. But it is not — indeed, the opposite is the case, pain is myopic and sees chiefly itself, which is one of the reasons it hurts. Finally we are all left with the modesty of our grasp. No whole classes of people are right and no whole classes of people are wrong.

The ineradicability of ambiguity from human relations, the ignorance of ourselves that accompanies our ignorance of others, the whole fallible heap, creates an urgent need for tolerance and, more strenuously, for forgiveness. Historians will record that in the early decades of the twenty-first century we became an unforgiving society, a society of furies, a society in search of guilt and shame, a society of sanctimonies and "struggle sessions" American-style. They will admire our awakening to prejudice but lament the sometimes prejudicial ways in which we acted on our progressive realizations. In this regard, America should become more Christian. (There, I said it.) For all our elaborate culture of self-knowledge, for all the hectoring articulateness of our identity vocabularies, we are still, each of us, our own blind spots. We should welcome every person we meet as a small blow against blindness.

The partiality of perspective: this is the great teaching of the contemporary tumult. The problem is that we have not only begun to acknowledge our partiality, and the partiality of others, we have also begun to revere it, and this is a mistake. If pain does not provide access to truth, neither does particularity. The worship of particularism is one of the great impediments to social justice, and in its exhilarating way it coarsens us all. In our moral and social thinking, our obsession with otherness has concealed that the foundation of moral and social action is sameness. The "other" is exotic, but there is nothing exotic about the homeless man on the street: he is the same as me, a human being, except that he is hungry and I am not. The difference in our circumstances is not a difference in our definition. When I hand him a few dollars I am not extending myself toward an alien being; I am practicing species solidarity. I am not discovering his humanity; I am responding to it. I am acting, in other words, universally, and none of the social problems that afflict us will be solved unless we recover the universalist standpoint that sees beyond the visible divisions, and is not trapped in, or enraptured by, the specificities of our tribes. Pluralism secures the right to turn inward, but it also broaches the duty to turn outward. By surrounding us with other partialities it legitimates our own partiality, but it also reveals that there is more to the world than what is merely ours.

A great deal has been written in recent years about the discovery of our commonplace biases and the techniques for overcoming them. Much of this literature is psychological, but some of it is political, and its aim is to confine us proudly within our limits and call them wonderful. In the name of authenticity, we are instructed that the partiality of our perspective is all we will ever have, and that the aspiration to impartiality is an aspiration to power, or a justification of power. Every view is a view from somewhere. Nobody escapes his or her position. We are all marooned in our respective glories. Objectivity, according to this advanced opinion, is an epistemological plot of the elites.

This inculcates a kind of localist arrogance that is fully the match of the globalist kind. Such "perspectivism" was one of Nietzsche's lasting provocations, and in American philosophy it was ringingly championed by Richard Rorty, who was the only man I have ever known to use the word "ethnocentrism" positively. He denounced objectivity in favor of solidarity, and his children are everywhere, in all the movements; and a similar war on truth flourishes, for less sophisticated reasons, also in the offices of prime ministers and presidents. The outlook for intelligence, as Paul Valery used to say in an earlier era of confusion and peril, is not heartening. Truth in America is a refugee, an undocumented immigrant. Philosophers and political operatives have joined together to proclaim the fictive nature of fact. About this there is no "polarization." It is not only policy over which we differ: we differ also over the description of reality. (And even if science is not all we need to know, is there any plainer measure of stupidity than the mockery of science?)

All these communitarianisms of the mind are absurd. If all one can express with one's beliefs is solidarity with one's community, then how is it possible to disagree with one's community, and what is the origin of dissent? If it is impossible for people of different backgrounds, or classes, or races, or genders, to understand each other, why are they disappointed or angry when they are not understood? If people who are white or male or rich cannot claim to comprehend people who are black or female or poor, how can people who are black or female or poor claim to comprehend people who are white or male or rich? Of course the world does not work this way, according to this Empedoclean epistemology, for which like can only know like. The startling reality — it is one of the tremendous features of human existence — is that, within societies and among societies, across nations and cultures, we manage to be intelligible to one another. If you don't *get it*, you *can* get it. As a strategy for thwarting human communication, Babel was a bust.

This everyday mental commerce, this regular passage through these permeable frontiers, sometimes needs the assistance of translation, and always needs the assistance of imagination, but it proves that the inherited perspectives may be enlarged and that the despair of a greater commonality is a self-inflicted wound. Perfect objectivity may never be attained, but that is no excuse to act like merry peasants. "Positional objectivity," as Amartya Sen has described the only plausible mitigation of our parochialism, will get us very far. Moreover, chafing against one's limits is a condition of ethical sensitivity: if I were to be content with what my own life has taught me, I could not recognize sufferings which I have not lived and against which I have a responsibility to act. All that I need to know I cannot learn in my town, even if I can learn a great deal there. We have moral obligations in unfamiliar situations.

I am not a woman and so I must imagine rape. I am not a black man and so I must imagine chokeholds. I am not a Syrian and so I must imagine that charnel house. I am not a Uighur and so I must imagine those camps. (But I am a Jew and so I expect others to extend the same imaginative respect to the fate of my people.) If victims were the only ones who understood oppression, who would help them? Often they insist that they must help themselves, which is correct, and evidence of their irreducible dignity, but there are limits to what they can do, and their "auto-emancipation" does not absolve the rest of us from the work of their emancipation.

This work involves shaking ourselves loose from the mental dullness that is the product of our distance. As Judith Shklar once observed, "it will always be easier to see misfortune rather than injustice in the afflictions of others."

Objectivity, in other words, is the sturdiest ground of justice, and the despisers of objectivity are playing with fire. Feelings are a reedy basis for reform. After all, the other side also has feelings — which is how we wound up with the revolting solipsist in the Oval Office. In a democratic society, reform comes about by means of persuasion, and the feelings of others may not do the trick. I may not feel what you feel. I will not be convinced that you are right by the fervor of your feeling that you are right. I need reasons to agree with you, that is, appeals to principles, to rational accounts of prefer-ences, to terms and values larger than each of us which, unlike feelings, we may share.

Without objectivity, without the practice of detachment that makes genuine deliberation possible, without tearing ourselves away from ourselves, justice in our society will mean only what the majority, or the crowd, or the media (all of them fickle) want it to mean. We will gag on our roots. We will continue to despise each other, some scorning the weak and others scorning the strong. Our system of disagreement will continue to be degraded into a system of umbrage, in which a dissenting opinion may be dismissed as "tone-deaf." Empathy, where it exists, will be remorselessly selective and most often reserved for one's own kind. (Down with himpathy! Up with herpathy!) We will remain stalled in our excitability. But none of the questions that we are asking as a society can be answered with a scream or a scowl.

Some of what I have written here will please progressives. Some of it will please conservatives. I call it liberalism.

"When the facts change, I change my mind. What do you do, sir?" Legend attributes that swaggering pronouncement to Keynes, and it has become the canonical formulation of the anti-dogmatic mentality, the credo of the open and empirical mind. It has always irritated me, and not because I have a complaint about the admiration for factuality. These days the facts are the front lines in the battle for reason in America. The power of the state has been pitted against them.

Keynes was an economist, and I have no doubt that the relation that he posits between facts and opinions is entirely appropriate for purposes of administration — say, setting an interest rate. As conditions change, policies must be adjusted. Only a fool would think otherwise. If you are not fascinated by the question of what works, stay away from government. (Or join up, because these days nothing gets done.) Practicality is always reactive; its timeline is short. Pragmatism waits on the news. There is even a current in modern American thought for which democracy is itself an exercise in unceasing pragmatism, in trial and error unto the generations. Its definitive statement can be found in the conclusion to Holmes' renowned dissent in *Abrams* in 1919. Immediately following his famous observation that "the best test of truth is the power of the thought to get itself accepted in the competition of the market," which was an important moment in the infiltration of the non-economic spheres of American life by the vocabulary of economics, Holmes went on to declare about the Constitution that "it is an experiment, as life is an experiment." Whatever the merits of such a philosophy of existence, the sense of the provisional championed by Holmes is admirable for the mental patience that it imparts, and for its revulsion from absolutism.

Yet Keynes' statement seems to be reaching for more than a merely managerial responsiveness. It appears to be making a more general claim about the dependence of beliefs on facts. There are many kinds of belief, of course. But there are some kinds of belief that do not originate in the facts, that are not hostage to changes in the facts, that exist prior to the facts and provide the framework within which the facts are understood and assessed. I cannot agree that moral opinions and philosophical opinions, if indeed Keynes had such opinions in mind when he made his remark, require such a tight association with fact. Even the belief that beliefs must be based in facts cannot be based on facts. There are views I hold about right and wrong, about the individual and the group, about ethical obligation, about the duties and the limits of power, about the nature of truth, about the nature of beauty, and about spiritual meanings that will not be revised by the morning paper, whatever it brings. Before tomorrow's bad news, I already know that the world is an unkind place and that there are a variety of ways to interpret its cruelty, and I have, to the best of my abilities, in ways that I can explain, already chosen an interpretation.

It is possible, over time and by means of careful reflec- 411 tion, taking your experience into account but not only your experience, to arrive at a view of life, a worldview, and to hold it continuously, through thick and thin, regardless of polls and presidents, without embarrassment at the steadfastness with which you maintain it, so long as you give reasons and present them for critical examination. There is no shame in intellectual constancy. It is nothing like dogmatism, if it is thoughtful. And the caprices of external events, even when they are cataclysmic, need not throw one into philosophical crisis. Especially in times of cataclysm, one should aspire to what Rebecca West called "an unsurpriseable mind."

I remember a conference, not long after the earthquake of 2016, where I was holding forth on the characteristics of populism. When it came time for questions, an acquaintance of mine, a fiendishly intelligent woman with a saturnine look on her face, a distinguished international civil servant, raised her hand. "After what just happened," she asked, "how should we revise our views?" It was not the first time that I heard this question in the aftermath of the Trump ascendancy. I disliked the question. It represented a fundamental misunderstanding about the formation of belief. We should not revise our views, I replied. The election did not prove that our views are wrong. It proved only that our views are unpopular. (And the well-named popular vote did not prove even that.) All that a poll can establish is the popularity of a belief, its distribution across a population. It has no bearing whatever upon its substance. What we believe may be wrong, but not because many people disagree with us. This is precisely the problem with Holmes' idea of verification, with his contention that truth will be established in the competition in the market: success in the market has nothing to do with truth. The interminable history of human illusion shows that the "marketplace of ideas" is like every other marketplace. It reflects only appetites and interests; it is easily manipulated; it is quantitative.

I may have been a little sharp in my reply to the questioner. My disrespect for her notion of intellectual flexibility must have showed. Politicians, of course, must evaluate ideas politically, but this was not an exchange about politicians. A losing side may need to revise its tactics, but beliefs are not tactics. There is nothing illegitimate or disqualifying about a minority position. A democracy, indeed, should be judged by how it treats its minorities, not least its intellectual minorities. There is honor in minority life. There is honor also in defeat, if one stands for something more than victory. If you stand for principle and you lose, you are equipped to fight again. Sometimes there is good company in the wilderness. In wondering whether defeat should inspire second thoughts about first things, my rattled interlocutor was skirting the problem known as the tyranny of the majority, which was long ago identified as one of the supreme abuses of democracy. When I assured her that the results of the election did not constitute a refutation of her views, I did not mean to lull her into a feeling of righteousness about what she — and I — believed. I wished only to draw a line between disappointment and crippling doubt.

Here is what I do, sir. When the facts change, I interpret the facts according to the methods and the assumptions in which I have the most intellectual confidence. If I can vouch for the integrity of those methods and assumptions, which in my case are liberal methods and assumptions, I will be reluctant to give them up — especially in a dizzying world, where the people with moorings will be better able to explain and to lead. I recognize that moorings come in many forms — evil, too, comes with intellectual frameworks; but those frameworks will be most effectively challenged and repudiated by those who have a different one of their own. As for the facts, I am all for them; but I am not sure they can do all the work that needs to be done. Will bigotry be vanquished by data? A hatred cannot be dispelled for being non-factual. Sooner or later we have to engage at the level of moral and philosophical principle. We must make ourselves competent in kinds of discourse that are not only empirical. We must not forget how to believe.

413

This journal begins its life in a time of breakdown and bewilderment, of arousal and expectancy. It is called *Liberties* because of all the splendid echoes of the word — liberty, liberal, liberate, liberality, even libertarian. It is both a grave word and a joyous word. The plural is a tribute to the plurality of freedoms that we enjoy as a matter of right, and also to the plurality of freedoms that the citizens of a growing number of countries are being ruthlessly denied. Above all, it is meant to announce that, in this universe of fascists and commissars, the objective of these pages will be, by argument and by example, in politics and in culture, the rehabilitation of liberalism.

The slander of liberalism is one of the spectacular idiocies of our age. The errors and the failures of the liberal order, at home and abroad, need to be acknowledged, but they do not need to be exaggerated. The pride of liberals deserves to be much greater than their guilt. A glance at history abundantly demonstrates this, as the issues of this journal will explain. But the historical events that provoked the social, economic, and moral achievements of the liberal order have receded in time, and the experience of time itself has been accelerated, so that historical memory can no longer be relied upon for the work of explanation and nothing is obvious anymore. The work of explanation, guided by reason and humaneness and the study of the past, needs to start again. There is nothing nostalgic about such a project. The restoration of liberal ideas and practices — a social equality based not on venerations of identity but on universal principles; an economic equality based not on a delusion of *dirigisme* but upon a rigorous regulation of capitalism; a faith in government as one of the great creations of human civilization and the protector of the weak against the strong; an affirmation of American power in the world because of the good that American power can do in the world — is entirely forward-looking. To curse liberalism is to curse the future.

It is no longer trite or tautological to say that a democracy is a place that behaves democratically. Within our democracy, and within other democracies, there are many leaders and movements who behave undemocratically or anti-democratically — who view democracy expediently, as an instrument for the acquisition of power and nothing more. For this reason, the philosophical grounds and political benefits of democracy also need to be re-clarified. In 1938, on a lecture tour of the United States, Thomas Mann observed to his American audiences that democracy "should put aside the habit of taking itself for granted, of self-forgetfulness. It should use this wholly unexpected situation — the fact, namely, that it has again become problematical — to renew and rejuvenate itself by again becoming aware of itself." He was speaking, of course, with the ruefulness of his German experience. Our situation is not as bleak and bitter, but an authoritarian temper is flourishing in our midst too, in the West Wing and the streets and the media and the platforms. We, too, have become self-forgetful. "No," Mann told the crowds from coast to coast, "America needs no instruction in the things that concern democracy...Europe has had much to learn from America as to the nature of democracy. It was your American statesmen and poets such as Lincoln and Whitman who proclaimed to the world democratic thought and feeling, and the democratic way of life, in imperishable words." It is bruising to read those sentences. We no longer offer such instruction to the world, or even care about the condition of freedom beyond our own borders.

The question of how to live is more than the question of how to vote. The liberal idea was never just a political idea. It is, more generally, a grand belief in human capacity, and in the obligation — exclusive to no group and no tradition — to cultivate it. When Henry James wrote about "the liberal heart," he meant a large heart, a generous heart, a receptive heart, an expansive heart, an unconforming heart, a heart animated by a wide variety of human expressions. Such an ideal of heartfulness pertains not only to politics but also to culture. The war against callousness cannot be won without the resources of culture. There is no more lasting education in human sympathy than an exposure to literature and the arts.

The dwindling position of the humanities in American society is one of its most catastrophic developments. This journal, an independent journal, will take a side in this struggle. It will champion sensibility as well as controversy, and attend to culture with the same ardor with which it attends to politics. But it will refrain from aligning cultural criticism with political criticism, in grateful awareness of the multiplicity of the realms in which we lead our lives, and in awareness also of the insidious history of the synchronization of culture with politics. Pardon the counter-revolutionary thinking, but culture must never become politics by other means. Of course this is precisely what culture is becoming, thanks not least to the hepped-up synchronizers at the *New York Times*. (And at *The New Yorker,* which is what *PM* would have been if it had the money.) The autonomy of art threatens nobody and enriches everybody. The social and political origins of artists vitiate the freedom of art about as much as the social and political origins of thinkers vitiate the freedom of thought. When art is weaponized, it is compromised. Racial justice does not require the racialization of all things. And culture harbors no dream of consensus. An aversion to controversy is an aversion to culture, just as it is an aversion to democracy.

Not least because it will appear only four times a year, this journal will not be in the business of rapid response to the emergencies and the imbecilities with which we are currently inundated. We will crusade, but slowly. There is a deeper reason for this counter-cultural pace. It is that the investigation into bigger ideas and larger causes takes time. If the sorting out of our intellectual pandemonium should not be conceived under the aspect of eternity, neither should it be conceived under the aspect of the news cycle. American journalists have brilliantly responded to an assault on their integrity and their legitimacy with a golden age of investigative journalism, but they cannot be expected to do more: the exposure of lies in a regime of untruth is as exhausting as it is essential. (How many synonyms are there for "madman"?) So in these pages we will be indifferent to the chyrons. There will be no quick takes and immediate reactions and emotional outbursts, nothing driven by velocity or by brevity. At this journal we are betting on what used to be called the common reader, who would rather reflect than belong and asks of our intellectual life more than a choice between orthodoxies. We are not persuaded that it is a losing bet. With a melancholy sense of the fragility of what we cherish, and with a bestirring sense of how much injustice there is in the country and the world, we wish to bring an old intellectual calling into in a new era and see what together we can learn. Nothing quickens the mind like hope.

Steadying

CONTRIBUTORS

MICHAEL IGNATIEFF is the president of Central European University. An earlier version of this essay was delivered as a lecture at the Nexus Institute in Amsterdam.

LAURA KIPNIS is a professor in the department of Radio/TV/Film at Northwestern University and the author most recently of *Unwanted Advances: Sexual Paranoia Comes to Campus.*

DAVID GROSSMAN's most recent novel is *A Horse Walks into a Bar.* The essay in this issue was translated by Jessica Cohen.

RAMACHANDRA GUHA is the author of *Gandhi: Before India* and *Gandhi: The Years That Changed The World.*

THOMAS CHATTERTON WILLIAMS is the author most recently of *Self Portrait in Black and White: Unlearning Race.*

HANNAH SULLIVAN is the author of *Three Poems* and *The Work of Revision.*

MARK LILLA is Professor of Humanities at Columbia University and the author of *The Once and Future Liberal.*

HELEN VENDLER is the A. Kingsley Porter University Professor Emerita at Harvard University, and the author of *Our Secret Discipline: Yeats and Lyric Form.*

SEAN WILENTZ is the George Henry Davis 1886 Professor of American History at Princeton University and the author most recently of *No Property in Man: Slavery and Antislavery at the Nation's Founding.*

CELESTE MARCUS is the managing editor of Liberties.

ADAM ZAGAJEWSKI's most recent book of poems is *Asymmetry.*

LOUISE GLÜCK is the author, among other books, of *Faithful and Virtuous Night* and *Poems 1962-2012*.

JAMES WOLCOTT is the author of *Critical Mass: Four Decades of Essays, Reviews, Hand Grenades and Hurrahs*.

ANDREA MARCOLONGO is the author of *The Ingenious Language: Nine Epic Reasons to Love Greek*.

ELI LAKE writes a column for Bloomberg Opinion.

SALLY SATEL is a visiting professor of psychiatry at Columbia University's Irving Medical Center and a resident scholar at the American Enterprise Institute.

MOSHE HALBERTAL's new book *Nahmanides: Law and Mysticism* will be published this fall.

JOSHUA BENNETT is the Mellon Assistant Professor of English and Creative Writing at Dartmouth College. He is the author of *Being Property Once Myself: Blackness and the End of Man* and *The Sobbing School*.

DAVID THOMSON is the author most recently of *Murder and the Movies*. His new books *A Light in the Dark: A History of Movie Directors* and *Disaster Mon Amour* will be published next year.

JULIUS MARGOLIN was the author of *Journey to the Land of the Zeks and Back: A Memoir of the Gulag*, translated by Stefani Hoffman, which will be published by Oxford University Press this fall.

CLARA COLLIER is a writer living in California.

SHAWN MCCREESH is a writer living in Washington, DC. The names in his essay have been changed out of respect for the privacy of its subjects.

LEON WIESELTIER is the editor of Liberties.

Thank You

Michelle Ajami, David Bradley, Erica Brown, Menachem Butler,
Angie Dickinson, Maureen Dowd, Yaacob Dweck, David Eliach,
Isabel Fattal, Joshua Fattal, Bradley Graham, Joel Grey,
David Grossman, Moshe Halbertal, Jennifer Homans, Robert Kagan,
Amy Kauffman, James Kirchik, Frederick Lawrence, Nicholas Lemann,
Catharine MacKinnon, Jerome Marcus, Lori Lowenthal Marcus,
Wynton Marsalis, Daphne Merkin, Martin Peretz, Richard Plepler,
Laurene Powell Jobs, Jomana Qaddour, Eveline Riemen, Rob Riemen,
Tom Sawicki, Will Schwalbe, Stephanie Solomon, Haym Soloveitchik,
David Thomson, Kenneth Weinstein, Matthew Wieseltier,
Thea Wieseltier, Sean Wilentz, Phil Zuckerman

Liberties, a Journal of Culture and
Politics, is published quarterly
in Fall, Winter, Spring, and Summer
by Liberties Journal Foundation.

ISSN 2692-3904

The insignia that appears throughout Liberties is derived from details in Botticelli's drawings for Dante's *Divine Comedy*, which were executed between 1480 and 1495.